New Narratives

Frontiers of Narrative SERIES EDITOR
David Herman *Ohio State University*

New Narratives

Stories and Storytelling in the Digital Age

EDITED BY RUTH PAGE
AND BRONWEN THOMAS

University of Nebraska Press | Lincoln and London

© 2011 by the Board of Regents of the University of
Nebraska. All rights reserved. Manufactured in the
United States of America.

Library of Congress Cataloging-in-Publication Data
New narratives : stories and storytelling in the digital
age / edited by Ruth Page and Bronwen Thomas.
p. cm.—(Frontiers of narrative)
Includes bibliographical references.
ISBN 978-0-8032-1786-7 (pbk.: alk. paper)
1. Mass media. 2. Narration (Rhetoric) 3. Discourse
analysis, Narrative. 4. Online authorship. I. Page,
Ruth E., 1972– II. Thomas, Bronwen.
P96.N35N49   2011
808.036—dc23
2011018072

Set in Minion Pro. Designed by A. Shahan.

Contents

Illustrations

Tables

New Narratives

Introduction

RUTH PAGE AND BRONWEN THOMAS

In recent years developments in digital technology have played a significant role in the transformation of narrative theory and practice. Stories
that exploit the capacity of digital media (that is, those that necessitate
the computer for their production and display) have provided vital new
territory against which the tools of narrative analysis could be tested and
refined. As such, technological innovations from the 1980s onward have
been pivotal in providing an alternative to the conventions of print media
narrative, allowing those working in narrative theory to scrutinize the
nature of narrative production and reception from a fresh perspective. By
the 1990s a wealth of criticism was available that made radical claims for
a narrative revolution in the light of hypertext, gaming, MUDs, and MOOs
(Douglas 1992; Aarseth 1997; Landow 1997; Murray 1997; Hayles 2001).
This criticism engaged with a range of narrative concepts, including questions about plot, event structures, and temporality, as well as questions
about how stories are produced and experienced, debated in relation to
matters such as interactivity, immersion, and agency.

At the start of the twenty-first century, much has changed both in
the kinds of narratives that are now available in digital media and in the
approaches taken to analyze them. The hypertexts of the 1980s published
on CD-ROM by Eastgate have acquired almost canonical status, and have
since been supplemented by "born digital" hypertext narratives, that is,
digital fictions that were created to use Internet applications to link to
sites beyond themselves. Meanwhile, the development of multimedia software such as Adobe's Flash in the mid-1990s enabled creators to integrate
an increasingly sophisticated multimodal range of resources into digital
texts. While visual and verbal elements have always been present in digital fiction—for example, in the use of icons, illustration, and layout—in
early hyperfiction the textual content remained central. Typically, narra-

1

tive was carried primarily in the verbal elements of the text, and navigation was enabled through hyperlinked words (illustrative examples are
found in Deena Larsen's *Disappearing Rain* [2001] and Geoff Ryman's *253*
[1997]). What Kate Hayles (2003) describes as the second wave of digital
fiction enriches the multimodal capacity of electronic literature. No longer are words so prominent, but graphics and animation are just as likely
to communicate story content or be used as part of the interactive interface. Contemporary examples include the quasi-cinematic qualities like
Pullinger and Joseph's ongoing work *Inanimate Alice*, or the visual richness of Fisher's *These Waves of Girls* (2001).

Increased access to and usage of the Internet has also influenced the
creation and reception of narratives in new media.[1] Where once the ability to create online text would have entailed specialist knowledge of programming techniques, the advent of what are popularly known as Web
2.0 technologies in the late 1990s has enabled users with relatively low
technical skills to upload and manipulate text with unprecedented ease.
The ability to harness the textual resources and networking capacities of
the World Wide Web has been exploited by a proliferation of storytelling communities. Such communities may explicitly foreground the act
of storytelling, as does the Center for Digital Storytelling, or archives like
Bubbe's Back Porch. Other communities have emerged within the wider
context of social networking sites, creating new and hybrid stories across
modes and genres. The photo-sharing application Flickr has been used to
push forward visual storytelling as its users are invited to "Tell a story in
five frames" ("Visual Story Telling" ongoing) or document their life story in pictures in the "365 Project." YouTube, the video-sharing website, is
fertile territory not just for audiovisual microclips but for fan-videos and
mashing movie trailers—examples that not only demonstrate the creative
endeavors of web users but contentious debates over intellectual property and copyright. Alongside this, sites like MySpace have provided platforms for individuals to narrate their life experiences on blogs, journals,
and discussion boards. Perhaps the most dominant social network site
to emerge in recent years is Facebook, which in 2010 boasted 500 million
users worldwide. Facebook is a multifaceted environment for collaborative storytelling ventures and for microblogging as its users narrate episodes of their life histories in status updates, wall posts, and comments.

The development of new narrative forms continues to expand as fast as technological innovation, and faster than can be documented by scholars and reviewers. We acknowledge that the range of texts interrogated by the authors in this volume will soon (if it has not already) appear not so very "new" at all. Instead, they might best be regarded as a selective snapshot of narrative practices—practices already significantly different from the hypertext fictions that were the focus of the first wave of digital narratology. Here we argue for a distinctive move forward into a fresh phase of digital narratology—one that revisits the relationship between narrative theory and digital technology but that explicitly grounds that relationship in a range of contextually oriented perspectives.

The intersections between theory and practice have always been central to the development of digital narratology. Many of the foundational writers in this field (such as Michael Joyce, Jane Yellowlees Douglas, and Shelley Jackson) continue to produce both creative and critical outputs that feed into each other synergistically. It might then come as no surprise to find that the continued innovation in narrative practice has gone hand in hand with profound challenges to the ways in which such texts can be theorized. Retrospectively, the radical claims of early 1990s theorists have been fiercely contested, with later commentators questioning the extent to which the digital forms are distinctive, emancipatory, influential, or narrative at all (Miall 1999; Aarseth 2004; Ryan 2004). However, rather than abandoning the project of digital narratology, recent work that extends narrative theory in the light of digital media has become finely nuanced. Through close readings of particular texts and detailed attention to the contextualized practices, digital narratology now seeks to identify what really is distinctive or innovative about "new" storytelling modes.

Narratology and Digital Media

This volume brings together diverse narrative practices and equally diverse ways of studying them, in a manner that both reflects and contributes to the polyvalent, expansive nature of contemporary narratology. While the evolution of narrative studies in recent years should not be presented as a simple story of progress toward a single, unified goal, it provides a critical context that illuminates key developments in research on digital narratives in particular.

Classical Narratology

The structuralist agenda for the formal study of narratology was laid out by francophone scholars such as Barthes (1977), Genette (1980), and Greimas (1966) as a transtextual project unconstrained by the particularities of media or culture. Conceptualizing the enterprise in such breadth facilitated later work on texts far beyond the literary canon, including those that would appear in digital media. However, the focus on investigating the underlying semiotic system of narrative resulted in models that tended toward abstraction rather than a full account of localized texts and contexts in which the processes of storytelling take place. By the late 1980s, the limitations of structuralist narratology had become well rehearsed (Brooke-Rose 1990), especially its problematic claims for universality. Nonetheless, the importance of the theoretical models emerging from classical narratology cannot be underestimated. Many of the concepts proved to be robust when put to work in the actual study of narrative practices, and these concepts continue to be fruitful for research on narratives in digital media, whether in conjunction with the study of narrative temporality (see Montfort, chapter 5) or in the rethinking of the nature of narrative grammar (as in Salway and Herman, chapter 6).

Situated Narratives

Shortly after the advent of structuralism, complementary narrative scholarship began to emerge in neighboring fields of inquiry: sociolinguistics, discourse analysis, and pragmatics. Focusing on conversational stories rather than literary texts, work on narratives of personal experience (Labov 1972) drew attention to stories as a form of social interaction, grounded in particular contexts and performing significant interpersonal and identity work for groups of speakers. Labov and Waletzky's (1967) pathbreaking study initiated a surge of research (see Bamberg 1997 for an overview) that continues to the present. Yet for the most part, sustained study of face-to-face narratives has remained in a parallel but separate domain from the literary theoretical study of storytelling (for exceptions, see particularly the work of Herman [2002], Fludernik [1996], and Toolan [2001]). Much online discourse is hybrid in nature, blending the written word with near-instantaneous communication, giving rise to what Ong (1982) described as secondary orality. In particular, the narratives that emerge in Web 2.0 environments where personal expression is inextricably interwoven with dialogue (for example, through the use of conversational metacommentary) require paradigms that account for both their interpersonal and expressive qualities. These emergent digital stories thus open further possibility for dialogue between researchers working in literary and linguistic narrative traditions.

Ideas deriving from the study of how narrative discourse is used in everyday interactions promise to throw light on stories told in online contexts. Specifically, earlier work identified narrative fragments in now familiar forms of computer mediated communication, such as e-mail exchanges (Georgakopoulou 2006) and discussion forums (McLellan 1997), illustrating how the fragmented, process-oriented, and communal nature of these forms extended our understanding of what narrative could be. However, as the online repertoire of communicative forums continues to widen to include blogs, wikis, and social networking sites, the central role of communities and the stories they tell comes further to the fore. For example, Page's analysis of personal blogs (chapter 12) shows how narratives of illness are reworked in gender-aligned ways to support those undergoing similar experiences. Storytellers might also form albeit temporary communities around particular collaborative storytelling ventures. Rettberg discusses several particular examples in chapter 10, including the project "Invisible Seattle" and the more recent "Million Penguins," a wikinovel experiment supported by Penguin publishing in 2007.

Likewise, this volume has contributions from practitioners who have experience of working within or alongside key projects that explore the implications of new digital narratives for specific localized, "real world" communities. Such work demonstrates the benefits of examining situated narrative practices, in contrast with constructing abstract models of the structuralist variety. For example, Brian Greenspan's chapter 8 outlines the development of the "Storytrek" prototype for digitizing aboriginal songlines. For her part, Heather Lotherington, in chapter 14, evaluates the effectiveness of the Multiliteracies project in addressing issues of cultural inclusion in Canadian elementary schools. In both chapters, the authors bring to light the cultural politics that lie behind the creation of new media narratives. Greenspan carefully argues that uses of virtual spaces are no more neutral than the appropriation of social or geographical spaces, and he points to the challenges of using geospatial information to configure itinerant hypertexts derived from Aboriginal songlines.

Lotherington's chapter showcases another, somewhat different instance of using technology for the benefit of minority groups. In her case, elementary-age children are enabled to retell traditional fairy tales using a range of digital technologies in a way that engages them successfully with storytelling practices beyond print literacy alone.

Postclassical Expansion

The diversity of contemporary narratology is characterized by expansion beyond classical narratology's literary perspectives and data set. For digital narratology, this is manifest in several ways. From the outset, integrating narrative and new media approaches has been by definition interdisciplinary, drawing on concepts from fields such as artificial intelligence and computer science and examining texts and practices that broaden the medial, generic, and modal range of data that might be considered storylike. This volume aims to expand the possibilities of innovative work in this area. Both Punday (chapter 1) and Joyce (chapter 4) reflect on the nature and influence of media and medial expansions. From another perspective, Salway and Herman's essay (chapter 6) explores how a freely available text-analysis software package can be used for the study of narrative corpora, demonstrating how technological advances might yield new tools for narrative analysis. On the other hand, contributions like Ensslin's study (chapter 7) of experimental hyperfiction and Lotherington's essay (chapter 14) on the images and movies created by schoolchildren suggest how the same digital technologies can be used to support multimodal narrative productions.

Furthermore, the augmentation of classical, structuralist narratology by critical perspectives from other fields has led to a heightened sensitivity to the political ramifications of narration, and indeed of narrative theory itself. While the practical outworkings of such politicization might remain a matter for discussion (Currie 1998), the apparent neutrality of narrative systems has in general been replaced by a critical narratology that draws attention to the ethics of storytelling and argues for the inherent value of narrative practices among formerly neglected minority groups. Within the study of digital narratives, we might now chart the emergence of a similar political sensitivity. Many of the studies included in this volume examine the formal qualities of digital narratives with critical perspectives that attempt to address inequalities relating to gender or cultural identity.

In this way, the essays demonstrate how contemporary narratology has moved beyond formalism to explore issues of gatekeeping and access (as in who gets to tell what kinds of stories, and in what contexts), and to interrogate the increasing corporatization of cross-media franchises such as Lucasfilm's *Star Wars* (discussed by Newman and Simons in chapter 13) or the Harry Potter phenomenon (discussed by Thomas in chapter 11). The influence of corporate practices on storytelling across media is also discussed in Cobley and Haeffner's work surveying changes in DVD formatting (chapter 9).

The critical and contextual breadth of digital narratology owes much to the tenets of new media theory, which concerns itself less with the stylistic or textual characteristics of new narrative forms than with the environments and social and cultural formations that produce and consume them, as well as the cultural uses to which narrative practices may be put. Wary of both technological determinism and crude progressivism, new media theory locates discussions of specific practices and communities within broader debates surrounding globalization and cultural imperialism. Attitudes toward new media practices may range from enthusiasm for the democratizing potential of interactive or participatory media to skepticism and suspicion of the economies of use that may marginalize and even exclude many social groupings. For some theorists, the transgressive potential of new media subcultures is something to be celebrated, and necessitates a rethinking of basic models and paradigms in the direction of hybridization rather than binary opposites—for example, mainstream versus marginal, or orthodox versus heterodox. Meanwhile, key concepts such as those of convergence (Jenkins 2006) and remediation (Bolter and Grusin 1999) demonstrate the need to move beyond fixed categories and boundaries in attempting to respond to the ever-shifting and evolving practices and affordances facilitated by new technologies.

Media theory and new media theory more especially view narratology's traditional focus on the text with some distrust. In turn, media theorists have been accused by narratologists of "text blindness" (Hausken 2004) both in their reluctance to engage in textual analysis and in their often cavalier disregard for the specific terminology and textual conditions of the kinds of narrative that they discuss. In both fields the challenge is to find a language to replace the concept of the text as a static object with the idea of texts as dynamic processes. By the same token, both media theorists and narrative theorists have recognized the need to view readers and audiences not as passive recipients of semantic contents but rather as participants in the coproduction of the text's meanings. Yet minor differences in terminological nuance continue to perpetuate a sense of divide, even where the object being scrutinized is similar. For example media theorists prefer to talk of transmedia storytelling (Jenkins 2007) while in narratology the term *transmedial* is usually preferred, both to highlight a concern with the materiality of different media, and to acknowledge the influence of semiotic theory (Ryan 2006). Likewise, in new media theory, cross-media texts or cross-media platforms both hold currency to describe what has been labeled in digital narratology as distributed narrative (Walker 2004).

More significantly, perhaps, attempts have been made to challenge the extent to which new media practices must be conceived of in narrative terms at all. Indeed, Lev Manovich (n.d.) charges that the word *narrative* is overused in relation to new media "to cover up the fact that we have not yet developed a language to describe these strange new objects." Instead, Manovich proposes the database or the algorithm as a way to better understand this emerging cultural sphere. Similarly, Espen Aarseth (1997; 2004) has contested the reliance on narrative models in relation to computer games, proposing instead the term *ludology* to foreground the importance of play and interplay between participants.

While this volume is generally enthusiastic about the affordances and possibilities opened up by new digital technologies and practices, it is important to recognize that voices have been raised against the cybertopianism found in much of the existing scholarship. In particular, literary critics such as Sven Birkerts (1994) have spoken out against what they see as an attack on print cultures and on established practices of critical reading and analysis. Meanwhile, David Miall has used empirical research on readers to demonstrate how hypertext fiction disrupts the experience of immersion and absorption that he argues is intrinsic to the literary experience, and to challenge the assumption that "literature can be made to dance to the multimedia tune" (Miall and Dobson 2001). Where new digital narratives explicitly intersect with questions of literariness (e.g., hypertext fiction, fanfiction), it becomes necessary to evaluate and explore the cultural place of such practices and the extent to which they can continue to offer the kind of affective engagement Miall and others see as so intrinsic to literature.

Central Concepts in Digital Narratology

As suggested in the previous section, the ongoing project of reworking and extending classical, structuralist models of narrative has been facilitated by the study of storytelling in digital media. A cluster of key concepts has emerged from this work—a cluster also explored by the contributors to this volume.

Narrative Progression: A Sense of an Ending

Early studies of digital fiction recognized the profound challenge that the associative qualities of hypertexts posed for narrative coherence (Landow 1997). The critics pointed to a central distinction between conventions of reading print narrative and reading stories told using the affordances of hypertext structures. Namely, print narratives are typically read from a series of consecutive pages whose sequence is determined by the author, while the lexias of digital fiction are navigated via a series of hyperlinked words or icons, the sequence of which is selected in part by the reader. Of course, there is no strict binary opposition between reading print and reading hypertext. Binding a sequence of print pages within a book cover does not preclude a reader indulging in a spoiler and reading the last pages of the story first. Conversely, digital fiction writers might be careful to arrange lexias in such a way that the segments of the story follow a strict chronological order. Nor should the reading conventions of particular media be conflated with narrative structure. Print narratives might contain extraordinarily complex temporal patterning and sophisticated configurations of possible worlds. Digital fiction need not. Nonetheless, the associative patterns typically exploited by the first-wave authors of digital fiction were theorized as generating a new spectrum of plot typologies (Ryan 2006, and chapter 2 of this volume), challenging theories of the nature of narrativity itself.

In particular, the multiple pathways characteristic of early digital fiction provided critics with fresh material against which to consider the forms and functions of narrative closure. Deferred endings or the possibility of multiple endings are not confined to narrative genres in digital media and can be found in offline stories from serial genres, such as the soap opera, through to postmodern fiction (for a discussion of hypertext's antecedents, see Landow 1997). Nor is the question of narrative closure related only to hypertextual fiction. In the essays that follow in this volume, deferred endings come in many guises and serve many functions. In Cobley and Haeffner's essay (chapter 9), DVD add-ons are seen as facilitating an immediate affective response to the text, while in Thomas's exploration of fanfiction (chapter 11), the capacity to endlessly update reworked stories is a source of readerly pleasure. In the case of the personal blogs considered by Page (chapter 12), the open-endedness comes in the episodic blog posts and their comments. Although deferred endings are in fact a concern of many of these essays, the authors are careful not to ascribe to such endings uniform character. As digital narratology becomes more contextually aware, it is clear then that we cannot conceptualize narrative in isomorphic terms where a single textual feature (here open-endedness) might signal a definitive relationship between form and function, a point that has been made in narratology more generally (Sternberg 1982).

Narrative, Fiction, and Identity

Hitherto, the impact of digital textuality on narrative theory has been concentrated for the most part on structural concerns. But narratives are not just sequences of events: those events are told by and about particular individuals. As the study of digital texts increasingly includes narrative practices, it is all the more pressing to reconsider how the relationship between narrative and self-representation might be reworked in the context of online environments.

It has always been acknowledged that storytelling, whether claimed to be fictional or not, is a selective and partial method of representation. As Bamberg reminds us, narrative analysis is not a transparent measure of identity but forms a "heuristic" for considering how the self comes into being (2004, 211). Assumptions about online representation further complicate debates about the relation between narrative, self-representation, and fictionality. On the one hand, the Internet is often perceived as an environment that enables apparently free identity play (for example, through adopting false and/or gender neutral pseudonyms, avatars, and other forms of role play). On the other hand, conventions of authenticity still prevail, such that notorious cases like Kaycee Nicole (a fictional person with leukemia created by Debbie Swenson in 2001) are rightly understood as hoaxes, and where enacting infidelity in a virtual world can be grounds for divorce in the offline domain.

The boundaries between these two positions are blurred by the uses of "fictional" representation across online genres. For example, autobiographical hypertexts such as Shelley Jackson's *My Body* (1997) weave together life story and artistic endeavor, making it difficult to isolate particular pieces of information about an individual that are deemed to be true in the real world. In contrast, danah m. boyd (2008) reports on American teenagers' use of "false" personal information on social networking sites as a deliberate strategy to be recognized as fictional by friends but to be taken as authentic and so ward off attention from unwanted lurkers.

The oscillation between the contradictory expectations of authenticity gives rise to an ambiguity that challenges the boundaries of fictionality (see Bell's chapter 3 for further discussion) and means that we cannot treat any discussion of narrative and identity work (for example, as seen in Page's essay, chapter 12) in essentialist terms. Rather, it forces us to consider the various ways in which narrators and readers treat stories told in digital media as bridges between their online and offline experiences.

Examining the relationship between identity in online and offline contexts is a salutary reminder that readers and writers are not abstract figures but actual individuals and that producing or processing narratives in digital media is an embodied experience. Far from viewing the online world in cybertopian terms as free from physical constraint, the essays in this volume include discussion of the human body as an important resource for readers and writers. In the chapter on blogging (chapter 12), the human body is a site for signification as bloggers construct narratives about their ongoing experience of illness. Meanwhile, Ensslin's chapter 7 examines the ways in which the human body interacts with a digital narrative. She takes as her subject an unusual subgenre of digital fiction: physio-cybertext, where the reader's navigation through the story is driven by his or her breathing pattern. Her analysis of Pullinger, Schemat, and babel's *The Breathing Wall* allows her to explore distinctions between corporeal and cognitive responses and so rework the concept of intentionality. In both essays, the relationship between the embodied experience of the reader/writer and the narrative is dynamic and mediated, allowing us to revisit readerly practices from a fresh perspective.

Narrative Interaction

The communicative interplay between a storyteller, an audience, and the story itself has long been a matter of interest to narratologists, and it is of heightened significance in relation to digital texts. Interactivity is repeatedly cited as the feature of digital media that most clearly distinguishes it from older, nondigital genres (Ryan 2004, 2006; Aarseth 1997; Walker 2003). How we define interactivity and its various forms remains a matter of debate, as Ryan explores in her chapter 2. She points out that neither traditional concepts of agency nor the idea of ergodism fully encapsulate what is entailed by the dialogical, reciprocal nature of interactivity.

In many of the essays that follow, concepts of interactivity (in its broadest sense) are reworked and extended in the light of recent technological and narrative developments. Both Montfort (chapter 5) and Bell (chapter 3) examine the possible worlds with which a user might interact via different digital genres. Bell's chapter explores early examples of hypertext fiction published by *StorySpace*, interpreting readerly navigational choices as moments where ontological shifts between different levels of possible worlds are foregrounded. In contrast, Montfort takes Interactive Fiction as his starting point. His chapter examines a technological architecture that forges new ground by enabling writers of Interactive Fiction to control event and expression levels of the narrative separately. Drawing on Genette's classical model, he demonstrates how users can enact variations in time and order, and points to future possibilities for automatic text generation.

Interactivity need not be considered a purely dyadic phenomenon between a single user and a single text. Rather, the networking capabilities of digital technology mean that textual interactivity can be coupled with the interaction between users. In turning the focus to actual communities of storytellers, this work marks a departure from textually oriented studies of interaction. Previously, typologies of interaction have tended to treat the figure of the reader in abstract, theoretical terms (for exceptions, see studies by Douglas 1992, 2000). In contrast, several of the writers in this volume ground their analyses in the empirical study of particular communities and collaborative projects. For example, Rettberg (chapter 10) surveys the history and methods of collaborative authorship, setting out different forms of conscious, contributory, and participatory user engagement demonstrated in various online projects. In so doing, he calls into question standard narratological concepts such as "narrator."

Collaborative interaction also bears on issues of plot development. Thus, Thomas (chapter 11) and Page (chapter 12) explore two different communities that evolve through writing about the same stories. In both fanfiction (Thomas) and blog writing (Page), interaction takes place in a mediated form through the collaborative construction of a metacommentary. The interaction here is clearly a dialogue between users rather than the navigation or authorship of a particular text. Analysts of digital storytelling need to develop ways of understanding the ongoing, process-centered nature of storytelling within such online interactions and also the genres thereby created and contested.

New Narratives: The Dialectic of Theory and Practice

This set of essays sets out to exemplify the breadth and flexibility of current approaches to the study of digital narrativity, and to demonstrate the usefulness of these approaches for understanding emerging forms and practices. The volume is structured such that it moves from suggesting new theoretical paradigms and conceptual frameworks for the analysis of digital narratives, toward exploring new architectures, uses, and platforms for narrative, and culminates in specific and detailed analyses of specific narrative practices and processes. However, there are many crosscurrents and commonalities between the chapters from each of these sections, and as suggested earlier, one of the defining concerns of the volume is to challenge the often arbitrary divisions made between theory and practice, or between theoretical frameworks and the modes of storytelling that complement rather than contradict one another. Each of the essays may be read individually as a contribution to the field in its own right, but when read in the context of the other contributions, each essay helps generate a rich dialogue about the interplay between the theories, practices and narratives that continue to evolve in digital media. It is our hope that the essays will advance our knowledge of these forms, stimulate new developments in narrative theory, and possibly even provide a springboard for new forms of narrative practice—both while the narratives discussed here are "new" and in the years to come when they will be augmented by storytelling possibilities not yet imagined.[2]

Notes

1. Discussion of narratives dependent on new technologies often uses the terms *electronic*, *digital*, and *new media* interchangeably. However, the term *new media* is usually employed to encompass the other two, and to suggest the ways in which computers have helped transform "old media," and in particular to move from analogue to digital technologies.

2. The authors wish to thank David Herman for his comments on an earlier draft of this essay. All errors, of course, remain our own.

References

Aarseth, Espen J. 1997. *Cybertext: Perspectives on Ergodic Literature*. Baltimore: John Hopkins University Press.

———. 2004. "Quest Games as Post-narrative Discourse." In *Narrative across Media: The Languages of Storytelling*, ed. Marie-Laure Ryan, 361–76. Lincoln: University of Nebraska Press.

Bamberg, Michael, ed. 1997. *Oral Versions of Personal Experience: Three Decades of Narrative Analysis*. Special issue, *Journal of Narrative and Life History 7*, nos. 1–4.

———. 2004. "Narrative Discourse and Identities." In *Narratology beyond Literary Criticism*, ed. J. C. Meister, T. Kindt, W. Schernus, and M. Stein, 213–37. Berlin: Walter de Gruyter.

Barthes, Roland. 1977. *Image-Music-Text*. Trans. Stephen Heath. London: Fontana.

Birkerts, Sven. 1994. *The Gutenberg Elegies: The Fate of Reading in an Electronic Age*. London: Faber and Faber.

Bolter, Jay, and Richard Grusin. 1999. *Remediation: Understanding New Media*. Cambridge MA: MIT Press.

boyd, danah m. 2008. "Taken Out of Context: American Teen Sociality in Networked Publics." PhD diss., University of California, Berkeley.

Brooke-Rose, Christine. 1990. "Whatever Happened to Narratology?" *Poetics Today* 11, no. 2:283–93.

Bubbe's Back Porch. Available at http://www.aboutus.org/Bubbe.com (accessed February 24, 2009).

Center for Digital Storytelling. Available at http://www.storycenter.org/ (accessed February 24, 2009).

Currie, Mark. 1998. *Postmodern Narrative Theory*. Basingstoke: Macmillan.

Douglas, Jane Yellowlees. 1992. "Print Pathways and Interactive Labyrinths: How Hypertext Narratives Affect the Act of Reading." PhD diss., New York University.

———. 2000. *The End of Books—or Books without End? Reading Interactive Narratives*. Ann Arbor: University of Michigan Press.

Fisher, Caitlin. 2001. *These Waves of Girls*. Available at http://www.yorku.ca/caitlin/ waves/ (accessed February 13, 2009).

Fludernik, Monika. 1996. *Toward a "Natural" Narratology*. London: Routledge.

Genette, Gérard. 1980. *Narrative Discourse: An Essay in Method*. Trans. J. E. Lewin. Ithaca NY: Cornell University Press.

Georgakopoulou, Alexandra. 2006. "The Other Side of the Story: Towards a Narrative Analysis of Narratives-in-Interaction." *Discourse Studies* 8:265–87.

Greimas, Algirdas J. 1966. *Structural Semantics: An Attempt at a Method*. Lincoln: University of Nebraska Press.

Hausken, Liv. 2004. "Coda: Textual Theory and Blind Spots in Media Studies." In *Narrative across Media: The Languages of Storytelling*, ed. Marie-Laure Ryan, 391–402. Lincoln: University of Nebraska Press.

Hayles, N. Katherine. 2001. "The Transformation of Narrative and the Materiality of Hypertext." *Narrative* 9, no. 1:21–39.

———. 2003. "Deeper into the Machine: The Future of Electronic Literature." *Culture Machine* 5. Available at http://www.culturemachine.net/index.php/cm/ article/viewArticle/245/241 (accessed December 2, 2010).

Herman, David. 2002. *Story Logic: Problems and Possibilities of Narrative*. Lincoln: University of Nebraska Press.

Jackson, Shelley. 1997. *My Body, A Wunderkammer*. Available at www.altx.com/ thebody/ (accessed November 20 2007).

Jenkins, Henry. 2006. *Convergence Culture: Where Old and New Media Collide*. New York: New York University Press.

———. 2007. "Transmedia Storytelling 101." Available at http://www.henryjenkins .org/2007/03/transmedia_storytelling_101.html (accessed February 3, 2009).

Labov, William. 1972. "The Transformation of Experience in Narrative Syntax." In *Language in the Inner City*, 354–96. Philadelphia: University of Pennsylvania Press.

Labov, William, and J. Waletzky. 1967. "Narrative Analysis: Oral Versions of Personal Experience." In *Essays on the Verbal and Visual Arts: Proceedings of the 1966 Annual Spring Meeting of the American Ethnological Society*, ed. J. Helm, 12–44. Seattle: University of Washington Press.

Landow, George P. 1997. *Hypertext 2.0: The Convergence of Contemporary Critical Theory and Technology*. Baltimore: Johns Hopkins University Press. (Orig. pub. 1992.)

Larsen, Deena. 2001. *Disappearing Rain*. Available at http://www.deenalarsen.net/ rain/ (accessed February 13, 2009).

Manovich, Lev. n.d. "Database as a Genre of New Media." Available at http://vv.arts .ucla.edu/AI_Society/manovich.html (accessed February 3, 2009).

McLellan, Faith. 1997. "'A Whole Other Story': The Electronic Narrative of Illness." *Literature and Medicine* 16, no. 1:88–107.

Miall, David S. 1999. "Trivializing or Liberating? The Limitations of Hypertext Theorizing." *Mosaic* 32, no. 2:157–71.

Miall, David, and Teresa Dobson. 2001. "Reading Hypertext and the Experience of Literature." *Journal of Digital Information* 2, no. 1. Available at http://journals .tdl.org/jodi/article/view/jodi-36/37 (accessed February 3, 2009).

Murray, Janet H. 1997. *Hamlet on the Holodeck: The Future of Narrative in Cyberspace.* Cambridge MA: MIT Press.

Ong, Walter J. 1982. *Orality and Literacy: The Technologizing of the Word.* London: Methuen.

Pullinger, Kate, and Chris Joseph. ongoing. *Inanimate Alice.* Available at http:// www.inanimatealice.com/ (accessed April 22, 2010).

Pullinger, Kate, Stefan Schemat, and babel. 2004. *The Breathing Wall.* CD-ROM. London: The Sayle Literary Agency.

Ryan, Marie-Laure. 2004. *Narrative across Media: The Languages of Storytelling.* Lincoln: University of Nebraska Press.

———. 2006. *Avatars of Story.* Minneapolis: University of Minnesota Press.

Ryman, Geoff. 1997. 253. Available at http://www.ryman-novel.com/ (accessed February 12, 2009).

Sternberg, Meir. 1982. "Proteus in Quotation Land: Mimesis and the Forms of Reported Discourse." *Poetics Today* 3, no. 2:107–56.

Toolan, Michael. 2001. *Narrative: A Critical Linguistic Introduction.* 2nd ed. New York: Routledge.

"Visual Story Telling." ongoing. Available at http://www.flickr.com/groups/visual story/ (accessed December 2, 2010).

Walker, Jill. 2003. "Fiction and Interaction: How Clicking a Mouse Can Make You Part of a Fictional World." PhD diss., University of Bergen.

———. 2004. "Distributed Narrative." Available at http://jilltxt.net/?p=931 (accessed December 2, 2010).

PART 1 | *New Foundations*

1 From Synesthesia to Multimedia

How to Talk about New Media Narrative

DANIEL PUNDAY

The title of Marku Eskelinen's controversial essay in the *Electronic Book Review*, "Cybertext Theory: What an English Professor Should Know before Trying," tells us a great deal about the problems of talking about new media narrative. Eskelinen offers the gamelike texts that Espen Aarseth calls cybertext as the *other* to the work that literature professors and narratologists usually discuss. For him, these games are the object of entrenched disciplines' "colonializing" gaze: cybertext theory must defend "its objects of study from various colonising enterprises from traditional literary institutions, whenever they'd become desperate enough to try" (Eskelinen 2001). According to this description, cybertexts (such as video games) are like some new species recently discovered; any attempt to impose traditional textual categories from other media (literature primarily, but also film) is by definition a misinterpretation of the form. The challenge of interpreting new media texts becomes one of developing native categories and terms that are fair to this new medium.

And yet, we all recognize that traditional and new media narratives are not really independent. When Katherine Hayles calls for a "medium-specific analysis," she is careful to explain that she "do[es] not mean to advocate that media should be considered in isolation from one another" (Hayles 2004b, 69). I am afraid, however, that Eskelinen's celebration of cybertexts encourages precisely this. Marie-Laure Ryan is surely right when she notes that each "narrative medium" will have a "unique combination of features" (2004, 19), among which are the senses that it stimulates, the way that it uses space and time, the technological and material basis for the work, and the cultural context for producing and disseminating the story. The danger of this flexible and powerful characterization, however, is that the word *unique* can make us forget the word *combination*, that our search for what is different about a medium distracts us from how much that medium shares features with others. In fact, media frequently achieve their identities in part by combining elements of other media that have complementary features, such as the use of music in a film, or newsprint in a collage painting.

Recently, there has been a growing interest in this mixture under the category of multimodality, which focuses on the way that communicational structures can invoke different senses (hearing, sight, touch) using different semiotic channels (text, image, audio recording, video). Analysis of sensory modalities has its roots in cognitive science and has been applied most extensively in work on interface design and pedagogy (see, for example, Selfe 2007). One limitation of such cognitive approaches to communication, however, is that they generally strip out cultural and material history to construct their models of the fundamental elements of human perception. Maribeth Back frames multimodal text design in such cognitive terms: "Multisensory reading relies on people's ability to collate and decipher multiple sensory streams simultaneously, much as we interpret the world around us through the use of multiple senses. This is more than a simple struggle between perceptual sensitivities, however; we use cultural cues and personal perceptual history as criteria to interpret sensory data" (2003, 161). Because of my desire to retain the history that cognitive theory can leave behind, I would like to resurrect a term that passed out of vogue some time ago, *multimedia*, which emphasizes existing cultural models of the various channels through which we encounter information. Early criticism usually described electronic textuality and digital images as multimedia. Some of the first new media texts that everyday consumers encountered were "multimedia" encyclopedias—published on CD-ROM and included with many new computer purchases in the 1990s. Although *multimedia* has remained a consumer buzzword, the term has fallen out of favor with critics who increasingly emphasize the unique qualities of digital works. The term *multimedia* has, however, two advantages that I want to emphasize in this essay. First, the multimedia work quite clearly combines several forms of already-existing media. In the popular consumer imagination, this usually means that multimedia products add additional layers of content onto a traditional media form. Thus, a book may come with a CD-ROM of music, or a DVD may come with production stills and on-screen games. Critics eager to see new media as an independent aesthetic form bristle at the implication that it has been cobbled together from previous media in the way that the "multimedia" DVD seems to be. And yet, the fact that the new media work comprises many different elements whose relationship can be altered is an obvious part of this medium. In a video game we might decrease graphics resolution to improve performance, on a website we might mute background music to avoid irritating the people around us, and so on.

The other advantage of the term *multimedia* is that it emphasizes that most electronic textuality is encountered through a personal computer or video game console (or, less commonly, through a mobile phone), and that such devices have multiple uses that we are all aware of even when those uses are not actualized by a particular electronic text. For all that new media critics have emphasized the role of interaction and even interface design, the fact that I play *Tetris* (for example) on my computer using keys and mouse buttons that a few minutes ago I was using to type a letter, or that one of the first decisions that a console game designer faces is how players will use the game controller, has virtually been unremarked by critics. This is not completely surprising, since this issue of hardware is the point at which new media criticism's exploration of the ergodic overlaps most uncomfortably with the celebration of consumerism implicit in the announcement of the newest electronic gadget each holiday season. To refer to new media independently of its hardware is, ironically, a mistake that academic critics are much more likely to make than commercial game reviewers—who rarely miss the opportunity to describe how well a particular game exploits the hardware on which it runs, be it the massive storage of the Blu-ray drive in Sony's Playstation 3 or the motion sensing of Nintendo's Wii. We can contrast our experience of new media with that of older media like film or print. Although I may have seen other films in a local theater, I am rarely aware of that space as having been put to different uses. Likewise, although I may notice the qualities of a printed book—a fuzzy or beautiful font, smeary or durable pages—books rarely call to mind other uses to which its components can be put.

New media, then, is multimedia both because it combines media with different sources whose relationship is manipulable, and because these media objects depend on the computer or game console through which we encounter them. The term *multimedia*, I will argue, offers a productive model for understanding the complex and overlapping relationships between media that make up the digital work.

Methods for Multimedia Positioning

The relationship between different media is an issue relevant to all art forms. The great accomplishment of Wendy Steiner in *The Colors of Rhetoric* is to have reframed discussion of "interartistic comparisons" in terms of rhetoric. In responding to the common definition of poetry as a "speaking picture," Steiner asks the question that critics so often overlook when trying to decide how one form of art differs from another: "Why should one want to think of a picture, on the one hand, as speaking, or of a poem, on the other, as being mute?" (1982, 5). More broadly, we can say that the tendency to associate or differentiate one medium from another is never unmotivated. She gives a more specific example a few pages earlier: "Literature is so often compared to painting, I believe, because painting has stood as the paradigmatic 'mirror of reality'; the 'sister arts' analogy thus permits literature as well to be considered an icon of reality rather than a mere conventional means of referring to it. The need to discover the mimetic potential in literature has been the underlying motivation for the long history of critical comparisons of the two arts. When the motivation disappears, as it did largely during the romantic period, so does the comparison" (Steiner 1982, 1–2).

Although some comparisons between arts and media are more common (writing and painting, writing and music) than others (music and film), these comparisons always reflect rhetorical goals. For this reason, I think, the claim that electronic narrative is "multimedia" cannot simply be a neutral description of qualities of the medium. Instead, the very idea of multimedia—which implies independent and equally valued media forms cooperating in a single work—is itself a rhetorical act that intervenes significantly into the whole history of interartistic comparisons.

Comparisons between the arts can emphasize either similarities or dissimilarities. The classic example of interartistic comparisons designed to differentiate media is Lessing's *Laocoön*. Lessing offers his distinction between temporal arts (writing and music) and spatial arts (painting and sculpture) as an attempt to get at "first principles": "if it is true that in its imitations painting uses completely different means or signs than does poetry, namely figures and colors in space rather than articulated sounds in time, and if these signs must indisputably bear a suitable relation to the thing signified, then signs existing in space can express only objects whose wholes or parts coexist while signs that follow one another can express only objects whose wholes or parts are consecutive" (Lessing 1984, 78). As an example of interartistic comparisons that emphasize the similarities between arts, we might think, for example of the late nineteenth-century interest in synesthesia as an artistic principle. Here is Charles Baudelaire's well-known poem "Correspondences," which exemplifies this principle:

Nature is a temple, where the living
Columns sometimes breathe confusing speech;
Man walks within these groves of symbols, each
Of which regards him as a kindred thing.

As the long echoes, shadowy, profound,
Heard from afar, blend in a unity,
Vast as the night, as sunlight's clarity,
So perfumes, colours, sounds may correspond.
(Baudelaire 1993, 19)

Baudelaire is drawing broadly on the romantic tradition that celebrates the associative power of the mind, which Steiner has already suggested is a point at which literary history breaks from the tradition of interartistic contrasts. Similar claims about the fundamental unity of the senses and thus of artistic media are a common feature of late nineteenth- and early twentieth-century art theory. Richard Wagner's manifesto "The Art-Work of the Future" claims that "Not one rich faculty of the separate arts will remain unused in the United Artwork of the Future; in *it* will each attain its first complete appraisement" (1993, 190). A few years later Wassily Kandinsky makes a similar point in *Concerning the Spiritual in Art*, which sees a coming fusion of the arts as a way to overcome the materialism of modern life: "In each manifestation is the seed of a striving towards the abstract, the non-material. Consciously or unconsciously they are obeying Socrates' command—Know thyself. Consciously or unconsciously artists are studying and proving their material, setting in the balance the spiritual value of those elements, with which it is their several privilege to work. And the natural result of this striving is that the various arts are drawing together" (2006, 40–41).

All these theories correlate artistic forms in terms of a fundamental and positive shared quality. However, it is also possible to emphasize the similarities between media in negative terms as well. This is the case in Dick

Higgins's well-known essay "Intermedia," which celebrates the breakdown of traditional art categories: "Much of the best work being produced today seems to fall between media. This is no accident. The concept of the separation between media arose in the Renaissance. The idea that a painting is made of paint on canvas or that a sculpture should not be painted seems characteristic of the kind of social thought—categorizing and dividing society into nobility with its various subdivisions, untitled gentry, artisans, serfs and landless workers—which we call the feudal conception of the Great Chain of Being" (Higgins 1978, 12).

According to Higgins, art categories blind us to the rich particularity of the work. Higgins is offering an interartistic synthesis but in very different terms than Baudelaire, Wagner, or Kandinsky do. Where these latter artists see various artistic media as united by a shared ability to represent different aspects of a whole social, psychological, and spiritual life, Higgins sees artistic media as united by their shared resistance to any institutional categorization. Rather than articulate a positive principle that every art form contributes to, Higgins instead describes a critical flaw that all art forms resist.

Positioning in the Multimedia Work

If my typology of media positioning is accurate, then, critics and artists seem to be faced with a relatively fixed set of choices in describing the relation between different artistic media (synthesis or difference on positive or negative grounds); that relation in turn will reflect cultural, institutional, and aesthetic goals.

Current "multimedia" websites generally depend on the differentiation of media and offer one medium as primary, to be supplemented by others. Many news websites, such as those associated with the *New York Times* (which describes itself as providing "Breaking News, World News & Multimedia") and CNN, are primarily textual but include sidebars with links to "multimedia" sections where additional photographs, video, or charts are stored. Here, text is taken to be the primary medium, and other media are defined as less essential resources. Even a website organized around a medium other than print depends on differentiation between media. YouTube, for example, is essentially a text page whose links then launch flash videos and provide a space for textual commentary from fans and critics. Here the difference between a video clip and its textual commentary is less a matter of supplementarity; the textual commentary that frames the clips is a much more essential element of the experience of the video. And even when this textual framework is hidden by the website, images will be sorted and categorized by textual "metadata" attached to each image file, providing information like its author, date, filename, and subject matter. Nonetheless, the difference between these media is what matters: it is only through text that these clips are sorted to be searched out, and it is only through such sorting that popular clips can be recognized and disseminated.

The rhetorical work of balancing media is evident in video games as well. Although most critics have focused on user interaction with these texts in terms of the player's ability to influence the outcome of the game and create (or resist) a feeling of immersion, I would suggest that at least as important is the way that users are able to modify the interface itself. In the case of 3D computer games, this modification is frequently necessary in order to achieve the right balance between graphics quality and smooth game functioning. But in nearly every case, players are given the ability to modify the way that they interact with the game. This can include "mapping" a command from one key to another to reflect personal playing style, showing subtitles for the spoken dialogue, or adjusting sound volumes so that background music is either a major part of the game or inaudible. In many games, this level of personalization treats the work as a kind of palimpsest of different media forms. For example, each year's edition of the wildly popular NFL football simulation program *Madden* comes with a new set of songs that provides the background music for the game. The announcement of who has been chosen to have their music on that year's *Madden* is a noteworthy event within the game community. Once published, the game in turn allows players to select some songs for play and to exclude others. This element of the *Madden* franchise is an excellent example of the way that a game includes a medium (music) that remains a relatively independent element of the playing experience.

In part, the ability to manipulate the relationship between media in such games simply reflects the general fact that digital media comprises objects with independent layers. One of the characteristics that Lev Manovich attributes to new media objects is "variability": "Old media involved a human creator who manually assembled textual, visual, and/or audio elements into a particular composition or sequence. This sequence was stored in some material, its order determined once and for all." In contrast, new media is characterized by variability: "Instead of identical copies, a new media object typically gives rise to many different versions. And rather than being created completely by a human author, these versions are often in part automatically assembled by a computer" (Manovich 2001, 36). Manovich's definition is flexible and powerful, and it very helpfully captures the difference between a digitally produced new media image and a superficially similar traditional photograph. I want to emphasize, however, that this variability extends to the interface through which we encounter these objects. In particular, my approach here leads to a way to read the rhetorical work that goes into defining the relationship between media in a particular text.

In a way, my focus on the rhetorical construction of media relations in these works simply emphasizes something that has already been implied by Bolter and Grusin's influential book *Remediation*. By *remediation* Bolter and Grusin mean "the representation of one medium in another" (1999, 45), and offer a broad application: "*all* mediation is remediation. . . . Our culture conceives of each medium or constellation of media as it responds to, redeploys, competes with, and reforms other media" (1999, 55). My return to the term *multimedia* is designed to emphasize the rhetorical construction of these "constellations," and to insist that this process is not just a broad condition of the contemporary "new media ecology" but also a quality that defines the success of individual works as they appear in the electronic medium. Espen Aarseth makes a relevant observation when he criticizes the idea that the computer is a new medium: "It cannot be repeated often enough that the computer is not a medium, but a flexible material technology that will accommodate many very different media. Hence, there is no 'computer medium' with one set of fixed capabilities, not [sic] is there 'the medium of the computer game'" (2004, 46). Aarseth wants to suggest that the category of *computer game* is less valuable than that of *game*, but I think he is missing an opportunity to consider the way that this mixture of media constitutes the forms of electronic textuality encountered through the computer. The multimedia experience of the computer, mobile phone, or game console is a sharp break from the more implicitly remediated nature of film and writing, because such multimedia devices make the relation between media a fundamental part of our interaction with the work.

The Example of *Lexia to Perplexia*

Let me explain what attention to media positioning might mean for how we read electronic texts by turning to a well-known work: Talan Memmott's *Lexia to Perplexia* (2000). First-time readers of *Lexia* are likely to be struck by the way that this work challenges our common interaction with the electronic screen. In particular, Memmott blurs the line between text and image on the screen, using both at different times as a trigger to alter the page. Memmott also changes the way that screen space responds to these triggers. Where most electronic works use links to load an entirely new page or to change the content of a section of the page, *Lexia* frequently overlaps new text and images onto existing images and text on the page. Indeed, it is not difficult to make the page unreadable with these different layers, and savvy readers of the work need to navigate to the same page several times in order to view all of the information on it before the layering of the text and images makes the page unreadable. In general, the effect is to emphasize the temporality of our navigation of these pages by making our choices on the page leave traces behind. Katherine Hayles claims that the work "hovers at the border of legibility, it hints that our bodies are also undergoing metamorphoses. What we read when we cannot read is not so much the disjunction between us and the computer (for it is always possible to access the underlying code and hack our way into a readable version of the nonreadable text). Rather, the occluded display signifies a trajectory in which we become part of a cybernetic circuit" (2004a, 293).

In terms of design, the major decision that Memmott appears to have made is to conflate text and image. Frequently, fonts are expanded to such a large size that they become visual elements in their own right. Likewise, small images become shorthand icons for ideas that might also be expressed textually, as for example, the way that Memmott uses the computer terminal in the screenshot shown in figure 1.

In this regard, it is no surprise that hieroglyphics emerge as an element of this work, since they embody this blurring between image and text. Likewise, large blocks of text placed onto the page often have as much a visual as discursive impact. The blurring of the line between text and image influences the way that space is imagined in *Lexia to Perplexia* as

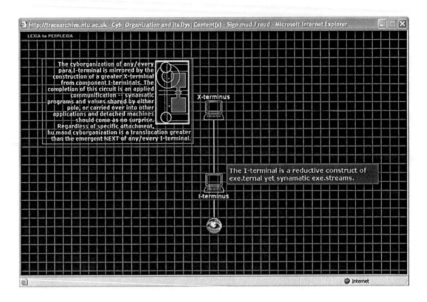

The cyborganization of any/every para,I-terminal is mirrored by the construction of a greater X-terminal from component I-terminals. The completion of this circuit is an applied communification -- synamatic programs and values shared by either pole, or carried over into other applications and detached machines -- should come as no surprise. Regardless of specific attachment, hu.mand cyborganization is a translocation greater than the emergent NEXT of any/every I-terminal.

X-terminus

The I-terminal is a reductive construct of exe.ternal yet synamatic exe.streams.

I-terminus

Internet

1. Screenshot from *Lexia to Perplexia*. Created by Talan Memmott.

well. The principal model for space is that of the diagram, which depends on the duality of the space. Although these spaces are abstract and conventional, the visual patterns described there have an iconic relevance to their subject matter. In other words, diagrams are both text and image.

This tension between text and image reflects ambiguities within our experience of the space of the computer screen. Like the television screen, this space is in some ways purely visual, but we understand that the *computer* screen is a metaphor as well as an image; the computer "desktop" is neither a real desktop, nor even a picture of a real desktop. Our experience of this computer space depends on negotiating the line between these two very different media—text and image. Indeed, the classic Apple desktop toolbar, which mixes words like *file* and *edit* with the visual icon , embodies this, as does the mixture of "folder" icons with labels (as well, at times, as visual "thumbnails" of the contents of the folder). This tension between text and image is always implicit within our experience of the multipurpose computer interface.

It seems to me that Memmott's work does not leave behind these older media categories to invent a new idiom but instead carefully works to develop a "multimedia" aesthetic. Our interaction with the text—

the way that information on the screen is both link and visual design—captures that balance between the two media. This is why, I think, Memmott rightly passes on the opportunity to integrate other media into this work. *Lexia* is concerned with themes of echoing, and the Greek nymph Echo is specifically mentioned in the story; it would have been an easy aesthetic choice to simply reflect this issue by creating echolike sounds in the work. And yet, Memmott rightly understands that the real tension in his work is not between the visual and the aural but between the medium of text and the medium of image.

Multimedia Narratology

I hope that my brief discussion of *Lexia to Perplexia* suggests the interpretive advantages of returning to the term *multimedia* and, in particular, of considering the way that electronic narratives are situated within the relations between many different media. This is, of course, a departure from the way that the multiple elements of electronic texts are usually studied. Most often, when critics refer to the multiplicities within the electronic text, they mean the way that a single program can manifest many different user events—what Aarseth captures in the distinction between *scripton* and *texton* (1997, 62), or what Hayles describes as the difference between "storage and delivery vehicles" (2003, 274). The media multiplicity that I have been describing instead defines the work's relation to its larger aesthetic, institutional, and cultural context.

Thus far I have addressed the overall design of the electronic text more than the way that it constructs narrative, but I would like to close by suggesting how such media positioning contributes to the relation between narrative and interactivity. The issue of whether an electronic text *is* narrative is of course vexed. As Jesper Juul (2005, 159–60) has rightly noted, the interactive structure of electronic texts in general and video games in particular makes it difficult to stage the distinction between story and discourse upon which our traditional understanding of narrativity is based. Eskelinen makes this point as well: "In games, the dominant temporal relation is the one between user time and event time and not the narrative one between story time and discourse time" (2004, 37). Nonetheless, only the most abstract games forego narrative appeals entirely. In this regard, we can follow Marie-Laure Ryan (2006, 7) and suggest that it is more accurate to speak of the *degree* of narrativity in a work. Such a shift seems to be occurring throughout the study of new media narrative. Henry Jenkins observes that "many games *do* have narrative aspirations. Minimally, they want to tap the emotional residue of previous narrative experiences" (2004, 119). Jenkins offers this observation as part of an explanation for "spatial stories," in which players participate in spaces that are drawn from narratives and animated by these "previous narrative experiences." Among Jenkins's primary examples are games based on *Star Wars*: "The *Star Wars* game may not simply retell the story of *Star Wars*, but it doesn't have to in order to enrich or expand our experience of the *Star Wars* saga. We already know the story before we even buy the game and would be frustrated if all it offered us was a regurgitation of the original film experience. Rather, the *Star Wars* game exists in dialogue with the films, conveying new narrative experiences through its creative manipulation of environmental details" (2004, 124). The narrativity of our experience in these spaces may thus not be so much a matter of a specific story that we string together through *our* actions but rather of stories glimpsed through spaces and objects familiar from film and print narratives. Juul, who has disagreed with Jenkins on his reading of the *Star Wars* games, nonetheless suggests something of this same structure himself when he notes, "one of the more interesting developments in recent years is that game designers have become better at creating games where objects *in* the game world point to past events. Modern adventure games tend to contain not only cut scenes but also artifacts in the game world (fictional time) that tell the player what happened at a previous point in fictional time" (2005, 148).

Jenkins seems to me to have pointed to the way that a large number of the most popular and best-known games introduce narrativity and at the same time to have recognized that this narrativity is a fundamental part of most players' pleasure with these texts. This hybrid textual object, in which play is coupled to narrative experiences drawn from other media, also happens to reflect the way that I have characterized the electronic text as multimedia. Indeed, many of the effects that Jenkins describes as part of "environmental storytelling" depend on media references. One of the striking things about every *Star Wars* game made in the last ten years—to take Jenkins's example—is the way that media elements have been imported directly from the films into the game. This includes the well-known music of John Williams, as well as familiar sounds of the "light saber" or laser "blasters." These elements are not simply imitations of the original sounds; they are the *same* sounds in that they have been produced from the same musical and special-effects sources. This aural framework is essential for being able to evoke the narrative experiences from the films. In this regard, the film score is much like the narrative objects that Juul describes; although it does not point to specific events in the past, it certainly evokes familiar narrative contexts. The role of these media elements is especially striking in the recent LEGO *Star Wars*, a very popular 3D game that retells the *Star Wars* film story using characters and environments built out of LEGO blocks. Visually, this game creates comic distance between the serious narrative of the films and the playful gameplay, where dying means exploding into a shower of LEGO blocks, and where players can create new characters by recombining the heads, bodies, and feet of characters from the films. However, the sounds and music of the game are not stylized at all but are identical to the films and to those 3D games that strive for realism. We could say that our visual interaction with these narrative environments is made possible by aural references, which suture us to the more serious narrative context for gameplay.

This rhetorical structure of sound and image is, of course, only one possible formulation. Consider the role of writing in *Myst* and its sequels. In contrast to the puzzles and exploration that make up the player's actions, the backstory in this game is conveyed in books that the player literally reads onscreen. Set side by side, these two media elements—writing in *Myst* and music in *Star Wars*—share the seemingly incidental quality of being imported more than imitated in the game. If we close our eyes we are actually listening to the music from *Star Wars*, and when we open a book in the *Myst* game we are simply reading in much the same way we might read any text—indeed, these books could just as easily have been actual texts scanned into a database like Google Books. These media elements help to set up the contrast between play and narrative, in which play is an imaged space invented within the game, and narrative is imported from elsewhere. These works depend for their whole design on the balance between what we could call *referential* and *play* media. Games can invoke this referential "other" medium even when that original medium is not itself prior to the environment in which play occurs. In the popular and highly narrative space-combat game *Homeworld*, for example, the cut scenes that provide the background for the story are rendered as rough pencil-sketches. In light of my discussion of *Myst* and LEGO *Star Wars*, we can see these drawings as a way of placing the backstory for the narrative beyond the scope of gameplay, making it faux-referential to an imported medium.

The balance between different media in games, then, will help to structure the interaction between narrative/referential and play elements. Of course, the balance between play and referential media will frequently be more complex. The recent *Madden* football games, for example, import not only music but player voices, statistics, and even scanned faces to provide on-the-field avatars; the balance between play and referential media will clearly be much more complex in this case. Nonetheless, I hope to have shown that the multimedia sources of these references form an important part of the construction of narrative in these texts. Eskelinen has rightly suggested that instead of distinguishing actions and happenings—as traditional narratology does—"games can be differentiated from each other on the basis of which events can or cannot be manipulated" (2004, 40). We can push this a step further and suggest that this balance between active and passive game elements will be entwined with the several media that make up the game. Aarseth comments again on this example: "While, as Jesper Juul has pointed out, the story of *Star Wars* is unextractable from the game of the same name, the setting, atmosphere and characters can be deduced. So, although nonnarrative and nonludic elements can be translated, the key elements, the narration and gameplay, like oil and water, are not easily mixed" (2004, 50–51). I have suggested that this combination of "unmixable" elements of the game text depends on the balance of the media from which they are drawn, and that one or another medium can be used to stand for narrative and ludic elements.

No doubt contributors to this volume will be quick to admit that we are only beginning to understand the nature of narrative and nonnarrative elements within the new media work. I hope to have shown that while rigorous narratological terms can help to clarify these texts, we should also not forget that the environment in which we encounter these works is first and foremost a multimedia space, and that the rhetorical work that goes into defining the relation between those media will in turn shape the way that such texts can tell a story.

References

Aarseth, Espen. 1997. *Cybertext: Perspectives on Ergodic Literature*. Baltimore: Johns Hopkins University Press.

———. 2004. "Genre Trouble: Narrativism and the Art of Simulation." In *First Person: New Media as Story, Performance, and Game*, ed. Noah Wardrip-Fruin and Pat Harrigan, 45–55. Cambridge MA: MIT Press.

Back, Maribeth. 2003. "The Reading Senses: Designing Texts for Multisensory Systems." In *Digital Media Revisited: Theoretical and Conceptual Innovation in Digital Domains*, ed. Gunnar Liestøl, Andrew Morrison, and Terje Rasmussen, 157–82. Cambridge MA: MIT Press.

Baudelaire, Charles. 1993. *The Flowers of Evil*. Trans. James McGowan. Oxford: Oxford University Press.

Bolter, Jay David, and Richard Grusin. 1999. *Remediation: Understanding New Media*. Cambridge MA: MIT Press.

Eskelinen, Markku. 2001. "Cybertext Theory: What an English Professor Should Know before Trying." Available at http://www.electronicbookreview.com/turead/electropoetics/notmetaphor (accessed January 19, 2010).

———. 2004. "Towards Computer Game Studies." In *First Person*, ed. Noah Wardrip-Fruin and Pat Harrigan, 36–44. Cambridge MA: MIT Press.

Hayles, N. Katherine. 2003. "Translating Media: Why We Should Rethink Textuality." *Yale Journal of Criticism* 16, no. 2:263–90.

———. 2004a. "Metaphoric Networks in *Lexia to Perplexia*." In First Person, ed. Noah Wardrip-Fruin and Pat Harrigan, 291–301. Cambridge MA: MIT Press.

———. 2004b. "Print Is Flat, Code Is Deep: The Importance of Media-Specific Analysis." *Poetics Today* 25, no. 1:67–90.

Higgins, Dick. 1978. *A Dialectic of Centuries: Notes towards a Theory of the New Arts*. New York: Printed Editions.

Jenkins, Henry. 2004. "Game Design as Narrative Architecture." In *First Person*, ed. Noah Wardrip-Fruin and Pat Harrigan, 118–30. Cambridge MA: MIT Press.

Juul, Jesper. 2005. *Half-Real: Video Games between Real Rules and Fictional Worlds*. Cambridge MA: MIT Press.

Kandinsky, Wassily. 2006. *Concerning the Spiritual in Art*. Trans. Michael T. H. Sadler. Boston: MFA Publications.

Lessing, Gotthold Ephraim. 1984. *Laocoön: An Essay on the Limits of Painting and Poetry*. Trans. Edward Allen McCormick. Baltimore: Johns Hopkins University Press.

Manovich, Lev. 2001. *The Language of New Media*. Cambridge MA: MIT Press.

Memmott, Talan. 2000. *Lexia to Perplexia*. Available at http://www.uiowa.edu/~iareview/tirweb/hypermedia/talan_memmott/ (accessed January 18, 2011).

Ryan, Marie-Laure. 2004. Introduction to *Narrative across Media: The Languages of Storytelling*, ed. Marie-Laure Ryan, 1–40. Lincoln: University of Nebraska Press.

———. 2006. *Avatars of Story*. Minneapolis: University of Minnesota Press.

Selfe, Cynthia L. 2007. *Multimodal Composition: Resources for Teachers*. Cresskill NJ: Hampton Press.

Steiner, Wendy. 1982. *The Colors of Rhetoric: Problems in the Relation between Modern Literature and Painting*. Chicago: University of Chicago Press.

Wagner, Richard. 1993. *The Art-Work of the Future and Other Works*. Trans. William Ashton Ellis. Lincoln: University of Nebraska Press.

2 The Interactive Onion

*Layers of User Participation
in Digital Narrative Texts*

MARIE-LAURE RYAN

Of all the properties of new media, interactivity is widely recognized as the one that marks the most significant difference from old media—think of movies versus computer games, drama versus Internet chat, and print novels versus hypertext fiction—but it is also the most difficult to define. Espen Aarseth (1997) finds the concept of interactivity too vague and wants to replace it with ergodism, while Janet Murray (1997) prefers agency. But as useful as the ideas of ergodism and agency are to the study of new media, they do not capture the same range of phenomena as interactivity. If we regard communication between intelligent agents as the prototypical form of interactivity, then neither ergodism nor agency will express its fundamentally dialogical nature. We can exercise agency by playing with a doll or a toy truck, and we can unfold many different sequences of signs out of an ergodic print text, but this does not make the toys or the print text interactive, because they lack the ability to modify themselves dynamically. Digital texts, by contrast, are operated by a program that reacts to the actions of the user by executing certain modules of code, thereby altering the global state of the computer, just as the behavior of the computer alters the global state of the mind of the user. A genuinely interactive system involves not only choice—dolls, toy trucks, and ergodic print texts also lend themselves to multiple uses—but also a two-sided effort that creates a feedback loop. The two sides can be two human minds, as in conversation or oral storytelling; they can be, more metaphorically, an agent and the world as a whole, because the world "kicks back" when the agent performs an action; or they can be a human and a programmable machine, because such a machine can simulate a mind or a dynamic environment.

Can this dialogue between mind and machine be put in the service of storytelling, the most powerful and the most widely distributed form of entertainment and information transmission? It all depends on whom you ask. In the years 2003 and 2004, four books were published on the topic of interactive narrative. Two of them—by Carolyn Handler Miller (2004) and Mark Meadows (2003)—regard the existence of interactive narratives as an indisputable fact. To make their case they boast about the existence, both on the Internet and elsewhere, of a wide variety of interactive texts that involve a story. For instance: computer games, interactive TV, interactive movies, smart toys (like talking dolls), augmented reality gaming, interactive cartoons, hypertext fiction, interactive fiction, websites devoted to history, people putting together digital autobiographies or family histories that combine pictures and text, even news stories on Google and CNN that let the user click and choose between audio, visual, and written documents pertaining to the story. Since interactive narrative is everywhere, Miller and Meadows do not regard the combination of narrativity and interactivity as a problem at all, and their books limit themselves to descriptions of projects, interviews with developers, and rather superficial advice on how to improve the design of digital stories.

Another author, Andrew Glassner (2004), believes that the purpose of interactive narrative is to be entertaining, and he finds that the only type of product that truly fulfills this goal is computer games. Hypertext, by contrast, only kills the narrative pleasure that we find in novels and movies. Glassner recognizes that there is ample room for improving game stories, but he concludes his book on an optimistic note: "One of the pleasures of thinking about story environments is that everything is still open: we haven't even begun to scratch the surface of what's possible" (2004, 469).

The fourth author, Chris Crawford, is much more pessimistic about both the past and the future. He claims that to date, "not a single interactive storyworld that commands wide respect has been created" (2003, 259) and he complains that game designers generally treat narrative as "just another tacked-on feature," like animation, sound effects, and music, instead of forming the defining aspect of games (2004, 69). After a successful career as a computer game designer, Crawford became dejected with the triteness and lack of variety of the stories found in computer games. He retired from the game business and has devoted the past thirteen years to designing a computer program, the Storytron, whose purpose is to generate interactive stories. But the Storytron is still in the development stage and has yet to produce a single *regular* story that meets Crawford's criteria of narrative excellence, much less an interactive one.

Who is right? The optimists or the pessimists? It all depends on what we mean by "interactive story." In this chapter, I would like to argue that digital texts are like an onion made of different layers of skin, and that interactivity can affect different levels. Those who regard the existence of interactive stories as a fait accompli are satisfied with an interactivity that operates on the outer layers; those who regard interactive stories as "an elusive unicorn we can imagine but have yet to capture," to quote Brenda Laurel (2001, 72), want interactivity to penetrate the core of the story. In the outer layers, interactivity concerns the presentation of the story, and the story exists prior to the running of the software; in the middle layers, interactivity concerns the user's personal involvement in the story, but the plot is still predetermined; in the inner layers, the story is created dynamically through the interaction between the user and the system. Here I propose to peel the interactive onion, by discussing texts that illustrate four different layers of interactivity (plus a fifth one that is not really a skin of the onion), all the way to the still resistant core.

Level 1: Peripheral Interactivity

Here the story is framed by an interactive interface, but this interactivity affects neither the story itself, nor the order of its presentation. I will discuss two variations on this idea.

My first example is the poem *Cruising*, by Ingrid Ankerson and Megan Sapnar (2001; figure 2). The "story" of the poem is a memory of growing up in a small Wisconsin town. It is not a fully fledged narrative, because it describes a somewhat repetitive action, and it does not reach any kind of narrative closure. But the reader can relate emotionally to the characters, and the setting sparks the imagination of anybody familiar with small towns in the Midwest. The user's action consists of controlling the display. By moving the cursor, the reader can make the text and its graphic background grow or shrink, move left or move right, and move at different speeds. The goal is to get a combination of size, speed, and direction that allows the text to be deciphered; most of the time, the letters are too small, and they move too fast for the eye to make out

2. Screenshots from *Cruising*. Created by Megan Sapnar.

the words. The user's control of the speed and direction simulates the driving of a car; and indeed, driving a car is what the text is all about. This creates a nice unity, not only of form and content but also of interface. But no matter how fast or slow the car moves, no matter whether it goes forward or backward, it is the same text that rolls before the reader's eyes. Sometimes we can read it, sometimes we cannot, but we cannot stop it, we cannot skip any of its parts, and we cannot change its internal order.

Viewing the text is turned into an even more challenging operation in my next example of interactive interface, *Marginal Effects* by Stuart

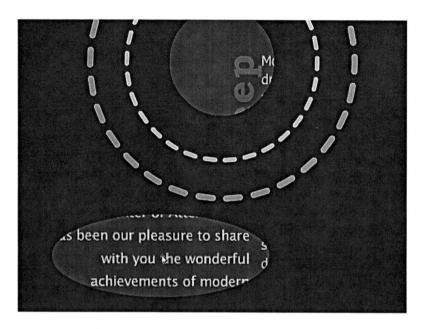

been our pleasure to share

with you the wonderful

achievements of modern

3. Screenshot from *Marginal Effects*. Created by Stuart Moulthrop.

Moulthrop (2005; figure 3). The text consists of a collage of story fragments that seem to be cut out from newspaper columns—an obvious allu-
sion to the cutout technique of William Burroughs. But the text is hidden
by an opaque cover. A hole in this cover travels on the screen, revealing
parts of the stories but without allowing the user to read them, because
it moves too fast and too randomly. The interactivity of the text depends
on a second hole whose movement can be fully controlled. By walking
this hole slowly over the screen, the user will be able to choose which
part of the hidden text to expose, and by moving it from left to right over
a fragment, she will be able to read it. When the controllable hole passes
over a certain hot spot, the page is replaced by another, but since the user
does not know where the hot spot is located, she has only indirect control over this event. Sometimes the text is instantly replaced, before the
user can read anything, sometimes it stubbornly refuses to give way to
the next page. The effect is like reading a book with a magnifying glass,
except that in this case the user is not free to turn the pages. In contrast to
Cruising, however, there is no obvious relation between the user's activity
and the particular themes of the text (mostly humorous and sexual), and I

cannot think of any other purpose for the interface than to bring attention to the reading process itself by de-automatizing the scanning of the text by the eye.

Level 2: Interactivity Affecting Narrative
Discourse and the Presentation of the Story

On this level, the materials that constitute the story are still fully predetermined, but thanks to the text's interactive mechanisms, their presentation to the user is highly variable. Narratologists would say that interactivity operates here on the level of narrative discourse, as opposed to the level of story. This form of interactivity requires what is known as a hypertextual structure: a collection of documents interconnected by digital links, so that, when the user selects a link, a new document comes to the screen. But the narrative forms of hypertext can rely on different configurations of links and nodes that embody different philosophies. Here I will discuss two of these philosophies and the designs that implement them.

My first type of design philosophy produces what Lev Manovich would call a database story. Actually, Manovich believes that "narrative and database are mortal enemies" (2001, 225), because narrative involves an implicit order dictated by chronology and causality, while a database is a collection of documents that can be consulted by the user in any order. But if the database is properly structured, and if its subject matter is appropriate, the free probes of the users and their always incomplete exploration will not prevent the retrieval of narrative meaning. Consider for instance the large website devoted to the Lewis and Clark expedition. The story of Lewis and Clark is known, in its broad outlines, to most users, and there is no need to follow it in chronological order. We can, for instance, read the diary entry that relates to the discovery of the Columbia River in Oregon before we read about the crossing of Montana. As the chronicle of an expedition, the story of Lewis and Clark is neatly divided into episodes that relate to the various stages of the journey. Thanks to this modular character, the reader can bring a magnifying glass to certain parts of the story without losing sight of the whole. The website is structured like a sea anemone (figure 4A) that allows the reader to retrieve more and more documents and to dig deeper and deeper into the database. With each of these probes the storyworld expands and reveals more stories, as the reader's attention shifts from the main characters to

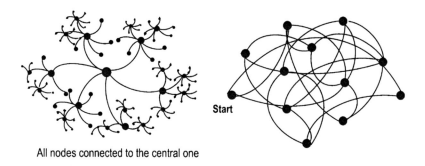

All nodes connected to the central one

A: Sea-anemone   **B: Network**

4. Structures for hypertext. Created by Marie-Laure Ryan.

the secondary characters, who then become main characters surrounded by their own casts of secondary characters, in a potentially infinite regression. But if we feel that we have strayed too far from the center, we can always return to the main menu with one click and reconnect with the diary of the expedition. With this type of interactivity, users are able to move freely around the story and to customize it to their own interests.

My second example of discourse-level interactivity is classical hypertext fiction, by this I mean a text based on a network or maze structure that looks like figure 4B. The best examples of this structure are the hypertexts produced in the early 1990s with the program Storyspace, for instance *afternoon* by Michael Joyce or *Victory Garden* by Stuart Moulthrop. (By contrast, more recent hypertexts, such as Shelley Jackson's *Patchwork Girl* and M. D. Coverley's *Califia*, have been influenced by the idea of the searchable archive, and they adopt the radiating design of the sea anemone, at least on the top level.) The formal characteristic of the network structure is the existence of loops that offer several different ways to get to the same node. These loops make it possible to circle forever within the network. This explains why the image of the labyrinth and J. Yellowlees Douglas's (2000) notion of "books without end" play such an important role in hypertext theory. To reinforce the reader's experience of being lost in a labyrinth, classical hypertext favors opaque links, which lead to random selection and blind navigation. In Michael Joyce's *afternoon* (1987), links are not visible at all.[1] In other texts, they are signaled by underlined words, but in contrast to the links of a database, the words themselves have no evident informational value, and the relation between the words that anchor the links and the text that comes to the screen is treated as a puzzle to be solved by the reader. Hypertext aesthetics favor the serendipitous emergence of meaning over a goal-oriented, deliberate retrieval of information. But is it possible to respect narrative logic under these conditions?

Early theorists like George Landow (1997) and Michael Joyce thought so. They claimed that hypertext is a storytelling machine that generates a different narrative with every run of the program. As Joyce put it, "every reading . . . becomes a new text. . . . Hypertext narratives become virtual storytellers" (1995, 193). Since there are an infinite number of different paths through a network, this means that hypertext can produce an infinite number of stories. For this to happen, the order in which the reader encounters the lexias would have to correspond rigidly to the chronological order of the events narrated in the lexias; for if the reader could mentally rearrange the lexias, different paths through the network could be read as the same story. Consider, for instance, a hypertext made of three text nodes that lets you visit every node only once, so that it will stop after all the nodes have been displayed:

Title (with links to 1, 2 and 3)
1. Mary marries Joseph (links to 2 and 3)
2. Mary loses her virginity (links to 1 and 3)
3. Mary has a baby (links to 1 and 2)

If the order in which you read events stands for their order in the story-world, this system yields six different stories. For instance, you could have an extension of the biblical story (3-1-2), or a perfectly bourgeois story (1-2-3) or the story of a shotgun wedding (2-1-3). But if you read in the order 3-1-2, and you decide that 3 is a flash forward, then 3-1-2 and 1-2-3 will tell the same story.

Now imagine that the system lets you loop around the network and revisit the same node over and over again. Then the sequence of lexias cannot be interpreted as a faithful image of chronological order. Consider the lexia in Joyce's *afternoon* where the narrator witnesses an accident, and fears the victims were his ex-wife and son:

Die?

I felt certain it was them. I recognized her car from that distance, no more than a hundred yards off along the road to the left when she would turn if she were taking him to the Country Day School.

Two men stood near the rear of the grey buick and a woman in a white dress sprawled on the wide lawn before them, two other men crouching near her. Another, smaller body beyond. (1987)

After reading a certain number of other lexias, you may return to this scene a second and perhaps a third time. How are you going to interpret this recurrence? There are, theoretically, four possibilities, though some of them are so contrived that they can be easily dismissed:

1. The narrator has seen two, three, or four similar accidents, depending on how many times the reader returns to the lexia. We are in a world where events strangely repeat themselves.
2. The narrator travels back in time, and sees the same accident over and over again.
3. The narrator is obsessed with the experience of the accident, and the return to the same lexia stands for the replaying of the scene in the narrator's mind. The text represents the narrator's stream of consciousness.
4. Return to the scene of the accident is nothing more than a return to the same chunk of text and has no significance within the storyworld.

The first two interpretations affect the level of story, but they involve a fantastic or science-fictional element that is totally absent from *afternoon*, and this makes them rather silly. The last two interpretations, which I find much more acceptable, involve the level of discourse: the inner discourse of the narrator in 3, and more abstractly, the discourse of the text in 4. In both of these interpretations there is only one accident, and interactivity provides many glimpses at the same scene, rather than creating different sequences of physical events within the storyworld. But interpretation 3 comes closer to affecting the level of story, because it naturalizes the text as the mental activity of a character who exists within the storyworld. In different runs of the text, the narrator's mind will consequently follow different paths and visit different memories. In interpretation 4, by contrast, the textual mechanisms are no longer interpreted mimetically. Interactivity becomes a game of putting a coherent story back together out of fragments that come to the reader in a variable order, like the pieces of a jigsaw puzzle.

For a hypertext to tell a different story every time, without losing narrative coherence, it would have to be organized on a tree structure that prevents loops. Since a tree structure offers only one way to reach a given node, it allows a strict control of the logical relations between lexias. Each branch on the tree can be made to correspond to a different development of events out of a common situation, and interactivity becomes a matter of choice between several predetermined stories. This structure has been implemented in the *Choose Your Own Adventure* children's stories. But since the branches of a tree eventually come to an end, the price to pay for guaranteed narrative coherence is the self-renewing power and the emergent meaning of classical hypertext fiction—for meaning in hypertext does not have to be narrative: relations between lexias can be analogical and lyrical, rather than standing for chronological and causal relations. The tree structure constitutes the easiest way to penetrate to the next layer of the onion, but it is also the least interesting, because the reader (or user) does not get more out of the system than what the author put into it. To take interactivity to the level of story without freezing the narrative content of the text, we need schemes that are more flexible.

Level 3: Interactivity Creating
Variations in a Predefined Story

On this level the user plays the role of a member of the storyworld, and the system grants him some freedom of action, but the purpose of the user's agency is to progress along a fixed storyline, and the system remains in firm control of the narrative trajectory. This type of interactivity is typical of computer games, such as adventure games, shooters, and mystery-solving games.

In the texts discussed so far, participation was external and exploratory: the user does not play the role of a member of the fictional world, and activity is limited to moving around a textual space. Here it is internal, and usually ontological.[2] In internal participation, the user has a body, or avatar, in the fictional world, and the actions available to him represent

Chronology

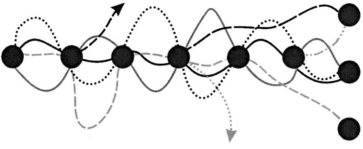

Avatar dies   **Game beaten**

5. Structure of a game with a predefined scenario and several endings.
Created by Marie-Laure Ryan.

a physical engagement of the avatar with the surrounding world, such
as moving, jumping, building, shooting, killing, picking up objects, and
looking around, rather than being abstract ways to see more of the text.
Ontological participation means that the life of the avatar is at stake: every
run of the program creates a new life story for the avatar and a new history for the fictional world.

The dominant narrative structure for ontological participation is the
archetypal story of the quest of the hero, as described by Vladimir Propp
(1968) and Joseph Campbell (1973). In a quest narrative, the hero fulfills
his mission by performing a series of tasks of increasing difficulty. The
game determines the theme of the mission and the sequence of the tasks,
but the player's performance creates variations on this fixed frame. These
variations differ from one another in how the avatar solves problems, in
the success or failure of his quest, and, in the case of failure, in the time
and manner of his death. The different ways to implement the same narrative arc are represented in figure 5. In this diagram, the player's actions
determine several different endings, but all the possibilities are scripted by
the system. To respect narrative logic, this type of structure should only
allow strands to merge when it no longer matters which route the avatar has taken. For instance, the hero may arrive at the dragon's lair with
or without a certain magic aid. This represents a merging of paths in the

physical space of the gameworld but not in the logical space of narrative possibilities, because without the magic aid, the hero cannot defeat the dragon. On a diagram like figure 5, branches can only merge when the actions of the past no longer cast a shadow on the future. Merging points are fresh starts that generally correspond to the various levels of the game.

The formula of layer 3 has been very successful, as the blockbuster sales of video games demonstrate. But the reason for this success may be the fact that game players are not very discriminating when it comes to narrative. Most players do not play for the story but for the adrenaline rush of competition and for the thrill of beating the game, and as long as they get stunning graphics, challenging problems, and their dose of fast action, they are satisfied with the same old storyline clad in different themes and visual motifs. It will take lots of imagination on the part of game designers to make games worth playing for the sake of the story. According to Chris Crawford (2004, 69), the standard practice so far has been to design action schemes and modes of interaction, and to hire a scriptwriter in the later development stages to wrap up the game in a story. The alternative would be to start with a narrative blueprint written by a talented author, and to create opportunities for user interaction within this blueprint, but I doubt that this approach would solve the problem of designing narratively compelling games, because it is not any easier to tack interactivity on a story than to tack a story onto a game. Both elements must be developed concurrently and in relation to each other. For a game to be worth playing out of narrative interest, storyline must grow out of opportunities for interaction, and vice versa, these opportunities must grow naturally out of the story. There is no recipe for achieving this feat.

The easiest way to combine narrative development and interactivity is to present the story by means of noninteractive movie clips known as "cut scenes." Cut scenes introduce into games the narrative power of film, and for many players they constitute a reward for being promoted to a new level, but if the story only moves forward during the cut scenes, the strategic significance of the player's actions is reduced to passing certain roadblocks in order to get more of the story. For the player who truly cares for the story, this necessity to pass tests of often dubious connection to the narrative theme can be exasperating. Crawford (2004, 131) calls this approach a "constipated story," and Steven Poole regards it as frustrating for both lovers of games and lovers of stories, "It is as if you were reading a novel and being forced by some jocund imp at the end of each chapter to go and win a game of table tennis before being allowed to get back to the story. Actually, with some games it's worse than that: it's the other way round. You really want a good exciting game of ping pong, but you have to read a chapter of some crashingly dull science-fantasy blockbuster every time you win a game" (2000, 109).

A more elegant and dynamic way to reveal the story than noninteractive cut scenes is to make the actions of the user contribute directly to the disclosure and development of the plot. This is not easy to do, but a fairly successful technique consists of sending nonplaying characters in the player's way and to have them converse with the player, telling him the backstory of the gameworld, giving advice, or instructing the player of his next task. In these conversations, the character generally uses spoken language, but the player communicates by means of a menu of possible questions to ask. Another "in-game" storytelling strategy consists of scattering documents within the gameworld that give information about its past history, such as books and signs, and have the player pick them up and read them. But this technique should not be overused (as it is in *Myst*), because playing a video game should be centered on user action, and not be turned into reading a novel.

A promising variation on the idea of built-in narrativity is to design what Henry Jenkins (2004) calls a narrative architecture: a rich gameworld brimming with hidden tales. In this architecture, every place would hold a story to be dug up, every object would offer opportunities for playful manipulation, and nonplaying characters would be full of witty gossip. The gameworld would tempt the user to pause, explore, visit roadside attractions, respond to affordances, gather stories, and set up his own goals, rather than being relentlessly driven forward by the desire to beat the game. By giving the user the option of freely exploring the virtual world and of deciding what tasks to perform, games such as *Morrowind* and *Grand Theft Auto* and online virtual worlds such as *EverQuest* take an important step toward implementing this design idea, though they remain dominated by the built-in scheme of progressing toward higher and higher status in the gameworld.

The main problem with current game design is its inability (or is it the unwillingness of developers?) to diversify the repertory of actions available to the player. Games of progression along a fixed script are very similar to one another on the level of the archetypal deep structure (the quest of the hero); reasonably varied on the level of the motifs that concretize the deep structure; but very similar again on the level of what the player can do. For instance, *Doom*, *Harry Potter*, and *Morrowind* create vastly different storyworlds, with different issues at stake, but the actions available to the player come from the same catalog: fighting, moving, dodging attackers, renewing one's health in order to fight more, solving puzzles to gain access to more spaces within the gameworld, and collecting objects to accomplish the various tasks. The similarity of these actions from game to game suggests their lack of deep connection with the narrative themes. Games won't be worth playing for the sake of the story until they introduce possibilities for actions that engage the player in strategic relations with other characters and require a construction of their minds: actions such as asking for help, forming alliances, betraying, deceiving, pursuing, breaking up with, threatening, flattering, seeking revenge, making and breaking promises, violating interdictions, convincing or dissuading.[3] Computer games have been very successful at enacting the fundamentally *solitary* quest of a hero in a world full of danger. But they have yet to tap—with a few exceptions described in the next section—into the mainspring of narrative interest: the evolution of a network of human relations.

Level 4: Real-Time Story Generation

On level 4, stories are not predetermined but rather generated on the fly from data that comes in part from the system and in part from the user. Every run of the program should result in a different story, and the program should therefore be replayable.[4] But to this day, we do not really have a story-generating system sufficiently sophisticated to produce a wide variety of interesting stories out of data internal to the system. Integrating the user's input in the generating process only raises the difficulty to a higher power.

The major obstacle to the development of truly interactive narratives is not technological but logical and artistic. How can the freedom of the user be reconciled with the need to produce a well-formed, aesthetically satisfactory story? VR researchers Ruth Aylett and Sandy Louchart refer to this problem as the "narrative paradox": "On one hand the author seeks control over the direction of a narrative in order to give it a satisfactory structure. On the other hand a participating user demands the autonomy to act and react without explicit authorial constraint" (2004).[5]

Another way to formulate the paradox is in terms of the discrepancy between the goals of authors and the goals of people engaged in living their own lives. This discrepancy is captured by the formula "Life is lived looking forward, but it is told looking backward." When we live our life we ask: what action can I take to solve my problems and reach a more satisfactory state of affairs in the future? But when we tell a story, we start from a situation that we find interesting, and we ask: what course of events led to this situation? Visitors to an interactive narrative system play the role of characters in a virtual world, and they adopt the forward-looking perspective of life. When we are faced with a problem in real life, we want to resolve it as quickly and as efficiently as possible. But the author who creates a story is more interested in actions that produce opportunities for interesting plot developments than in efficient problem solving.

A particularly telling example of the conflict between character goals and authorial goals is the story of *Little Red Riding Hood*. When the hungry wolf meets the little girl in the forest, why doesn't he eat her on the spot, rather than waiting until she reaches the house of the grandmother? He is taking the risk that Little Red Riding Hood will never find the grandmother's house, or that another wolf will eat her in the meantime. But from the perspective of the storyteller, the plan of the wolf is infinitely superior to the practical solution, because it prepares the highly dramatic episode of the wolf tricking the heroine by taking the place of the grandmother in bed and the climactic event of their confrontation. *Little Red Riding Hood* is not a very promising scheme for interactivity of level 4, because the other options that offer themselves to the wolf or to the little girl are vastly inferior in terms of dramatic interest and tellability to the actual tale.[6] The most sophisticated AI and VR technology will not help conquer the inner layer of the onion if designers do not come up with stories that truly benefit from active user participation. Aristotle (1996) wrote the rules for traditional drama in his *Poetics*, but there is to this day no poetics and no set of guidelines for interactive drama.

A story can be generated in two ways: top-down or bottom-up—or more precisely, bottom-along. The top-down direction reflects the perspective of the author, while the bottom-along direction reflects the perspective of the characters. A top-down system would operate a little bit like Chomsky's generative grammar. Chomsky-style grammars are able to generate the syntactic structure of all the sentences in a given language by means of a finite collection of rewrite rules that create a tree-shaped diagram. In a narrative application of the grammar, the top rules may read:

Story = Beginning + Middle + End.
Beginning = Exposition.
Middle = Complication + Crisis.
End = Resolution of crisis + Epilogue.

The product would be a strictly author-controlled Aristotelian plot, though I don't know how we could rewrite the rules that expand "complication," "crisis," and "resolution" to ensure both narrative coherence and narrative diversity. Chomsky-type grammars have been occasionally used for the computer generation of texts, for instance in Jean-Pierre Balpe's novel *Trajectoires*, but these texts are not truly interactive,[7] and they do not offer a great deal of narrative variety, because the rules prescribe the development of the plot very narrowly.

A bottom-up system, by contrast, would start from the detailed description of the initial state of a world and of its characters, specifying their desires, their fears, and their disposition. The database of the system would consist of a very large number of rules made of three components: a set of prerequisites, specifying under which conditions—in which state of the world—the rule can apply; an "action" part, describing what happens in the storyworld when the rule is chosen; and a "consequences" part, which would describe the changes in the world effected by the event that forms the kernel of the rule. The application of a rule would lead to a new state of the storyworld, and another group of rules would become applicable. Figure 6 shows how the rules would be formulated. The system's selection of one of many applicable rules in a given state would generate different sequences of events, and consequently, different stories. Thanks to the prerequisites, the selection of rules would always respect logical coherence. In such a system, the generation and presentation of the story would follow the chronological order of its events and reflect the temporal experience of the characters. It would be, in a full sense, a forward-looking simulation of life.

Rule 1	Rule 2	Rule 3
Preconditions	*Preconditions*	*Preconditions*
x near y	x's love for y>50	y feels harassed by x
(x loves y) OR	x believes y loves x	y's love for x<-5
(x wants to flirt)	*Action*	*Action*
Action	**x proposes marriage**	**y sues x for sexual harassment**
x kisses y	**to y**	*Postconditions*
Postconditions	*Postconditions*	decrease x's love for y by 0
if (y's love for x>0) then	if (y's love for x>50) then	select random number
increase y's love for x by 1	y agrees to marry x	if (random number is odd) then
y is happy	x is happy	x is convicted
x believes y loves x	y is happy	y is happy
if (y's love for x<0) then	if (y's love for x <50) then	if (random number is even) then
decrease y's love for x by 5	y rejects x	x is acquitted
y feels harassed by x	x is unhappy	y is mad

6. Rules for a bottom-up generative system. Created by Marie-Laure Ryan.

This type of system could be made interactive by handing over some decisions to the user. The user and the system could take turns generating events, and the story would be the product of their collaboration. The balance of control could be adjusted by giving more turns to the user or to the system. From a narrative point of view, the main drawback of this approach is its lack of teleology. Since both the system and the user produce events in response to the current state, the storyworld will evolve somewhat randomly, rather than striving toward a global narrative pattern.

A compromise between top-down and bottom-up (or rather, bottom-along) generation could be achieved by making the system consult global templates before deciding which rule to implement. The template could, for instance, tell the system that after a certain number of events it is time to introduce some surprise, or to conclude the story. The system would then have to evaluate each rule with respect to two criteria: how well it fits with respect to the current situation; and how well it satisfies the top-down requirements. This is much easier said than done because it doubles the task of the system. Imagine, for instance, that our top-down template tells the system: now generate a surprising action or a sudden turn of events. We cannot tag the rules in the database as inherently "surprising" or "sudden-turn producing," because these effects depend on the context. It would consequently take a fairly complicated process of evaluation to decide which events, in the current situation, will produce the desired narrative effect.

Yet despite the difficulties of combining top-down guidance with bottom-level simulation, many designers believe that without the former, interactive narrative systems would put an excessive burden on the user. The systems must be *authored*, and users should respond to affordances built into the virtual world and programmed into the system, rather than being entirely responsible for the construction of the story. Not many of us prefer writing plays and novels to watching and reading them; by the same reasoning, most users of interactive narrative systems would rather be invited into a story than have to create it from ground zero. Nicolas Szilas, developer of the system IdTension, advocates, for instance, a module he calls the "Virtual Narrator," whose function is to guarantee "storiness" by selecting rules and events on the basis of their effect on the user rather than (exclusively?) on the basis of the behavior of characters (n.d., 3). Aylett and Louchart (2004) believe that narrativity in VR systems should "emerge directly from the interactions between the protagonists," rather than from a scripted plot, but they still recommend a "drama manager" function, inspired by the game master of tabletop role-playing games, who monitors the story though indirect communication with the players, such as sending nonplaying characters in the player's way to influence their decisions.

All this explains why there aren't many systems in existence that both generate stories on the fly and allow active user participation. Here I would like to discuss two projects that represent the state of the art in interactive narrativity, and illustrate widely different design philosophies.

Façade

Façade, by Michael Mateas and Andrew Stern (2005), is a project in interactive drama that combines the top-down and the bottom-along approach (see screenshots in figure 7). *Façade* is designed for a short but intense fifteen-minute experience, rather than for the extended sessions that players devote to their favorite online role-playing games. The authors believe that the best way to fill the short duration of the drama is through a condensed action sequence that follows an Aristotelian pattern of exposition, complication, and resolution. Here is how Mateas and Stern describe the plot:

> In *Façade*, you, the player, play the character of a long-time friend of Grace and Trip, an attractive and materially successful couple in their early thirties. During an evening get-together at their apart-

7. Screenshots from *Façade*. Michael Mateas and Andrew Stern, 2005.

ment that quickly turns ugly, you become entangled in the high-conflict dissolution of Grace and Trip's marriage. No one is safe as the accusations fly, sides are taken and irreversible decisions are forced to be made. By the end of this intense one-act play you will have changed the course of Grace and Trip's lives—motivating you to replay the drama to find out how your interaction could make things turn out differently the next time. (2002, 2)

The user interacts with the characters by typing text, and the characters respond through spoken dialogue. Since the spoken dialogue must be entirely prerecorded, the narrative is assembled during run-time out of fairly large units of text, and the combination of these units does not allow a great deal of variation. The user hears about 30 percent of the available dialogue during each run, and after five or six runs, the database is exhausted. All the plot variants follow the same global pattern:

Exposition: Grace and Trip welcome the visitor to their apartment, and engage in small talk with their guest.

Crisis: The small talk degenerates into an argument between Grace
and Trip that exposes the disastrous state of their marriage.

Denouement: The visitor is asked to leave.

Whether or not replaying the drama affects the course of Grace's and Trip's lives—as the authors intend—is a matter of interpretation, rather than a matter of generating significantly different sequences of events. In all versions the couple fights bitterly, and the only open question is the survival of their marriage: in some runs the user leaves under the impression that Grace and Trip will stay together despite the disastrous state of the marriage, because fighting is essential to their personal relationship, while in other runs, the user may leave the apartment convinced that Grace and Trip will break up, because the evening has brought to light deep resentments that the dysfunctional couple had denied until then. But these variations are subtle and very subjective.

The natural language interface represents an elegant way to participate in the action, and it gives unlimited freedom of expression to the user, but the drawback of this freedom is the system's inability to process more than a small proportion of the user's input. With a language-understanding system, a large number of possible user actions must be mapped onto a small number of different system options, and many of these options are not logically compatible with the user's input. For instance, if Grace asks the user, "How are you," and the user replies, "I feel terrible," the system understands that the user expressed unhappiness, and it will make Grace respond with a sad expression. When the user types "I feel great," Grace will respond with a smile. But when the user types "I feel terrific," she understands "terrible," and she frowns. When the system cannot parse the user's input, it simply ignores it, and it selects from its database a response that may or may not make sense in the current situation.

But the frequent incoherence of the dialogue does not lead to a serious loss of credibility, because it can be explained by the self-centered personalities of Grace and Trip. As the conversation turns into a domestic fight, it is not too surprising that Grace and Trip increasingly ignore the visitor. With its theme of marital feud, *Façade* is very successful at minimizing the limitations of its AI module. Grace and Trip control the flow of the conversation, and the user's contribution to the development of the action is largely limited to answering questions. For instance, the user can say "you" or "Trip" when Grace asks who is responsible for the deterioration of the marriage. The user's response will influence the development of the dialogue, but he or she cannot predict in which way. By making Grace and Trip run the show, and by limiting the user to a marginal role, *Façade* is able to generate dialogue sequences on the fly, while remaining in control of the general direction of the plot. A "drama manager" ensures that each successive dialogue unit (called "beat" by the designers) increases the tension of the previous unit, until a climax is reached. At this point the drama manager switches to units that decrease tension and lead to the resolution (Crawford 2004, 319). In its combination of top-down design and bottom-along user input, *Façade* heavily favors the top-down direction. The user can say whatever he or she wants, and sometimes Grace and Trip will listen but with next to no predictable influence on the narrative arc.

The Sims

A totally different design is found in the computer game *The Sims*, perhaps the most powerful interactive narrative system in existence today, at least for those who do not insist on Aristotelian form and narrative closure. *The Sims*, as most readers already know, is a life simulation game in which the user creates a family and controls the behavior of its members. Thematically patterned after TV soap operas, *The Sims* is played on a PC, and it is designed for lengthy playing sessions that create never-ending stories. The principal mode of interaction is the selection of items from a menu. For instance, if the user is currently controlling Dina, and if she mouses over her sister Nina, a menu will appear that shows a list of behaviors that Dina can adopt toward Nina: appreciate, entertain, irritate, play, hug, dance together, kiss, and talk (figure 8). Or if she mouses over the TV set, the menu will offer the choice of making Dina exercise (good for her athletic shape) or having her watch a soap opera (good for her mood). While menus are a far more restrictive, and a far less immersive mode of participation than natural language, they present the significant advantage of allowing a coherent response of the system for every choice of the user.

The generative algorithm of *The Sims* operates from a strictly bottom-along perspective. When the user selects an action, the system computes its consequences and updates the current state of the gameworld, opening up a new set of possible actions. The system also plays the role of blind

8. Menu from *The Sims*. Screenshot.

fate, by occasionally throwing in random events, such as a burglar stealing objects from the house, neighbors dropping by unexpectedly, the house catching fire, or Death taking a character away. These random events occasionally take the form of mini narrative scripts. For instance, a male character can be kidnapped by space aliens and return pregnant with a monstrous hybrid, or a burglar may be arrested by the police but escape from the police car. Yet, even when the system takes a turn at implementing events, it does not operate on the basis of narrative templates. The game simulates the randomness of life, rather than the teleology of narrative. But in life as in stories, people must learn to deal with the accidents of fate, and this is why *The Sims* is both a believable simulation of life and a powerful story-generating system. Thanks to the top-down interventions of the system, which take away control from the player, the pleasure of the game lies as much in discovering the possible stories embedded in the system as in managing the life of the Sims family members according to the goals set for them by the player.

The implicit goal of the game is to make the Sims climb the social ladder by acquiring more and more commodities, but the player must also take care of the daily needs of characters, such as hunger, rest, bladder, entertainment, and social life. It can be argued that because of the importance of these daily needs, *The Sims* is more a game of resource management than a narrative system. *The Sims 2*, which appeared in 2004, tries to enhance the narrative interest of the game by placing a greater emphasis on interpersonal relations and on the mental lives of characters. The Sims now have memories, fears, and personalized life goals ("aspirations"), but except for the aspirations, which are selected by the player at character creation time out of a fixed menu, these aspects of mental life are all determined by the system. Yet even though players cannot specify the content of the characters' minds, they are able to take physical actions that lead to certain mental and emotional states or that implant certain memories. For instance, kissing or arguing has obvious effects on the degree of love of the patient for the agent. In other words, the player cannot make Nina develop a sudden crush on Jim—she must patiently build up this love by having Jim take appropriate actions toward Nina. Through this indirect control of minds, players can spice up the biographies of their characters with stories of love, hate, betrayal, and jealousy—the proper stuff of soap operas.

Here is an example of the kind of story that the player can produce by activating the narrative affordances inherent to the gameworld (in italics: system-generated events):

The Noovorich family started from nothing, but now they live in a large mansion. They are slightly dysfunctional—father Paul has his eyes on Jenni, one of the Boob sisters who live across the street; mother Linda is a frustrated novelist; and Britney, the daughter, has been known to skip school in order to go shopping at the Community Ground, where she spends inordinate amounts of the family money. Paul sells all of her clothes to pay the monthly bills, and Britney is quite mad at her dad. One day the Noovorich house is robbed, but the burglar, Chris, is arrested. As the police car is about to take him to jail, Britney opens the back door *and he escapes.* He now becomes a regular guest in the Noovorich household. Britney seduces Chris and she becomes pregnant. Chris moves in with the Noovoriches, but when the baby is born, *the house becomes overcrowded. Exasperated with the situation, Linda decides to move out.*

Marie-Laure Ryan   57

This is just what Paul wanted—he invites the Boob sisters to a party, hoping to start something with Jenni. Meanwhile, Britney fails to take proper care of her baby, and *the social worker places the baby in a foster home.* (To be continued indefinitely.)

Not a literary masterpiece, admittedly, though no worse than a TV soap opera. (But this is a deceptive comparison, because soap operas, being human-generated, are capable of far greater complexity and variation.) What my summary leaves out, however, is the repetitive actions that must be performed to keep the Sims alive between the highlights of the plot. As Chris Crawford writes, "Players of *The Sims* guide their characters in going to the bathroom, taking showers, preparing and eating meals, cleaning the dishes, taking out the garbage, cleaning house, sleeping, and earning a living. This is not drama; this is a housekeeping simulation. Alfred Hitchcock once described drama as 'life with the dull bits cut out.' The Sims is life with the dramatic bits removed" (2004, 143). Crawford makes an important point about the difference between raw life and its narrative shaping, but he underestimates the potential of *The Sims* for dramatic (or rather, melodramatic) events. For those who want to play the game for the sake of the stories, the main problem with the current version is that it tries to be three different things at the same time: resource management game, construction game (the user can build fancy houses for his family), and story-generating system. The game will not improve its narrative appeal until it downplays the simulation of everyday life, and offers richer possibilities of interaction between the characters. What the system most urgently needs is a way to compress and expand time, so that the Sims can spend less time washing dishes, and more time building the networks of interpersonal relations that produce dramatic situations.

In the final analysis, the prospects for interactivity on the inner layer of the onion are not as bleak as Crawford suggests, because the thrill of being in a virtual world and of interacting with it, or, in the case of *The Sims*, of discovering its affordances, relieves some of the burden that falls upon narrative aesthetics. As Kelso, Weyrauch, and Bates have argued (1993), a plot that seems trivial when watched by a spectator becomes exciting when experienced by an interactor. The good news is that we may not need characters as complex as Hamlet, dialogue as witty as Jane Austen's, or a plot as thrilling as *The Da Vinci Code* to enjoy active participation in a fictional world. In an interactive setting, narrative follows different aesthetic rules than in literature, and these rules are slowly being discovered through trial and error in projects like *Façade* or *The Sims*.

Level 5: Meta-Interactivity

On this level, the interactor is not consuming the onion but rather preparing new ways to cook it for other users, such as designing a new level for a computer game, creating new costumes for the avatar, introducing new objects, associating existent objects with new behaviors, and generally expanding the possibilities of action offered by the storyworld. To constitute a genuinely "meta" interactivity, this must be done by writing code and patching up the source, rather than by using tools internal to the game, such as the house-building module of *The Sims*. It is on this level that the idea of the user as coauthor becomes more than a hyperbolic cliché, but the two roles do not merge, since users cannot simultaneously immerse themselves in a storyworld and write the code that brings this world to life.

Conclusion

The inner layers of the onion are much harder to conquer than the outer layers, but we should not confuse problem-solving difficulty with aesthetic value. There is a tendency in digital culture to evaluate a work as a feat of programming virtuosity. I call this the anti-WYSIWYG aesthetics,[8] because you have to imagine the code that lies behind the screen to appreciate the text. By these standards, a work of level 4 is automatically superior to a work of level 1, regardless of its narrative quality, because it constitutes a much more impressive programming feat. If we applied this aesthetics of difficulty to print literature, a palindrome story or a novel written without the letter "e" (such as Georges Perec's *La disparition*) would automatically represent a greater artwork than a novel like Marcel Proust's *À la recherche du temps perdu*, which was written without stringent formal constraints (though certainly not without form).

Another aesthetic criterion popular in digital culture that favors the work of the inner layer is the idea of emergence and self-renewability. *Façade* can be replayed half a dozen times with different results, and *The Sims* virtually endlessly, while the texts of level 3 will rarely be replayed once the game has been beaten. And while it is possible to fiddle for a long time with a hypertext of level 2 like *afternoon*, the works of level 1 quickly yield all of their substance. But for the reader who truly cares for the story, an interactive work that produces a relatively fixed plot but gives intense pleasure during its unique run is not inherently inferior to a system that creates a wide variety of mediocre stories. I am not saying that diversity of output does not contribute positively to aesthetic value but rather that a work can compensate for lack of replayability with other qualities. There are consequently good and bad solutions, success and failure, entertainment and boredom on all the layers of the interactive onion.

Notes

1. At least not visible to the neophyte. Readers familiar with the Storyspace system know that when a certain key is pressed, the words with links will appear surrounded by boxes. This kind of esoteric trick raises for the critic the question of whether the text should be discussed from the point of view of a naïve reader who encounters such a system for the first time (a type of reader that is rapidly disappearing), or from the point of view of an expert user who knows all the idiosyncrasies of the interface.

2. See Ryan 2006, chap. 5, esp. 107–8, on the concept of internal, external, exploratory, and ontological interactivity.

3. Some of these actions are available in multiplayer online role-playing games (MMORPGS), because players interact with other human beings, rather than with system-created characters of limited intelligence.

4. Without different replays, users would be unable to find out if the program really listens to their input. There are indeed some examples of fake interactivity, where the system asks the user questions but disregards the answers, and tells the same story every time.

5. On the paradox of interactive narrative, see also Ryan 2001, 319–20.

6. There have been several interactive texts based on *Little Red Riding Hood*, for instance Donna Leishman's *Red Ridinghood* (2001) and the video game *The Path* (2008), but if a text satisfies any of the following conditions (as I believe to be the case with the above-mentioned works), it will not represent level 4 interactivity: all the variations are prescripted rather than being generated in real time (that is, during the run of the program), interest lies in the graphics and not the story, or one of the plot lines is clearly superior to the others.

7. *Trajectoires* is reactive rather than interactive: the use of movement back and forth among the pages triggers replacements on the level of words and sentences, so that the text is ever changing, but the user has no control over the changes.

8. WYSIWYG stands for What You See Is What You Get, the slogan of GUI (graphic user interface).

References

Aarseth, Espen. 1997. *Cybertext: Perspectives on Ergodic Literature*. Baltimore: Johns Hopkins University Press.

Ankerson, Ingrid, and Megan Sapnar. 2001. *Cruising*. Available at http://www .poemsthatgo.com/gallery/spring2001/crusing-launch.html (accessed December 6, 2010).

Aristotle. 1996. *Poetics*. Trans. Malcolm Heath. London: Penguin.

Aylett, Ruth, and Sandy Louchart. 2004. "The Emergent Narrative: Theoretical Investigation." In *Proceedings of the Narrative and Learning Environments Conference*, 25–33. Available at http://www.nicve.salford.ac.uk/sandy/ENFrame setPage.htm (accessed May 5, 2005).

Balpe, Jean-Pierre. *Trajectoires*. Computer-generated novel. Available at http:// trajectoires.univ-paris8.fr/ (accessed May 19, 2005).

Campbell, Joseph. 1973. *The Hero with a Thousand Faces*. 2nd ed. Princeton NJ: Princeton University Press. (Orig. pub. 1968.)

Crawford, Chris. 2003. "Interactive Storytelling." In *The Video Game Theory Reader*, ed. Mark J. P. Wolf and Bernard Perron, 259–73. New York: Routledge.

——. 2004. *Chris Crawford on Interactive Storytelling*. Berkeley CA: New Riders.

Douglas, J. Yellowlees. 2000. *The End of Books—or Books without End? Reading Interactive Narratives*. Ann Arbor: University of Michigan Press.

Glassner, Andrew. 2004. *Interactive Storytelling: Techniques for 21st Century Fiction*. Natick MA: A. K. Peters.

Jenkins, Henry. 2004. "Game Design as Narrative Architecture." In *First Person: New Media as Story, Performance, and Game*, ed. Noah Wardrip-Fruin and Pat Harrigan, 118–30. Cambridge MA: MIT Press.

Joyce, Michael. 1987. *afternoon, a story*. Hypertext software. Cambridge MA: Eastgate System.

——. 1995. *Of Two Minds: Hypertext, Pedagogy, and Poetics*. Ann Arbor: University of Michigan Press.

Kelso, Margaret, Peter Weyrauch, and Joseph Bates. 1993. "Dramatic Presence." *Presence: Teleoperators and Virtual Environments* 2, no. 1:1–15.

Landow, George. 1997. *Hypertext 2.1: The Convergence of Contemporary Critical Theory and Technology*. Baltimore: Johns Hopkins University Press.

Laurel, Brenda. 2001. *Utopian Entrepreneur*. Cambridge MA: MIT Press.

Leishman, Donna. 2001. *Red Ridinghood*. Electronic Literature Collection, Vol. 1. Available at http://collection.eliterature.org/1/works/leishman_redridinghood .html (accessed December 6, 2010).

Lewis and Clark Expedition Website. Available at http://www.lewis-clark.org (accessed October 27, 2008).

Manovich, Lev. 2001. *The Language of New Media*. Cambridge MA: MIT Press.

Mateas, Michael, and Andrew Stern. 2002. "*Façade*: An Experiment in Building a Fully-Realized Interactive Drama." Available at http://www.quvu.net/inter activestory.net/papers/MateasSternGDC03.pdf (accessed December 6, 2010).

———. 2005. *Façade*. Interactive CD-ROM. Available at http://interactivestory.net/ download (accessed December 6, 2010).

Meadows, Mark Stephen. 2003. *Pause and Effect: The Art of Interactive Narrative.* Indianapolis: New Riders.

Miller, Carolyn Handler. 2004. *Digital Storytelling: A Creator's Guide to Interactive Entertainment.* Amsterdam: Focal Press/Elsevier.

Moulthrop, Stuart. 2005. *Marginal Effects.* Available at http://www.tekka.net/07/ marginal/mfx01.swf (accessed December 6, 2010).

Murray, Janet. 1997. *Hamlet on the Holodeck: The Future of Narrative in Cyberspace.* New York: Free Press.

The Path. 2008. Computer game. Available at http://thepath-game.com/ (accessed December 6, 2010).

Poole, Steven. 2000. *Trigger Happy: The Inner Life of Video Games.* New York: Arcade Publishing.

Propp, Vladimir. 1968. *Morphology of the Folktale.* Trans. L. Scott. Revised by A. Wagner. Austin: University of Texas Press.

Ryan, Marie-Laure. 2001. *Narrative as Virtual Reality: Immersion and Interactivity in Literature and Electronic Media.* Baltimore: Johns Hopkins University Press.

———. 2006. *Avatars of Story.* Minneapolis: University of Minnesota Press.

The Sims. 2000. Designed by Will Wright. Maxis.

The Sims 2. 2004. Designed by Will Wright. Maxis.

Szilas, Nicolas. n.d. "A New Approach to Interactive Drama: From Intelligent Characters to an Intelligent Virtual Narrator." Available at http://www.idtension.com/ (accessed December 6, 2010).

3　Ontological Boundaries and Methodological Leaps

The Importance of Possible Worlds Theory for Hypertext Fiction (and Beyond)

ALICE BELL

Introduction

This essay sets out an ontologically centered approach to Storyspace hypertext fiction by applying Ryan's (1991) model of Possible Worlds Theory to two canonical texts. It begins by showing how different waves of hypertext theory have sought to understand the narratological peculiarities of Storyspace hypertext fiction. It then argues that Possible Worlds Theory not only provides an essential means of conceptualizing the ontological domains that are so crucial to an understanding the reader's experience of the texts, but it also offers a fitting vocabulary with which to label them. The efficacy of a Possible Worlds Theory approach is shown through its application to Shelley Jackson's *Patchwork Girl* (1995) and Stuart Moulthrop's *Victory Garden* (1991). The analyses show how the Possible Worlds Theory method allows the study of hypertext fiction to move away from the chronological focus of traditional narrative theory to address the ontological mechanics of hypertext narratives. The chapter closes by suggesting ways in which Possible Worlds Theory might also be used as an analytical tool for other forms of digital literature.

From First- to Second-Wave Theory

Hypertext theory has always accompanied hypertext novels. Many hypertext fiction authors, including Joyce and Jackson, have also written a number of critical essays to accompany their fictional works (e.g., M. Joyce 1987, 1988, 1996, 1997; Jackson 1995, 1998). However, some of the primary or what has recently been termed "first-wave" (Bell 2010; Ciccoricco 2007; Pang 1998) hypertext theory has been scrutinized by a second wave of hypertext theory for its theoretical and methodological limitations (see Bell 2007, 2010; Ciccoricco 2007; Ensslin and Bell 2007). As the following discussion shows, second-wave hypertext theory addresses two central limitations of the first wave: a reliance on abstracted theoretical models and an unrealistic conviction in the power of the reader.

Initially, first-wave theory explored some attractive associations between the hypertext form and poststructuralist textual models such as Barthes's (1990) "writerly" text, Deleuze and Guattari's (1988) "rhizome," and Derrida's (1979, 1981) theory of "deconstruction" (for full accounts, see Bolter 2001; Burnett 1993; Delany and Landow 1991; Landow 1994, 1997, 2006). Perhaps most famously, hypertext has been described as "an almost embarrassingly literal reification or actualization" (Delany and Landow 1991, 10) of contemporary literary theory. While potentially appealing, the association of hypertextuality and particular theoretical models has not necessarily led to literary-critical readings of individual hypertext fictions. Rather, the metaphoric mapping of theory and textuality has remained mostly at an abstract level, a blueprint from which few, if any, analyses have since materialized.

In what has proved to be a more influential approach, first-wave approaches situate hypertext fiction readers in a binary relationship with their print counterparts (e.g., Coover 1992; Douglas 1992; Liestol 1994). The role of the reader represents an important and distinguishing facet of hypertext fiction and its reception and, as this essay will demonstrate, the reader's position in the text is crucial to second-wave analyses. However, overambitious claims have been made in first-wave theory that dispro-portionately elevate the authority of the hypertext reader. For example, Douglas, in her article "What Hypertexts Can Do That Print Narratives Cannot," argues that "in print narratives our reading experience begins with the first words of the narrative and is completed by the last words on the last page" (1992, 2). The rigidity of print and the lack of choice that Douglas believes it offers is contrasted with the apparent freedom that hypertext permits. "In *Victory Garden*," she notes, "readers are unable to begin reading without . . . making decisions about the text—where their interests lie and which pathways through the text seem most likely to sat-isfy them" (2–3). Douglas's observations are accurate insofar as the reader is granted a choice of paths through any hypertext fiction. However, in a hypertext fiction, the reader is often ignorant of which paths are "most likely to satisfy them." As Landow notes, "few [examples of hypertext fiction] grant readers the kind of power one expects in informational hypertext" (2006, 215–16) so that in "fictional hypertext . . . readers cannot make particularly informed or empowered choices" (222).

The difference between informational and literary hypertext is revealed by comparing the function of hyperlinks in each respective environment (see Pajares Tosca 2000 and Parker 2001 for comprehensive studies). In an informational hypertext, structural clarity is usually part of the design, but in a literary hypertext, the same principles do not always apply. For instance, in an informational hypertext, the linked term is more often than not suggestive of what the reader will find at the destination screen. It is chosen because of its capacity for indicating, in advance of the destination screen, what the reader will find if he or she follows it. However, in a hypertext fiction, the linked term or icon does not necessarily directly indicate what will be found at the destination lexia. While readers might surmise where the link will lead, they often must decipher figural connections between link and lexia content after the link has been followed. Thus, while semantic associations in informational hypertext systems are usually correctly predicted in anticipation of the destination screen, in hypertext fiction they are often authenticated in retrospect. Hypertext fiction does allow the reader a choice of reading routes via a choice of links, but the reader's knowledge of and associated power within hypertext fictions is sometimes exaggerated in first-wave theory.

Despite some of the limitations identified in first-wave theory, later theorists have further refined observations about the role of the reader. In second-wave theory, the reader's interactive role in a hypertext is perceived not necessarily as powerful but rather as one of the defining characteristics of reading in a digital context. The most influential work of this kind is Aarseth's *Cybertext* (1997), which is a study of digital textuality more generally but within which hypertext forms an integral part. In his introduction, Aarseth outlines the category of "ergodic literature," which he defines as any kind of literature that is categorized by the "nontrivial effort [that] is required to allow the reader to traverse the text" (1997, 1). While Aarseth's definition does not explicitly exclude print texts, his concept of nonergodic literature shows why a print text does not satisfy the criteria associated with ergodic literature. In nonergodic literature, he states, "no extranoematic responsibilities [are] placed on the reader except (for example) eye movement and the periodic or arbitrary turning of pages" (1–2). The nontrivial effort that Aarseth identifies in ergodic literature generally is characterized in hypertext more specifically by the role that readers have to play in its navigation. In a hypertext fiction, readers make choices by moving a mouse, clicking a button, or typing on a keyboard. Consequently their reading experience is much more active or "nontrivial" than that associated with their print counterparts.

Affirming Aarseth's conviction that reading hypertext fiction requires nontrivial effort, Ryan (2001, 2006) links the hypertextual reading context to the reader's experience of hypertext narratives. Ryan's work is particularly influential within both hypertext theory and Possible Worlds Theory, and in the analysis below, I will use the framework that she has developed in the latter context. The ontological focus of Ryan's work can be detected in the general observations that she makes about hypertext fiction and its reading. She suggests that readers of hypertext fiction are continually alerted to their ontological position relative to the fictional world because their absorption in the narrative is periodically disrupted by the proactive role they are required to play. In *Narrative as Virtual Reality*, she shows that varying degrees of what she defines as "spatial," "temporal," and "emotional" immersion apply when reading digital works, and in so doing she highlights some anti-immersive attributes found across different types of electronic literature. With regard to hypertext, she notes that "immersion remains a rather elusive experience" (2001, 19) because "every time the reader is asked to make a choice she assumes an external perspective on the worlds of the textual universe" (20). In a later study, Ryan affirms that the reader is inevitably held back from the narrative because the hypertext's "external/exploratory interactivity . . . promotes a metafictional stance, at the expense of immersion in the virtual world" (2006, 109). In both investigations, she identifies an almost inevitable partnership among the hypertext form, the role of the reader, and the associated ontological alienation that the reader experiences.

Both Aarseth and Ryan either implicitly or explicitly focus on the reader's role in the fiction-making process. While in any reading experience, readers are ontologically separated from the fictional domain that is described, as Ryan notes, readers of hypertext fiction are alerted to this external position explicitly. Using Aarseth's observations, this is because they have a "nontrivial" role in the fictional world's construction. More specifically, readers have a consistently material and tactile relationship with the machine that displays the text, and this foregrounds the fact that the fictional world that the computer generates is ontologically distinct to them. They may be able to influence the order in which the fictional world is described, but they can only do this from an external ontological position.

Aarseth's and Ryan's work can be seen as bridging the gap between the first wave of hypertext theory, which made ambitious and therefore overly exaggerated observations, and the second wave of hypertext theory, which seeks to link more general theoretical conjectures to the analysis of individual digital works. In studies that focus more specifically on the narrative devices contained within hypertext fictions, theorists have shown how the interactivity of the hypertext medium is often coupled with self-reflexive devices so as to compound feelings of ontological alienation. Moving further away from the first wave, which emphasized the uniqueness of the medium from a material perspective, these studies consider how the medium affects or corroborates with narratological features inside the texts. Drawing similar conclusions to Ryan, for example, Bolter recognizes that the hypertext medium causes feelings of estrangement because "whenever the reader comes to a link and is forced to make a choice, the illusion of an imagined world must break down, at least momentarily, as the reader recalls the technical circumstances of the electronic medium" (2001, 138). However, he also points out that the narrative devices *within* hypertext novels are often used to intensify that experience. In particular, he suggests that while "it may be possible for a reader to ignore these [reading] circumstances, . . . interactive fictions are [usually] calculated to make the reader aware of their links, their technical circumstances" (138). Focusing on Storyspace novels, he suggests that an increased sense of ontological detachment is achieved by metafictional devices such as contradictory narratives, nonchronological ordering of events, overtly visible navigation tools, and the use of explicit intertextual references (121–38). In each case, he argues, "rhetorical displacement draws attention to itself and therefore away from any simple illustration the narrative might create" (138), so that the reader is always aware of the inherently artificial nature of the fictional world that they are exploring.

As the preceding discussion shows, estrangement in hypertext is usually a consequence of two separate but integrally related characteristics.

First, since readers have a nontrivial, corporeal role in hypertext reading in which they are often required to choose from a number of different structural possibilities, they are habitually reminded that they are involved in the construction of an artifact. In addition, as Bolter in particular notes, because hypertext readers often experience a range of self-reflexive devices within Storyspace novels, their attention is drawn to the artificiality of the narratives that the hypertexts contain. While these two attributes of hypertext are distinct, they happen simultaneously and are intrinsically linked. They mutually foreground the ontological divide between the world in which the reader resides and the world described by the text.

From Theory to Method

While some theoretical consistencies have been identified in second-wave hypertext theory—most notably the importance of alienation in hypertext fiction—the field currently lacks methodological coherence. In addition, while conclusions about the corporeality of the hypertext reading experience are significant because they isolate particular generic features that might potentially apply to all hypertexts, without indicative examples of how and where such displacement operates within individual hypertext fictions, any potential alienating effects are attributed solely to the neoteric status of the hypertext medium rather than the narratives that it is used to display.

As a consequence of the ontological self-reflexivity that theorists observe in Storyspace hypertext, a number of studies (e.g. Bell 2007, 2010; Koskimaa 2000; Ryan 2001, 2006) have shown that Possible Worlds Theory provides a suitable analytical framework through which such texts can be analyzed. The most significant advantage of a Possible Worlds Theory analysis is the spatial as opposed to temporal emphasis that it facilitates. As a theory that is founded on propositional modal logic, it is fundamentally concerned with the relationship between different worlds—both real and imaginary—and their respective constituents. More specifically, Possible Worlds Theory in literary studies (e.g., Dolezel 1998; Pavel 1986; Ronen 1994; Ryan 1991) appropriates concepts of ontology, reference, and modality from possible-worlds logic (e.g., Hintikka 1967; Kripke 1972; Lewis 1973; Plantinga 1974) and applies them to the worlds built by fictional texts. As a methodological approach it is extremely proficient at simplifying very complex ontological configurations and also has the necessary terminology for labeling different ontological domains.

Perhaps because of the apparent fragmentation within Possible Worlds Theory in philosophical logic (for particular criticisms, see Bell 2010; Ronen 1994), narratological applications of the theory are sometimes inconsistent. Similarly, while most theorists working within the context of Possible Worlds Theory recognize either implicitly or explicitly that fictional texts generate ontological networks (e.g. Pavel 1979; Dolezel 1998), few theorists have developed such observations into an imitable analytical method. Ryan's (1991) seminal work is one, if not the only, exception.

In her extensive elucidation of Possible Worlds Theory in a literary context, Ryan offers a framework that respects the capacity of narrative discourse to construct alternative worlds by distinguishing between two systems of modality: the "system of reality," which is the system in which we live, and a "textual universe," which is a modal system projected by a text. Ryan asserts that in our system of reality, the "Actual World" forms the center; in the context of a literary analysis, it is the domain to which the reader belongs. In this modal universe, "possible worlds" represent alternatives to the Actual World and are indefinite in number. These domains are created by the wishes, fears, imaginings, and so forth of the inhabitants of the Actual World. In the context of any "textual universe," Ryan asserts, sits a "Textual Actual World." This is a particular kind of possible world, which is described and thereby constructed by an individual fictional text, and it is the domain to which the characters of that text belong. Paralleling the ontological configuration of our system of reality, the textual universe also comprises two types of ontological domain. The Textual Actual World is surrounded by numerous "Textual Possible Worlds," which represent alternatives to that respective Textual Actual World and, again, are formed by the dreams, wishes, and imaginings of the inhabitants—in this case the characters—of that domain.

As the categories above show, Ryan's (1991) Possible Worlds Theory provides terminology that can be used to label different types of ontological domain. In the context of hypertext fiction analysis, its ontological focus is particularly useful because it can be used to systematically map the ontological relationship between the reader and the hypertext in the real world and the fictional agents, such as characters and narrators, in the fictional world. It can also be used to show how readers can experience different events, different versions of events, or contradictory events in the same text, which, as has been noted above, is a common experience in hypertext reading.

It is precisely because of its capacity for modeling modal structures that Koskimaa (2000) finds Possible Worlds Theory particularly effective for the analysis of hypertext fiction. He argues that while all texts construct alternatives and thereby always implicitly construct an alternative modal system—or, in Ryan's terms, a "textual universe"—hypertext fictions make that system of reality very explicit by literalizing the alternative possibilities. "In hypertext fiction" Koskimaa argues, "we have to take the possible worlds model . . . for granted—instead of simply imagining that this or that event might have happened in several ways resulting in potentially very different consequences, some of events really do happen in more than one way" (2000). According to Koskimaa, because Storyspace hypertext fictions contain narrative contradictions, Ryan's model can be used as a means of categorizing and therefore legitimizing conflicting narrative events.

Like Koskimaa, Ryan (2001, 2006) uses Possible Worlds Theory as a means of modeling ontological configurations and of legitimizing ontological contradictions in hypertext fiction. In her application, she maintains that "every lexia is regarded as a representation of a different possible world, and every jump to a new lexia as a recentering to another world. . . . This approach is a way to rationalize the texts that present a high degree of internal contradiction" (2001, 222–23).

While Koskimaa and Ryan advocate an ontological approach to hypertext fiction in general, this chapter will show how Possible Worlds Theory can be applied to two texts in particular. Similarly, while their studies focus on narrative contradictions, this chapter will focus on the reader's ontological position relative to the two hypertexts. Like Koskimaa and Ryan, the analyses presented in this chapter do not attempt to determine a definitive chronological order through a particular hypertext, because this represents an attribute of traditional narrative analysis that is incredibly hard to justify in texts that inherently house a range of different and sometimes contradictory narrative possibilities. Instead, using the beginnings of two Storyspace novels, the analyses will show how each text deploys ontologically self-conscious narrative devices that work in conjunction with the hypertext medium to create a distinctive reading situation. From a methodological perspective, the discussion will show how Possible Worlds Theory can be used to analyze different manifestations of self-reflexivity, so that this selective analysis can be replicated in other parts of each text and also in other hypertext fictions in general.

Victory Garden

Victory Garden (Moulthrop 1991) is a historical novel, set at the beginning of the first Gulf War and located in both the Persian Gulf and the imaginary University of Tara in the United States. As is typical of Storyspace hypertext, it utilizes the potential of the hypertext form and structure to offer a number of competing narratives that sometimes contradict one another or re-represent events that may have already been presented. Consequently, it is difficult to determine a comprehensive or definitive description or outline of the Textual Actual World because its representations change frequently and unpredictably, often corresponding to how it is viewed by different characters.

Most readings of the text focus on the association between the fiction's multiple paths and the theme of "representation" within *Victory Garden* as a whole (e.g., Ciccoricco 2004, 2007; Gaggi 1997; Koskimaa 2000). Critics note that the many different reading paths literalize the epistemological multiplicity that is found both within and outside the text. The following analysis will show, first, how the reader is alienated from the fictional world from the very beginning of the text and, second, how Possible Worlds Theory can be used to explain the ontological mechanics of such alienation.

In line with the narrative multiplicity found within the novel, *Victory Garden* offers multiple entrances to the text from which the reader must choose. As shown in figure 9, the overview map posits thirty-nine distinct areas, each acting as an entrance to a different part of the text. This large map further subdivides into thirds, so that each distinct area is labeled with words that correspond to the title of the lexia that is accessed (see figure 10).

As noted by Douglas (1992), the map in *Victory Garden* dictates that readers make a choice on their first encounter with the text. Yet while this endows the reader with a role, it also means that some degree of alienation is achieved before any of the paths have been unearthed. As a navigational tool, the map grants the reader a panoramic view of the Textual Actual

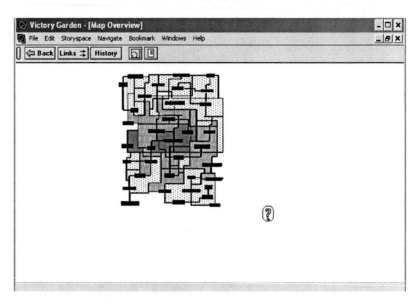

9. Map overview of *Victory Garden*. Screenshot. Courtesy of Mark Bernstein.

World that he or she is about to explore. Crucially, however, although the link titles provide some detail, they actually reveal very little about the contents of the destination lexias or the length and duration of the onward reading paths to which they lead. In fact, they often reveal nothing more than the chapter headings of print fictions might—perhaps even less because the absence of numerical sequencing does not show how they might fit together chronologically. For example, the links titled "The War Channel" or "Thea's War" are fairly indicative of their content—a collection of quotations from media representations of the war and the war as focalized through the character Thea. However, these associations can only be confirmed in retrospect, after the path has been explored. Other links, such as "Latticework" and "JSN" are less revealing and demand that the reader access the lexia in order to interpret any semantic connections. The reader can experiment with the links, accessing different parts of the text and experiencing different parts of the Textual Actual World, before deciding which part to explore further and/or beginning to understand how the different parts function collectively.

Similarly, because readers must return to the map once the end of each reading path is reached, they must regularly retract from the Textu-

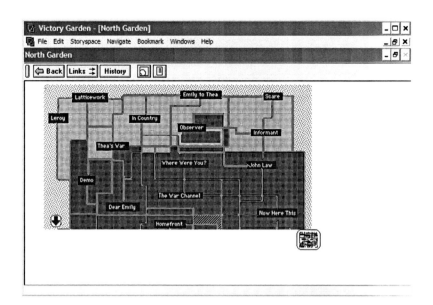

Back Links History

Latticework   Emily to Thea   Scare
Leroy   In Country
Observer
Informant
Thea's War
Where Were You?   John Law
Demo
The War Channel
Dear Emily
Now Here This
Homefront

10. Close view of map in *Victory Garden*. Screenshot. Courtesy of Mark Bernstein.

al Actual World to peruse the options. Structurally, therefore, while each link offers the reader choice, ontologically they also emphasize the multiplicity to be found once readers have entered the Textual Actual World. Each reading path and therefore each experience of the text can always be replaced with another reading path and another narrative so that the temporariness and contrived nature of all of the narratives within the novel are foregrounded. The links show that the text is composed of a number of possible reading paths. The reader must therefore operate at a metafictional level where attention is drawn to their role in the fiction making process as well as their inherent separation from the Textual Actual World.

In his discussion of *Victory Garden*, Koskimaa suggests that "the use of a representational map is, of course, one way of making the interface 'fuse' to the represented fictional world" (2000). Koskimaa's use of the verb *fuse* is notable because it implies that complete cohesion exists between the physical representation of the novel in the Actual World and the fictional representation of events, characters, and locations in the Textual Actual World. However, rather than the map causing complete amalgamation or unification between one space and another, somewhat paradoxically it actually accentuates the ontological divide between the Actual World and the Textual Actual World. Maps in the Actual World may depict a space, but they do not provide direct access to the world that they portray; they are simply a representation. In the hypertext *Victory Garden*, however, the representation of the world—the map—also provides access to the space—the Textual Actual World. Thus, the relationship between map and space in this case is ontologically distinctive.

In contradiction, despite the ontological occlusion that the map dictates, the entrance map does provide access from one domain to another. Furthermore, the reader's physical presence is signified, metonymically, on screen by the cursor that he or she uses to select links. While readers are alerted to the fact that they exist in a space separate from Textual Actual World, the hypertextual map also shows that they are able to influence their experience of that domain.

Thus, the map in *Victory Garden* performs a number of different functions. From a navigational point of view, it invites readers to take a panoramic view of the text, encouraging them to explore its contents. From a metafictional point of view, it acts as a multifarious entrance to the Textual Actual World, thereby overtly displaying the text's multiplicity. Ontologically, it displays a space that is distinct from the Actual World. Visually, it provides an area in which the reader and his or her movements can be observed. The map offers relatively little information about the narratives to which it provides access, but it does typify the relationship between reader and text that is sustained throughout.

Patchwork Girl

As a Gothic novel, *Patchwork Girl* (Jackson 1995) is very different from Moulthrop's historical narrative; a graveyard provides the setting, and the protagonist is a supernatural creature. Yet the reader is just as much the ontological outsider in both texts, and a similar ontological foregrounding to that shown at the beginning of *Victory Garden* is also achieved in *Patchwork Girl*. In a textual entrance that mimics the conventions of print fiction, the full title, authorship, and individual sections of *Patchwork Girl* are listed on its title page (see figure 11). As figure 11 shows, the text contains a number of different sections, ranging from "a graveyard" to "broken accents." Just as in *Victory Garden*, readers are responsible for their own journey through the text from the very beginning.

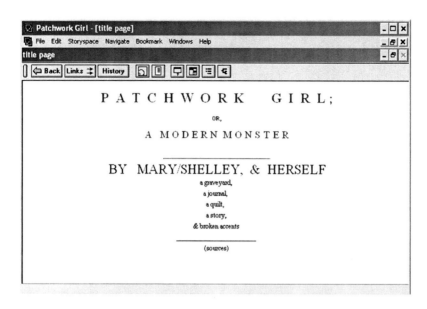

PATCHWORK   GIRL;

OR,

A MODERN MONSTER

BY MARY/SHELLEY, & HERSELF

a graveyard,
a journal,
a quilt,
a story,
& broken accents

(sources)

11. Title page of *Patchwork Girl*. Screenshot. Courtesy of Mark Bernstein.

Entering *Patchwork Girl* at "the graveyard," the main protagonist introduces herself in first person: "I am buried here. You can resurrect me, but only piecemeal. If you want to see the whole you will have to sew me together yourself"{graveyard}. In what is quite a mysterious instruction, the protagonist indicates that someone is responsible for her reconstruction. In the next lexia, {Headstone}, various body parts are listed (see figure 12); the typology, textual structure, and lexia title all imply that the lexia is designed to resemble a graveyard headstone.

The reader can learn about the origin of each body part by clicking on the respective links. Selecting "trunk," for example, leads to a lexia in which the background to the torso's donor is offered. The text tells the tale of "Angela, a woman of low birth and high sights, and a mimic ear for the accents of the upper class" {trunk}. However, it is not only contextual information that is provided. The lexia also offers details about the donor's temperament: "my body is both insinuating and naïve" {trunk}. Using the metaphor of the patchwork, this section asks the reader to stitch together the text, connecting pieces of information about the protagonist from a host of female contributors. Many of the donors are presented as willing providers, rather than victims of a grotesque experiment, and numerous

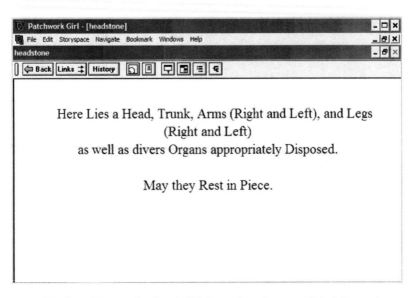

The image content (window):

Patchwork Girl - [headstone]

File Edit Storyspace Navigate Bookmark Windows Help

headstone

Back | Links | History

Here Lies a Head, Trunk, Arms (Right and Left), and Legs
(Right and Left)
as well as divers Organs appropriately Disposed.

May they Rest in Piece.

12. {Headstone} lexia in *Patchwork Girl*. Screenshot. Courtesy of Mark Bernstein.

voices emerge from the gravestone to detail the history of both the monster's limb and organs.

Most readings of the text note an association between the structure of the text and the patchworked body of the protagonist (e.g. Hayles 2000; E. Joyce 2003). Analyzing the {Headstone} lexia using Possible Worlds Theory, this analysis will show how the piecing together of the protagonist draws attention to the ontological separateness of the Textual Actual World while simultaneously asserting the reader's presence therein.

As the reader unveils the links in {Headstone}, a number of different and sometimes contradictory effects result. First, as the reader selects each link and destination lexia, he or she is given information about the patchwork girl and her temperament. The links therefore have a functional role in terms of their ability to depict the patchwork girl as a fictional agent with the Textual Actual World and introduce her to her Actual World audience. In addition, because the protagonist must be resurrected textually, the reader is simultaneously aware of the protagonist's status as an artificial construction. That is, while the patchwork girl appears to be aware of the reader's existence, she is a fiction as opposed to real being. Her fictional status is foregrounded by the fact that the reader is responsible for rebuilding her "piece by piece." The reader can gather information about the protagonist, but this can only be achieved by remaining external to the ontological domain that the patchwork girl occupies. While in the {Headstone} lexia the reader is invited to take part in the process of construction, requiring some degree of responsibility within the Textual Actual World, the reader's role in the reconstruction of the protagonist requires an ontological separation from it. The hypertext medium thus has both a communicative and metafictional function. It transmits information about the Textual Actual World to the reader but it also signals the domain's ontological status.

The preceding analysis shows how the reader of *Patchwork Girl* is alerted to the ontological status of the patchwork girl and the world to which she belongs by the role he or she has to play. It also shows how the relationship between the two agents is complicated by the fact that the reader must construct the protagonist by reaching into the context in which she is displayed. Inevitably, the reader cannot and therefore does not materially enter the Textual Actual World, but he or she is represented on the screen, metonymically, by the cursor's icon. Thus, while a clear boundary is asserted between the two agents and their respective domains, as was shown in *Victory Garden*, the reader's relationship to the Textual Actual World of *Patchwork Girl* is complicated by the "nontrivial" role that he or she is required to play within the text.

Future Worlds

As the analyses above show, *Victory Garden* and *Patchwork Girl* each contain devices that concurrently alienate and embrace the reader so as to simultaneously assert and collapse the ontological boundary that surrounds each Textual Actual World. Methodologically, the analyses have shown that Possible Worlds Theory is effective at analyzing the ontological origin of the text's estrangement by providing an appropriate analytical framework and accompanying terminology. This essay has offered an initial application of the theory to two Storyspace hypertext fictions, but more analyses are required to establish and refine the approach.

First, self-reflexive devices are certainly not exclusive to digital texts. Estrangement can be found throughout print fiction, from the self-conscious playfulness of Laurence Sterne's eighteenth-century novel *Tristram Shandy* to the more experimental strategies that McHale (1987, 1992) identifies in postmodernist print fiction (cf. Waugh 1984). Deploying

Possible Worlds Theory in his study, McHale focuses on the relationship between readers and fictional worlds, defining the ontological boundary that divides them as a "semipermeable membrane" (1987, 34). His conceptualization, like that offered in the analyses above, maintains that an ontological boundary exists, but it also concedes that the boundary is passable. Yet while similarities can be drawn between self-reflexive print and self-reflexive digital narratives, each reading experience is inevitably different. As this chapter has shown, the hypertext reader has a physical role and an associated visual presence in digital texts that intensifies and complicates the ontological relationship between reader and text, reader and machine, and reader and fictional world. The media specifics of each reading environment must therefore be taken into account in the analysis of any type of fiction (cf. Hayles 2002).

In a digital context, while the analyses above concentrate on the self-reflexivity of Storyspace hypertext novels, the application of Possible Worlds Theory may prove equally useful for the analysis of other types of electronic literature. The emergence of hypermedia narratives, which incorporate sound and image, will likely benefit from the approach demonstrated here. Disk-based texts, such as M. D. Coverley's *Califia* (2000) and Steve Tomasula and Stephen Farrell's *TOC* (2009), as well as web-based fictions, such as Stuart Moulthrop's *Reagan Library* (1999) and Lance Olsen and Tim Guthrie's *10:01* (2005), utilize the form and structure of the hypertexts analyzed above; they contain multiple paths, demand reader agency and therefore exhibit a degree of self-reflexivity produced in their hypertext cousins. Yet they also contain extensive visual images as well as sound and sometimes film. In addition to the narratological capabilities of Possible Worlds Theory, therefore, the multimodal attributes of these texts will likely require additional media-specific tools for their analysis.

Ryan (2006) notes that features of estrangement, found in the hypertext fiction novels above, are also apparent in other digital genres. In particular, she suggests that Code Poems, such as Talan Memmott's *Lexia to Perplexia* (2000), incorporate program code within the poem itself, representing "a new twist . . . on self-reference" (Ryan 2006, 219). By openly displaying the program code in which they are written, Code Poems inevitably foreground their ontological status and further analysis would help to establish whether such self-reflexivity is also exhibited within the content of the works. According to Ryan, computer games can also "play with the levels of world and code" (2006, 224) as well as "exploit the contrast between the player's real and fictional identities" (224). An accurate means of examining the relationship between real and fictional identities would further verify this conjecture. In both cases, Possible Worlds Theory could be used as a means of differentiating between the various ontological domains that are constructed within them.

Applying Ryan's (1991) Possible Worlds framework to one adventure game in particular, *Myst* (Miller and Miller 1994), Van Looy (2005) demonstrates the flexibility of the theory's narratological remit. Focusing on the immersive capacity of computer games, as opposed to features of estrangement and alienation, Van Looy interrogates Possible Worlds Theory and thereby establishes a clear analytical agenda. While he recognizes that the use of "narratological concepts and theory to describe digital media is not always unproblematic," he does conclude that "it can deliver valuable insights," and as such advocates similar experimentation in other areas of digital media analysis generally.

As this brief survey suggests, the analysis of a number of different text types may well benefit from a Possible Worlds Theory approach; self-reflexivity, reader alienation, and immersion can each be analyzed using its ontologically centered framework. However, general conclusions must not be made about its benefits for entire genres without the accompanying analyses of individual works necessary to substantiate such claims. First-wave theory stands accused of fostering a schism between theory and practice (e.g., Bell 2010; Ensslin 2007). In order to ensure that is not continued into the second wave, substantiating analyses must accompany all second-wave accounts of hypertext fictions. Despite this note of caution, the progress made within second-wave hypertext theory generally and in Possible Worlds Theory more specifically might well prove useful in the enviable task that we, as new narrative theorists and analysts, have ahead of us.

References

Aarseth, Espen. 1997. *Cybertext: Perspectives on Ergodic Literature.* Baltimore: Johns Hopkins University Press.

Barthes, Roland. 1990 [1974]. *S/Z.* Trans. Richard Miller. Oxford: Blackwell.

Bell, Alice. 2007. "'Do you want to hear about it?' Exploring Possible Worlds in Michael Joyce's Hyperfiction, *afternoon, a story.*" In *Contemporary Stylistics*, ed. Marina Lambrou and Peter Stockwell, 43–55. London: Continuum.

———. 2010. *The Possible Worlds of Hypertext Fiction*. Basingstoke: Palgrave-Macmillan.

Bolter, Jay David. 2001. *Writing Space: Computers, Writing, and the Remediation of Print*. 2nd ed. Mahwah NJ: Lawrence Erlbaum Associates Publishers.

Burnett, Kathleen. 1993. "Toward a Theory of Hypertextual Design." *Postmodern Culture* 3, no. 2. Available at http://www3.iath.virginia.edu/pmc/text-only/issue.193/burnett.193 (accessed February 3, 2010).

Ciccoricco, David. 2004. "Tending the Garden Plot: Victory Garden and Operation Enduring . . ." *Electronic Book Review*. Available at http://www.electronicbookreview.com/thread/internetnation/operational (accessed February 3, 2010).

———. 2007. *Reading Network Fiction*. Tuscaloosa: University of Alabama Press.

Coover, Robert. 1992. "The End of Books." *New York Times Book Review*, June 21, 1992, 23–24.

Coverly, M. D. 2000. *Califia*. CD-ROM. Watertown MA: Eastgate Systems.

Delany, Paul, and George, P. Landow. 1991. *Hypermedia and Literary Studies*. Cambridge MA: MIT Press.

Deleuze, Gilles, and Felix Guattari. 1988. *A Thousand Plateaus: Capitalism and Schizophrenia*. Trans. Brian Massumi. London: Athlone Press.

Derrida, Jacques. 1979. "Living On." In *Deconstruction and Criticism: A Continuum Book*, ed. James Hulbart, 75–176. New York: Seabury Press.

———. 1981. *Dissemination*. Trans. Barbara Johnson. Chicago: University of Chicago Press.

Dolezel, Lubomir. 1998. *Heterocosmica: Fiction and Possible Worlds*. Baltimore: John Hopkins University Press.

Douglas, Jane Yellowlees. 1992. "What Hypertexts Can Do That Print Narratives Cannot." *Reader: Essays in Reader-oriented Theory, Criticism, and Pedagogy* 28:1–22.

Ensslin, Astrid. 2007. *Canonizing Hypertext: Explorations and Constructions*. London: Continuum.

Ensslin, Astrid, and Alice Bell, eds. 2007. "New Perspectives on Digital Literature: Criticism and Analysis." Special issue, *dichtung-digital* 37. Available at http://www.brown.edu/Research/dichtung-digital/index.htm (accessed February 3, 2010).

Gaggi, Silvio. 1997. *From Text to Hypertext: Decentering the Subject in Fiction, Film, the Visual Arts, and Electronic Media*. Philadelphia: University of Pennsylvania Press.

Hayles, N. Katherine. 2000. "Flickering Connectivities in Shelley Jackson's *Patchwork Girl*: The Importance of Media-Specific Analysis." *Postmodern Culture* 10, no. 2. Available at http://www.iath.virginia.edu/pmc/text-only/issue.100/10.2hayles.txt (accessed February 3, 2010).

———. 2002. *Writing Machines*. Cambridge: MIT Press.

Hintikka, Jaakko. 1967. "Individuals, Possible Worlds, and Epistemic Logic." *Nous* 1:33–62.

Jackson, Shelley. 1995. *Patchwork Girl; Or, A Modern Monster*. CD-ROM for Windows. Watertown MA: Eastgate Systems.

———. 1998. "Stitch Bitch: The Patchwork Girl." *Paradoxa* 4, no. 11:526–38.

Joyce, Elisabeth. 2003. "Sutured Fragments: Shelley Jackson's *Patchwork Girl* in Piecework." In *Close Reading New Media: Analyzing Electronic Literature*, ed. Jan Van Looy and Jan Baetens, 39–52. Louvain: Leuven University Press.

Joyce, Michael. 1987. *afternoon, a story*. CD-ROM. Watertown MA: Eastgate Systems.

———. 1988. "Siren Shapes: Exploratory and Constructive Hypertexts." *Academic Computing* 3:10–14.

———. 1996. *Twilight, a Symphony*. CD-ROM. Watertown MA: Eastgate Systems.

———. 1997. "Nonce upon Some Times: Rereading Hypertext Fiction." *Modern Fiction Studies* 43, no. 3:579–97.

Koskimaa, Raine. 2000. "Digital Literature: From Text to Hypertext and Beyond." PhD diss., University of Jyvaskyla. Available at http://users.jyu.fi/~koskimaa/thesis/thesis.shtml (accessed February 2, 2010).

Kripke, Saul. 1972. *Naming and Necessity*. Oxford: Blackwell.

Landow, George P. 1994. "What's A Critic to Do? Critical Theory in the Age of Hypertext." In *Hyper/Text/Theory*, ed. George P. Landow, 1–48. Baltimore: John Hopkins University Press.

———. 1997. *Hypertext 2.0: The Convergence of Contemporary Critical Theory and Technology*. Rev. ed. Baltimore: John Hopkins University Press.

———. 2006. *Hypertext 3.0: Critical Theory and New Media in an Era of Globalization*. Baltimore: John Hopkins University Press.

Lewis, David. 1973. *Counterfactuals*. Oxford: Blackwell.

Liestol, Gunnar. 1994. "Wittgenstein, Genette, and the Reader's Narrative in Hypertext." In *Hyper/Text/Theory*, ed. George P. Landow, 87–120. Baltimore: John Hopkins University Press.

McHale, Brian. 1987. *Postmodernist Fiction*. London: Routledge.

———. 1992. *Constructing Postmodernism*. London: Routledge.

Memmott, Talan. 2000. *Lexia to Perplexia*. Available at http://www.uiowa.edu/~iareview/tirweb/hypermedia/talan_memmott/ (accessed February 2, 2010).

Miller, Rand, and Robyn Miller. 1994. *Myst*. Computer game. Broderbund.

Moulthrop, Stuart. 1991. *Victory Garden*. CD-ROM for Windows. Watertown MA: Eastgate Systems.

———. 1999. *Reagan Library*. Available at http://iat.ubalt.edu/moulthrop/hypertexts/rl/ (accessed January 17, 2011).

Olsen, Lance, and Time Guthrie. 2005. *10:01*. Available at http://www.lanceolsen.com/1001.html (accessed January 17, 2011).

Pajares Tosca, Susan. 2000. "A Pragmatics of Links." *Journal of Digital Information* 1, no. 6. Available at http://journals.tdl.org/jocu/article/view/23 (accessed January 17, 2011).

Pang, Alex Soojung-Kim. 1998. "Hypertext, the Next Generation: A Review and Research Agenda." *First Monday* 3, no. 11. Available at http://131.193.153.231/www/issues/issue3_11/pang/index.html (accessed February 3, 2010).

Parker, Jeff. 2001. "A Poetics of the Link." *Electronic Book Review*. Available at http://nww.ahx.com/ebr/ebr12/park/park.htm (accessed January 17, 2011).

Pavel, Thomas, G. 1979. "Fiction and the Casual Theory of Names." *Poetics* 8:179–91.

———. 1986. *Fictional Worlds*. Cambridge MA: Harvard University Press.

Plantinga, Alvin. 1974. *The Nature of Necessity*. Oxford: Clarendon Press.

Ronen, Ruth. 1994. *Possible Worlds in Literary Theory*. Cambridge: Cambridge University Press.

Ryan, Marie-Laure. 1991. *Possible Worlds, Artificial Intelligence and Narrative Theory*. Bloomington: Indiana University Press.

———. 2001. *Narrative as Virtual Reality: Immersion and Interactivity in Literature and Electronic Media*. Baltimore: John Hopkins Press.

———. 2006. *Avatars of Story*. Minneapolis: University of Minnesota Press.

Tomasola, Steve, and Stephen Farrell. 2009. *TOC: A New Media Novel*. DVD. Tuscaloosa: University of Alabama Press/Fiction Collection Two.

Van Looy, Jan. 2005. "Virtual Recentering: Computer Games and Possible Worlds Theory." *Image and Narrative* 12. Available at http://www.imageandnarrative.be/tulseluper/vanlooy.htm (accessed February 3, 2010).

Waugh, Patricia. 1984. *Metafiction: The Theory and Practice of Self-Conscious Fiction*. London: Methuen.

4 Seeing through the Blue Nowhere

On Narrative Transparency and New Media

MICHAEL JOYCE

But I'm not interested in transparent forms, language that
dissolves and leaves a dream of the real world: in books as well
as in hypertexts, I like to run up against the written thing,
bruise myself on its edges. I like writing that's a little hard to
swallow. And I'm not impressed by the difference between
theory and fiction, anyway. All ideas about reality are fictional,
and some of them are beautiful, too.

SHELLEY JACKSON (1998)

By now we have a reasonably long history of considering the questions of
what we mean by transparency in narrative, and how, if it is, is it threat-
ened (or perchance enhanced) by new media forms. Almost a year before
Shelley Jackson proclaimed her loyalty to written things that bang against
the shins (and a decade before this essay), Paul Harris suggested that the
transparent narrative was an illusion you could bang into:

> But once transparency appears on the screen or the net, once trans-
> parency is projected onto a network, it becomes curiously opaque
> . . . it quickly becomes apparent that we are nodes in the network,
> that the network as such will remain an unknowable system—an
> invisible territory . . . which will remain several dimensions beyond
> our ken. The opacity of the network persists in more visceral ways
> than its merely implicit invisibility—it comes home to us when we
> experience the alternating ecstasy and frustration of reading hyper-
> texts, writing with new softwares, or exploring the web. [There is]

. . . an irreducible bluntness, a resistance of the medium, that we like to overlook when our jack-in glasses fit snugly or when we theorize transparency in sweeping terms. (Harris 1997)

Yet it is just that I propose here, a sweep through notions of transparency, a sort of metanarrative meant to theorize narrative and yet just as likely to leave narrative and theory behind, a shin-bangers'—rather than a head-bangers'—ball. The method is what I have long since called theoretical narrative, a narrative of theory, theory as narrative; in this case proceeding by way of a series of more or less quirky encounters with the notion of transparency in technology and in global society alike.

Looking into transparency you quickly find a mixed history. I had already framed the previous sentence in my mind when I realized that it hid (or disclosed—I will try before long to explain why I have always thought that hiding and disclosing are related) a fairly simplistic play on words.

We are always looking into a transparency. The blue nowhere we know as the sky is an illusion of light not unlike the surface of representation, interface, and interaction that we imagine we see on a computer screen. Nor is it unlike what we claim not to see in traditional narrative. What we see the blue through is the transparency, the vitreous eye and I alike, wherein we live and breathe and move and love and make art, love, life, light, and breath.

Worse than a play on words perhaps is this, beginning with poetry. When my former student Vanessa Chang taught English to Chinese students, she sent an e-mail to me telling the story of a conversation session with her students where she asked "what language was for, i.e., beyond communication, the stock answer," and where her students' responses "turned to trade and whatnot."

We will mark for a moment that Vanessa's question, too, has its roots in the history of transparency, soon enough coming back to a consideration of how seeing or not seeing the surface of language—and thus what language is for—has intimately informed our understandings of narrative and technology alike.

As a matter of fact the in-between, which is to say the time taken up by Vanessa's story, may not occupy all that much space between this momentary bracketing mark and the coming back, from the deferral to destiny.

As such, it is nearly transparent, with emphasis on the near. Though China sometimes still seems a world away, it is no longer far from the dreams of my childhood where a hole dug in a backyard could get you there, the child's shovel giving way to a cursor and now yielding what we have come to know as a wormhole, a space through time. Or how is it the Tori Amos lyrics go?

> China all the way to New York
> Maybe you got lost in Mexico
> (1991)

Worse than beginning with a play on words or poetry is perhaps a series of interlinked stories, not to mention a feint toward the space–time continuum, but these at least are transparent gestures for someone who is a known hypertextualist. And so, speaking of wormholes—and still deferring the pleasure of Vanessa's story, I would call the reader's attention in passing to the unconsciously but eponymously punning Faile effect, named after Dr. S. P. Faile, "a semi-retired materials research engineer and scientist," according to the more than quirky website devoted to him and to his effect, who "in 1997 and early 1998 . . . began recording observations of a curious effect witnessed by him around his home. The effect seemed to mainly consist of occasional circumstances where common, normally opaque objects ranging from one's forearm, to sheet metal, to furniture, would seem to turn partially transparent. More distant objects seemed to be visible through these structures, even to the extent of such details as printed characters" (Reiter 1999).

I will leave it for the reader's later researches to discover what connection there is, at least in the mind of the writer of the web essay, between the Faile effect and LED lanterns. However, I will point out that the essay is housed on the site of "the Avalon Foundation for paranormal investigation and research," where according to the Avalon mission statement they "stand on the shore, peer through the myst [sic], and glimpse that mysterious realm [and t]he quest is to open minds by bridging the gap between science and spirituality" (Reiter 1999).

Whether or not we are as quirkily paranormal in our concerns here, gaps (or their lack, which is itself a gap) are what we are confronted with in any consideration of transparency. Nicholas Reiter, the earnest LED lantern investigator and author of this web essay on the so-called anomalous transparency of the Faile Effect, does report having "considered a number of theoretical models for the phenomenon, such as coherence of short to medium length wormhole pairs in the quantum foam of space," noting sadly, however, that "the Faile Effect . . . requires far greater definition and characterization than exists currently" (1999).

Yet it is not so far from the quantum foam of space to the classroom in Dalian, China, where Vanessa and her students conducted their own inquiry into the mist of what language hides as it discloses. In the gaps of their fledgling conversation regarding trade and whatnot, Vanessa reports that "a woman named Helen, who never speaks, never, held a long pause and then said: 'Language is to express pain, but the pain is too complicated to express.'"

Poor Doctor Faile found himself reading through sheet metal, the unspeaking Helen found words for herself through pain. Nothing stays still, as Heraclitus taught us, which makes the world of our experience a transparent place, a blue nowhere where—since the comic and tragic flow together—they are apt quickly to intermix.

Let's propose this then as a principle of transparency, narrative or otherwise: hiding is disclosing, disclosing hiding, and a gap or its lack alike is a gap.

"It was quite a moment," Vanessa's e-mail continued, "although at first I thought she said 'paint' [rather than pain] which didn't really make much sense . . . but it sent the next 30 minutes spiraling into the poetic."

I often ask my hypertext students to think about how you would know you were in the nautilus shell spiral of the classic labyrinth. Almost always someone suggests you would sense that you keep turning in the same direction, but it takes a while for someone to "see" that to really know the form you would have to put yourself in the perspective of a god, goddess, flying saucer, police helicopter, or surveillance satellite and thus intuit the form from above. However, it is only an occasional rare genius who suggests that we might be able to feel the spiral proprioceptively, forming it from within so to speak, whether from intestinal loop, brain coil, fingertip whorl, or a dervish sense of the blood flow of our gyroscopic, constantly spinning equilibrium.

Ever more a tale-spinner than in any sense an historian, I will here briefly turn to the maze of various notions of transparency, attending to what common directions we feel, what privileged views we come to see, and what embodied forms we recognize from within ourselves and the labyrinth alike, hoping in passing to contrarily say something about (new) narrative forms.

It is almost surely a generation marker that for many of us transparencies summon the 35-millimeter slides that artists once (*still* really, since the art world of galleries, curators, and dealers only slouches slowly toward the digital) labored to shoot just so and then ever after lugged along in a small narrow box along with huge portfolios in hopes of gaining a seeing if not a showing. Many of us also had a family relation, usually he was called Uncle Ned, who insisted vehemently upon the virtues of transparencies over snapshots as the preferred medium for recording everything from still lives to the blowing out of birthday candles. The result of course was that the images never went into circulation, although on regular occasions we all were forced to sit in the impromptu theater of Uncle Ned's living room while he fussed with the Kodak carousels trying to unjam badly dropped slides before they melted in the heat of the projector lamp, thus providing a vivid demonstration of the fleetingness of surface transparency.

On its face I think we are inclined to think well of the word *transparency* at least in its musicality, its traversal softened by the lapsing (if not lisping) sound of the sea at its end, the *para* rising above its center in a billow and gently drifting down. It evokes images of a certain softness and erotic mystery: the dragonfly's wing, the ballerina's tutu, or that which the graphic artist and *Watchman* writer Alan Moore describes in the introduction to his poem/performance piece *Birth Caul* as "a bellflower membrane blossomed from the amnion that masks the newborn head. Its presence occasional. Its purpose obscure, a vestment signaling involvement in some silent and unfathomable elite; some sect of Trappist embryos that dream the Absolute beneath these wan, translucent hoods" (Moore and Perkins 1995).

We will look soon enough at the engines of hell sometimes found under such translucent hoods, but for now we'll consider more benign, even idealized views of transparency.

To continue for awhile with the quirkily technological as found on the world-weary web, Brad McCormick EdD, in an essay titled "The Crown and the Cross: An Essay on Transparency and Light, *and Heart*" (the last two words set off and italicized for emphasis: *and heart*), launches himself from the high board of Heidegger's *Being and Time* to "propose a continuing role for fine mechanical timepieces as inspirational or 'evocative' objects" (2000). To think of the encrustations of the Rolex as a kind of transparency has a certain charm, as does McCormick's html-encrusted, gif-animated, blatantly boldfaced and italicized yet nonetheless sweet meditation. While it might be tempting to smile at his memoir of how "through the transparency of a department store glass display case and the intervening air, . . . those Rolex watches . . . appealed to me . . . as light reaching me across the open" there is, at end, a certain compelling poetry to his account of "examining my new Patek's movement through the crystal back . . . [and] how fragile and vulnerable the small balance wheel looks as it so rapidly oscillates back and forth . . . [reminding] me eerily of the vulnerable fragility of the beating of a human (or animal's, e.g., one of my cats' . . .) heart" (2000).

It may perhaps disclose a lack of will to turn so quickly from this survey of benign views of see-through machines to Marcel O'Gorman's earnest critique of how "the more aesthetically pleasing our hardware becomes—pleasing by means of transparency, that is—the more ignorant we become about what is actually making it tick" (2000). Talking about the briefly popular translucent iMac O'Gorman says it "creates a visual register of the industry's drive to veil computing processes from the user" acting as "a hypericon of computer marketing strategies . . . designed to reduce the consumer's level of control over information systems." He hints vaguely but forebodingly that such transparency may be complicit with a movement toward involuntary cyborgization wherein "transparent hardware would allow for a seamless transition between the real and virtual," a condition he sees as "the stuff of biotechnological implants, but . . . more readily apparent in the constant miniaturization of digital devices, which relentlessly pushes hardware toward the immaterial" (2000).

Already we are some distance, as far away as China, from McCormick's Patek Philippe Aquanaut sports watch as cute as a kitty memento mori. The question at hand—forgive the wristwatch pun and did someone mention Heidegger?—is literally one of life and death, which is to say our own inevitable push toward the immaterial. McCormick waxes poetically about the symbolic value of the "*reserve de marche* . . . or power reserve indicator" in high-end wristwatches, which marks our waning, serving "the useful function of telling how long the watch has to go until it stops working unless rewound . . . [but] perhaps even more important symbolically . . . as a reminder that time does not only 'go on' (as in the eternally repeated circular motions of the starry heavens) . . . [but]—at least for us mortals—also 'winds down' and 'runs out'" (2000).

If death is present, love, of course, cannot be far behind, an inversion I offer in keeping with my provisional principle of transparency that hiding is disclosing, disclosing hiding. McCormick cites as an epigraph to his essay a fairly representative formulation of longing from pioneer of media archeology Erkki Huhtamo: "Technology is gradually becoming a second nature, a territory both external and internalized, and an object of desire. There is no need to make it transparent any longer, simply because it is not felt to be in contradiction to the 'authenticity' of the experience" (1995, 171). If our desire takes us into the machine—transparently (the subtitle of Huhtamo's essay speaks of the Quest for Total Immersion)— our immersion seems to promise a kind of ecstatic *petit mort*, an undifferentiated post-orgasmic sleep.

Thus inevitably we return to what stand-up comics call the old in and out, whether of consciousness or body, of silence and pain or language, (someone did mention Heidegger, no?). Gianni Vattimo, the Heideggerian philosopher of transparency, is conspicuously also a philosopher of a variety of ecstatic in-and-out or "oscillation." In the emergence of a networked "society of generalized communication," Vattimo sees a lighted clearing wherein "cultures and subcultures of all sorts" can emerge into the "limelight of public opinion" (1992, 5). For Vattimo this "giddy proliferation of communication" holds the promise of a truly "transparent society" different from the Habermasian self-transparency, which as it "becomes possible from a purely technical point of view . . . is shown to be an ideal of domination and not emancipation . . ." (23). Against a self-transparent public sphere, Vattimo proposes a giddily transparent polyvocal bubble of babble, wherein our "'Emancipation' . . . consists in disorientation, which is at the same time also the liberation of differences, of local elements, of what could generally be called dialect" (8). My colleague Heesok Chang describes this dialect-filled, if not dialectical, and transparent limelight as "a constant oscillation between revelation and concealment" (1993).

"If, in a world of dialectics, I speak my own dialect," Vattimo writes, "I shall be conscious that it is not the only 'language,' but it is precisely one amongst many" (1992, 8). Thus for him, "to live in this pluralistic world means to experience freedom as a continual oscillation between belonging and disorientation" (10). It is a disorientation Heesok Chang finds wanting, an oscillation in which differences "can only appear as trembling versions of themselves—as different or 'contaminated' identities" (1993).

This cry against a contaminated disorientation is a cry for dis-orientalization as well, and as such it echoes Gayatri Spivak's famous denunciation of a "denegated" transparency in "Can the Subaltern Speak?" There she speaks of intellectuals who are neither upper-nor lowercase S/subjects—she has in mind Deleuze and Foucault—who "become transparent in the relay race, for they merely report on the nonrepresented subject and analyze (without analyzing) the workings of (the unnamed Subject irreducibly presupposed by) power and desire" (1988, 279). For Spivak, "the produced 'transparency' marks the place of 'interest'; it is maintained by vehement denegation," a sort of redoubled negative whose formulation of false innocence Spivak as something of a ventriloquist puts as an indictment in the mouths of the intellectuals she condemns, having them say "'Now this role of referee, judge, and universal witness is one which I absolutely refuse to adopt'" (1988, 279–80).

The exempting of oneself from witnessing or judging by assuming a mantle of shining transparency perhaps sheds light on the formidable listing of arenas for transparency described in the Organisation for Economic Co-operation and Development's formidably titled policy paper "Public Sector Transparency and International Investment Policy," whose abstract describes "transparency [as] a core principle of international investment policy and rules . . . good for societies at large as well as for international investors" (2003). Transparency has indeed become a buzzword of globalization (and database keyword). In this OECD document a sidebar (box 2, p. 21) lists definitions of transparency ranging from a political science dictionary ("openness to the public gaze"); to a Price Waterhouse Coopers statement on business consultancy ("the existence of clear, accurate, formal, easily discernible and widely accepted practices"); to a litany of others from the International Monetary Fund, the Draft Multilateral Agreement on Investment, the World Trade Organization, and so on.

All this supposed openness makes one suspect that there's more to this transparency than fails to meet the eye. What we have here is the flasher who hopes you don't see his real gun. We could dust off Foucault long enough after Spivak's drubbing of him a moment ago to note his classic formulation from "The Eye of Power" of how the panopticon "provided a formula applicable to many domains, the formula of 'power through transparency'" (1980, 154).

That is, if I show you my power, in time you won't see it any longer. Better still, you will come to see it as your own power. This was a danger noted by earlier hypertext theorists, who warned that the illusion of (narrative) choice could be transparently wielded by malign powers turning our every click into complicity. This is a capability taken, cynically and fascistically, to extremes by contemporary imperial powers, here and elsewhere, who believe that atrocity eventually becomes transparent once the media tires us of it through repeated seeings. Seemingly more benignly, the same line is taken—apparently unselfconsciously, even idealistically—by Digital Equipment Corporation computer scientists Karen A. Holtzblatt, Sandy Jones, and Michael Good in their paper "Articulating the Experience of Transparency" (1998).

Like the OECD transparency policy paper, they begin the section "Transparency: An Example of a Usability Concept" with a survey of the term's widespread usage. Here we might remind ourselves that such surveys and genealogies are, as Foucault or Bruno Latour tell us, transparent claims themselves: "transparency," Holtzblatt, Jones, and Good assure us, "is not a new concept" (1998). Rutkowski (1982) proposes that transparency is the ideal relationship between user and tool, with the tool seeming to disappear. Winograd and Flores (1986) relate this aspect of computer system design to Heidegger's principle of readiness-to-hand. Similar concepts are first-personness (Laurel 1986) and direct engagement (Hutchins, Hollan, and Norman 1985).

This quoted batch of internal citations in their parenthetical mustering and march of years seem to an ear or eye to warrant the claim for the not new, despite the fact that on closer notice the citations cluster around a midpoint equidistant from the first of them and the date of first publication of this paper. Holzblatt et al. go on to claim that "we see the experience of transparency when users remain in the flow of their work and are not disrupted by the computer system. Users of more transparent systems focus on the accomplishment of their tasks, and feel satisfied with how their work is moving along. The focus of users' attention is not diverted to the use of the interface" (1988).

Afloat in the workflow, up the transparent creek without an apparent paddle, feeling satisfied if not sated by how the work is moving along, we are had by others right where they would have us think we want and are wanted to be. Derrida has warned that these seemingly benign flows "through a translating medium that would claim to be transparent, meta-linguistic, and universal" while seemingly "pleading for transparency . . . for the univocity of democratic discussion, for communication in public space, for 'communicative action,'" sink us by keeping us from seeing the language within which we float, flow, and, in turn, tumble in turbulence (1992, 54–58). In such a flow there are no edges of the written thing to run up against or bruise ourselves against; everything flows smoothly through predetermined courses. "Claiming to speak in the name of intelligibility, good sense, common sense, of the democratic ethic," Derrida writes, "this discourse tends, by means of these very things, and as if naturally, to dis-credit anything that bends, overdetermines, or even questions, in theory or in practice, this idea of language" (1992, 55).

To be sure, the crusade for democracy has become the dominant impe-rialist mythos, and therefore an informing notion in new media narra-tive, in our time. Scott Robert Olson's highly influential *Hollywood Planet: Global Media and the Competitive Advantage of Narrative Transparency* describes a media strategy utterly coincident with Derrida's fears.

Working from a definition of transparency as "luminous and lucid, penetrating and clear, both in its literal sense of enabling something to be seen through and its figurative sense of the understandable manifesta-tion of meaning," Olson identifies "the capability of certain texts to seem familiar regardless of their origin, to seem a part of one's own culture, even though they have been crafted elsewhere" (1999, 18). Within these medial "texts"—among which we might cluster action movies, sports, celebrity, as well as games and other online entertainments—their (often literally) cartoon figures are not merely readable across borders but easily become (sometimes cyborgized) figures of identification. "Although those imag-es are American, they are not shaping recipients into Americans," Olson suggests in a language sure to please, if not explicitly crafted to appeal to, a polity resistant to the influx and immigration of anything but cheap Chinese goods to Walmart. Instead, Olson suggests, the images and, one supposes, the global audience that fashions themselves upon them "are merely the icons of more complex hybridization" (1999, 168).

In the realm of media transparency the sacred text is, of course, Frank Baum's Oz. Pay no attention to the man behind the scrim of his own complex hybridization. As David Bolter, a sometime latter-day Ozian, puts it in *Remediation*, "virtual Reality, three-dimensional graphics, and graphical interface design are all seeking to make digital technology 'transparent.' In this sense, a transparent interface would be one that erases itself, so that the user is no longer aware of confronting a medium, but instead stands in an immediate relationship to the contents of that medium" (Bolter and Grusin 2000, 3).

The longing to stand in immediate relation to reality is a longing for contamination by transparency, to lose yourself in the moment, the map, the medium itself, erasing all traces of the unwieldy body and its haunting and haunted mindfulness. Yet as Albert Borgmann argues, "transparency, however, is anything but transparent and casts its own shadows of enigma and confusion" (1999, 175). Noting that "transparency as a norm of clarity and presentation . . . has no intrinsic points of rest or satisfaction," Borgmann spells out what we might call the contamination of transparency, of interface, and thus of our own self-narratives, by information itself. "If you imagine yourself in control of a perfect GIS (Global Information System)," Borgmann writes, "nothing any longer presents itself with any authority. Anything might as well be an impediment to inquiry. Pollution obscures the vegetation, vegetation hides the soils, the soils conceal the geology, the geology obstructs a view of the magnetic field. And all the information about the physical makeup of the globe may be thought of as getting in the way of social reality, the latter as crowding out information about the arts and sciences, and so on" (1999, 177).

This is to say that what we know about the world gets in the way of the world we know even as it is going away from us. In *What Is Called Thinking*, Heidegger sees the moment in which "drawn into what withdraws, drawing toward it and thus pointing into the withdrawal, man first is man." For Heidegger our "essential nature lies in being such a pointer. Something which in itself, by its essential nature, is pointing, we call a sign . . . man is a sign" (1968, 9).

Not a man pointing to loss, but Lev Manovich, upon whom—at least by his own reports—nothing seemingly is lost, points to not the world but the World Wide Web as a "hypertext model . . . [of] the world as a non-hierarchical system ruled by metonymy" and where "far from being a transparent window into the data inside a computer, the interface brings with it strong messages of its own" (2001). Let us put aside the question of how, short of using LED lanterns, the interface brings these messages along by itself, and what its ownness *is* exactly as opposed to, for instance, our own. No matter, since Manovich argues against (or seems to, one is never quite sure with him) so-called "modern thinkers, from Whorf to Derrida, [who] insisted on [the] 'non-transparency of a code' idea." Instead Manovich emerges with what he thinks he sees as "an interesting paradox." The so-called "'informational dimension' . . . [of] new media objects[, which] includes retrieving, looking at and thinking about quantified data" justifies our "separating the levels of content and interface" (2001). Yet, says Manovich, "new media artworks have more traditional 'experiential' or aesthetic dimensions, which justifies [*sic*] their status as art rather than as information design." These aesthetic dimensions he lists as "a particular configuration of space, time, and surface articulated in the work; a particular sequence of user's activities over time to interact with the work; [or] a particular formal, material and phenomenological user experience."

Here he's got himself (or is it me?) in a muddle over surface that a modernist thinker, say Clement Greenberg for instance, might have helped with. Arguing that "the work's interface . . . creates its unique materiality and the unique user experience," that is, that the material is constituted by its transparency, Manovich says, "to change the interface even slightly is to dramatically change the work . . . [and] to think of an interface as a separate level, as something that can be arbitrarily varied is to eliminate the status of a new media artwork as art." This is a transparent claim for transparency, a sort of negative theology—possibly if not positively a tautology, wherein what is there is so fundamental to the work that it cannot be seen and yet its removal, through contamination or alteration, is to be guarded against.

An interesting paradox indeed. Transparency on the one hand is not to be read aesthetically, and on the other it is how we read something as having an aesthetic dimension. Hiding is disclosing, disclosing hiding, and a gap or its lack alike is a gap.

We have been this way before. Looking at the language of new media—in this case the interface of the alphabet—as a lens into the real, Richard Lanham notes how Eric Havelock "stressed that an alphabet that could support a high literate culture had to be simple enough to be learned easily in childhood. Thoroughly internalized at that time, it would become a transparent window into conceptual thought. The shape of the letters, the written surface, was not to be read aesthetically; that would only interfere with purely literate transparency" (1963, 4). Havelock's genius lay in seeing how, according to Lanham, "unintermediated thought . . . was both possible and democratizable" in an "unselfconscious transparency [that] has become a stylistic, one might almost say a cultural, ideal for Western civilization" (1963, 4).

Over against this supposedly democratizing transparency we have the shin-banging or blurring recognition of individuality and specificity. Thus, in a canny, media-specific reading of Mark Z. Danielewski's novel *House of Leaves*, albeit one deeply dependent upon Lanham's notions of transparency (as well as N. Katherine Hayles's [2002] reading of the novel), Sonya Hagler speaks of those "texts that have been influenced by the advent of electronic publishing" that "reject the traditional transparency of the page, forcing the reader to first look at the textual surface before looking through it to the content" (Hagler 2007, 5). Referring to Lanham's looking *at/through* distinction, Hagler notes that "whereas before, a reader simply looked through the text into its content, readers in our postmodern age must first look at the text, acknowledging the physicality and aesthetics of the text on the page. . . . Danielewski constantly forces an awareness of the book's physical existence . . . [and] manipulates the conventions of print space in order to blur the boundaries between traditional print and hypertexts" (Hagler 2004).

The most recognizable embodiment of transparency in our time—and the penultimate in this essay—is the figure against the blue screen: the weatherman floating like a balloon in the blue nowhere above a city, the anchorwoman superimposed on a mappemunde. Because I am told that he spent several years in Poughkeepsie after his retirement from Yale while his wife still taught there, I sometimes think of Eric Havelock as a figure against a blue screen, superimposed along Raymond Avenue in the vicinity of Vassar where I teach. What I know of him comes out of the blue as well, from rumor and passing recollection. He is said to have been a womanizer, to have haunted the libraries, to have been amusing at parties. I like the idea of the great pre-Socratic professor passing largely unnoticed among the coeds, transparent if you like, a mere year after Vassar decided to sever its sister school relation with Yale.

Michael Joyce 95

Of course, rumor and reputation are themselves both sorts of interfaces, and in Greek mythology a single goddess serves both. Pheme or Fama, fame or rumor, according to Ovid's *Metamorphoses*, makes "her chosen home set on the highest peak constructed with a thousand apertures and countless entrances and never a door. Open night and day and built throughout of echoing bronze; it all reverberates, repeating voices, doubling what it hears. Inside, no peace, no silence anywhere, and yet no noise, but muted murmurings like waves one hears of some far-distant sea" (2000, ll. 39–63).

Ovid means this description as a disavowal if not a condemnation. What we see through reverberates. Yet seeing through is a phrase I love, having written before about its doubleness: how seeing through suggests both lens and persistence. Like "still flowing," another favorite meditative phrase, seeing through releases as it contains, an oscillation put in play in what Gianni Vattimo (1992) sees as the defining characteristic of transparency. It is this (doubleness, putting into play, oscillation, shin-banging) that perhaps forms (and reinforms) our understanding of narrative in a world of putatively new media.

There is a dilemma that lingers after charged language like the smell of ozone after lightning. Clarity once one is clear of the thicket seems a refutation ("if you can say it directly, and it appears that you can, why not do so?"), as if all that went before was laziness and not the work of getting here.

If the dreamer awakes, was the dream false? If the feverish child no longer raves, was nothing uttered? Is the blue nowhere nowhere at all?

I once thought to give a talk for which I might wear a particular grey Italian suit that I bought a long time ago to attend La Scala. My idea was to have myself filmed against a blue screen and then project the image of myself reading the talk, like a one-to-one map, against myself reading it live before the audience in the same grey suit. Not the unintermediated but the hypermediated man. I had in mind the extraordinary and much richer version of such an effect that I had seen in a recent revival of Robert Whitman's *Prune Flat* (2003) performance piece at the DIA Beacon museum, New York. Seeing that performance in which two women dressed in white walked in and out of images of themselves, nude, clothed in flowers and leaves, or the same white dresses, I was struck by the materiality and mortality of the film that clattered through dual 16-millimeter projectors. There was a materiality and mortality also in the gap between the women depicted in the projected images of thirty years ago, their bodies now surely aging and perhaps even gone to earth, and the women who performed the piece now, lithe and light, the flesh and fur of thirty years ago ripe upon them. They moved in a light we might now perhaps construct better and more swiftly from transparent Photoshop layers adrift above the film of interface that floats upon the river of still more transparent digits the pre-Socratic Greeks knew long before us. Seeing them, I recalled the many pleasures of seeing and seeing through, walking through imaginary gardens with long gone ladies and gentlemen, celebrating our persistence in the blue nowhere, our muted murmurings like the waves one sometimes sees from afar.

References

Amos, Tori. 1991. "China." *Little Earthquakes*. New York: Atlantic Records.

Bolter, David, and Richard Grusin. 2000. *Remediation: Understanding New Media*. Cambridge MA: MIT Press.

Borgmann, Albert. 1999. *Holding on to Reality: The Nature of Information at the Turn of the Millennium*. Chicago: University of Chicago Press.

Chang, Heesok. 1993. "Postmodern Communities: The Politics of Oscillation." *Postmodern Culture* 4, no. 1. Available at http://muse.jhu.edu/journals/postmodern _culture/v004/4.1r_chang.html (accessed January 12, 2011).

Derrida, Jacques. 1992. *The Other Heading*. Trans. Pascale-Anne Brault and Michael B. Naas. Bloomington: Indiana University Press.

Foucault, Michel. 1980. "The Eye of Power." In *Power/Knowledge: Selected Interviews and Other Writings, 1972–1977*, ed. Colin Gordon, 146–65. Sussex: Harvester.

Hagler, Sonya. 2004. "Mediating Print and Hypertext in Mark Danielewski's House of Leaves." MODE. Available at http://www.arts.cornell.edu/english/publications/ mode/documents/hagler.html (accessed January 12, 2011).

Harris, Paul. 1997. "HYPER-LEX: A Technographical Dictionary." *Electronic Book Review*. Available at http://www.altx.com/ebr/ebr4/harris.htm.

Havelock, Eric A. 1963. *Preface to Plato*. Cambridge MA: Harvard University Press.

Hayles, N. Katherine. 2002. *Writing Machines*. MIT Press: Mediaworks Pamphlets.

Heidegger, Martin. 1968. *What Is Called Thinking*. Trans. J. G. Gray and F. Wieck. New York: Harper & Row.

Holtzblatt, Karen A., Sandy Jones, and Michael Good. 1988. "Articulating the Experience of Transparency: An Example of Field Research Techniques." *SIGCHI Bulletin* 20, no. 2:46–48. Available at http://home.earthlink.net/~goodclose/sigchi 88.html (accessed January 7, 2011).

Huhtamo, Erkki. 1995. "Encapsulated Bodies in Motion: Simulators and the Quest for Total Immersion." In *Critical Issues in Electronic Media*, ed. Simon Penney, 159–86. Albany: SUNY Press.

Hutchins, Edwin L., James D. Hollan, and Donald A. Norman. 1985. "Direct Manipulation Interfaces." *Human-Computer Interaction* 1, no.4:311–38.

Jackson, Shelley, and Mark Amerika (interview). 1998. "Stitch Bitch: The Hypertext Author as Cyborg-Femme Narrator." *Amerika Online* 7. Available at http://www .heise.de/tp/r4/artikel/3/3193/1.html (accessed January 7, 2011).

Lanham, Richard. 1993. *The Electronic Word: Democracy, Technology, and the Arts.* Chicago: University of Chicago Press.

Laurel, Brenda K. 1986. "Interface as Mimesis." In *User Centered System Design*, ed. Donald. A. Norman and Stephan W. Draper, 67–85. Hillsdale NJ: Lawrence Erlbaum Associates.

Manovich, Lev. 2001. "The Interface." Excerpted from *The Language of New Media.* Cambridge MA: MIT Press. Available at http://interface.to.or.at/levmessay.html (accessed January 7, 2011).

McCormick, Brad. 2000. "The Crown and the Cross: An Essay on Transparency and Light, *and Heart.*" Available at http://www.users.cloud9.net/~bradmcc/lux .html (accessed January 19, 2011).

Moore, Alan David J., and Tim Perkins. 1995. *The Birth Caul.* Staged in Newcastle upon Tyne, November 18. CHARRMMCD22.

O'Gorman, Marcel. 2000. "You Can't Always Get What You Want: Transparency and Deception on the Computer Fashion Scene." *CTHEORY Theory, Technology and Culture* 23, no. 3, Event-Scene 94. Available at http://www.ctheory.net/text _file.asp?pick=227 (accessed January 7, 2011).

Olson, Scott Robert. 1999. *Hollywood Planet: Global Media and the Competitive Advantage of Narrative Transparency.* Mahwah NJ: Lea.

Organisation for Economic Co-operation and Development. 2003. "Public Sector Transparency and International Investment Policy." Available at http://www .oecd.org/dataoecd/45/22/2506884.pdf (accessed January 7, 2011).

Ovid. 2000. *Metamorphoses.* Trans. Sir Samuel Garth, John Dryden, et al. Book 12. The Internet Classics Archive. Available at http://classics.mit.edu/Ovid/ metam.12.twelfth.html.

Reiter, Nicholas. 1999. "Observations of Anomalous Transparency: The Faile Effect." Available at http://www.theavalonfoundation.org/docs/faile.html (accessed December 23, 2010).

Rutkowski. Chris. 1982. "An Introduction to the Human Applications Standard Computer Interface, Part I: Theory and Principles." *Byte* 7, no. 10:291–310.

Spivak, Gayatri. 1988. "Can the Subaltern Speak?" In *Marxism and the Interpretation of Culture*, ed. Cary Nelson and Lawrence Grossberg, 271–313. Urbana: University of Illinois Press.

Vattimo, Gianni. 1992. *The Transparent Society*. Trans. David Webb. Baltimore: Johns Hopkins University Press.

Whitman, Robert. 2003. *Prune Flat*. First performed in the Expanded Cinema Festival at the Film-Makers Cinematheque, New York City, December 1965. Restaged at DIA: Beacon, and DIA: Chelsea, September 5–7 and 10–12, 2003.

Winograd, Terry, and Fernando Flores. 1986. *Understanding Computers and Cognition: A New Foundation for Design*. Norwood NJ: Ablex.

PART 2 : *New Architectures*

5 Curveship

An Interactive Fiction
System for Narrative Variation

NICK MONTFORT

Interactive fiction is a venerable, well-defined category of computer programs that includes the canonical *Adventure* and *Zork* as well as work by established literary authors: *Mindwheel* by Robert Pinsky, *The Hitchhiker's Guide to the Galaxy* by Douglas Adams and Steve Meretzky, and *Amnesia* by Thomas Disch. These programs are often correctly called games, but they can also be rich text-based computer simulations, dialog systems, and examples of literary art.

Unlike many other new media forms, interactive fiction (often called "IF") computationally simulates a world underlying the textual exchange between computer and user. Theorists of narrative have long distinguished between the level of underlying content or story (which can usefully be seen as corresponding to the simulated world in interactive fiction) and that of expression or discourse (corresponding to the textual exchange between computer and user). While IF development systems have offered a great deal of power and flexibility to author/programmers, they have not systematically distinguished between the telling and what is told. Developers have not been able to use separate modules to control the content and expression levels independently, so there has been no easy, general way to control narrative style and create variation in the narrative discourse.

This chapter reports on a new interactive fiction system, called Curveship, which does allow this sort of control. (The system was originally called "nn," and early writing about the system refers to it as such.) First, I provide a brief introduction to interactive fiction, as a particular form with a history. Then, I describe how ideas from narratology can be applied to interactive fiction. After that, I sketch a new architecture for interactive fiction that abstracts the expression level from the content level by specifying different modules. The Teller module, which is responsible for producing different sorts of narrative discourse based on the underlying simulation of the IF world, is described in detail. Although implemented in the context of interactive fiction, this module was designed to offer a general way of narrating in natural language. It is hoped that it will provide insight into how computers can automatically narrate in other, nontextual modalities and in other contexts. The Teller module is offered as a concrete example of how narratology can inform and improve the generation of natural language by computer.

Some Interactive Fiction Essentials

Interactive fiction is an intriguing digital media form with a rich history. It may be less familiar than hypertext to many people in the humanities, but it was very popular among minicomputer users and early home computer users. Because it involves the explicit computational simulation of the content or story level, it is particularly interesting to those who study narrative theory.

As a brief example of how interaction in interactive fiction works, a transcript of few interactions from Michael Gentry's *Anchorhead* (1998), a large-scale interactive fiction work that draws on the mythos of H. P. Lovecraft, is supplied below. There are only two actions carried out in this excerpt, but they are very representative ones: moving objects around and interacting with characters accounts for much of the activity in interactive fiction generally, and this often reveals interesting information. This part of the transcript occurs after the player character (the character controlled by the user's typed input) walks into the vacant lot, encountering an old man she had previously met. It is important to know here that the player character is wearing a coat and that she is holding a newspaper and has a gold locket in her pocket, items that have only been obtained after exploration of the environment and some effort on the user's part.

Vacant Lot

Where once a building stood, there is now only cracked pavement and rampant weeds. A high chain-link fence surrounds this vacant lot; the only breaks lie to the west and southeast.

The old man looks up at you with fawning admiration.

>show the gold locket to the man

(first taking the gold locket)

(slipping the newspaper into the pocket of your trenchcoat to get a hand free)

The bum starts to reach for the locket, but his hand stops a few inches away. His fingers are trembling. He gazes at the woman's picture with grief and regret, and a hint of something akin to love. "Why," he whispers, "that's the very likeness, so it is. That's my Anna. Pretty little Anna . . ."

>ask man about anna

Tears stream unchecked down the old man's face. "Shouldn't have happened to the girl. Only seventeen, she was, still a child when he . . . when that red-eyed monster took her . . ." His eyes suddenly darken, his fists clench. "HIS OWN DAUGHTER, GODS FUCK'EM! SHOULDN'T HAVE DONE THAT TO HIS OWN DAUGHTER! GODS FUCK 'EM ALL!!"

The ">" character is a prompt provided by the program; what follows are commands typed by the user. The user initially types "show the gold locket to the man," which results in the player character trying to take it out of her pocket. This requires that the player character put the newspaper away, which is done automatically. Then the locket is shown to the man, who reacts.

The next command is "ask man about anna." Proper capitalization, punctuation, and articles such as "the" and "a" are usually optional in commands. Although the actions taken here are typical ones, and it is usual for actions to reveal new information, the information that comes to light here has a rather different emotional impact on the old man—and likely on the user—than did the light, humorous events often associated with interactive fiction in the late 1970s and early 1980s.

Interactive fiction originated in 1976 with Will Crowther's *Adventure*, a game for the PDP-10 that was expanded into its canonical form by Don Woods. The text adventure (a designation that means almost the same thing as interactive fiction) and the "adventure game" genre both take their names from this program. There were antecedents, including the conversational character *Eliza*, which Joseph Weizenbaum developed in

1966; Gregory Yob's 1973 cave-crawl game *Hunt the Wumpus*; and Terry Winograd's AI system SHRDLU of 1968–70, with its natural-language interface to a simulated robot. Early interactive fiction was developed at universities in the United States and abroad; the University of Cambridge produced many games. An important follow-up to *Adventure* was developed by four programmers at MIT: *Zork*, which was commercialized at the company Infocom.

Infocom broke out of the fantasy genre with the 1981 detective story *Deadline* and became the most prominent U.S. developer of interactive fiction. Adventure International had made it to market first; many other companies, including several in the United Kingdom and Australia, produced and sold games, such as Melbourne House's text-and-graphics adventure *The Hobbit*. The market for interactive fiction waned in the late 1980s as the first relevant academic effort began: Carnegie Mellon University's Oz Project, which ran from 1989 until 2002.

As companies folded or moved on, individuals turned to creating their own interactive fiction. New development systems came about: TADS (Text Adventure Development System) by Mike Roberts was released as shareware in 1987; Graham Nelson's Inform was released for free in 1993 along with Nelson's game *Curses*. In 1995 the first Interactive Fiction Competition was held. The 1998 winner, Adam Cadre's *Photopia*, portrays several scenes from a girl's brief life and rich imagination and demonstrated to many that these games could use literary modes and deal with serious issues. In 2000 Emily Short's *Galatea* offered an animated statue, capable of conversation and driven by topic-based and emotional models. For more on recent and historical interactive fiction work, see Montfort's "Riddle Machines" (2007b) or the more thorough treatment in *Twisty Little Passages* (Montfort 2003).

The discussion so far has outlined the way interactive fiction appears from the user's perspective. It is also useful to mention certain essential formal aspects. A work of interactive fiction is characterized by being:

- A text-accepting, text-generating computer program. There are interactive fiction programs with multimedia elements; graphical adventure games also share many features with standard, text-based IF. The term is typically used to indicate programs that accept natural language textual input, however, and that produce textual output in reply.

- A simulation of an environment, which can also be called a world, since it is complete and systematic. When the player character is directed to move to a new location in an interactive fiction program, the system does not just cause a new hypertextual lexia to appear on the screen. A simulation runs, and the world is updated to reflect the movement of that character from one place to another. This may have consequences—perhaps different ones, based on different states of the world. Other characters may also act during this turn, and consequences of earlier events may ensue.
- A structure of rules in which an outcome may be sought. If there are outcomes that are preferred (ones corresponding to a higher score, or ones in which the player character triumphs), this makes the program a game in the strict sense of the word. It is not essential that an interactive fiction program is a game. Most are structured as games, however—as is *Anchorhead*—just as most works of hypertext fiction are not.
- Not a narrative but a *potential narrative*. That is, the program itself is not a representation of a sequence of events. By analogy to the Oulipian concept of potential literature (Mathews and Brotchie 1998), a given work of interactive fiction is instead a potential narrative—something that can produce many different narratives depending on what a person types into it. (Different narratives might also arise as a result of randomness or other actors, but it is essential that the output is conditioned on input from the user— this is what makes interactive fiction interactive.) IF can also be seen as producing small-scale narratives during each turn in reply to the user's input.

A Potential Narratology

To understand interactive fiction deeply, I have worked to develop a *potential narratology* of the form. This involved identifying categories of narrative variation that are possible in IF, an effort that was based mainly on Genette's *Narrative Discourse* (1980) and his further writing on the system introduced there in *Narrative Discourse Revisited* (1988). In part, a formalization of Genette's system was necessary so that the result would be precisely defined from a mathematical or computational standpoint and could be effectively implemented in a natural language generation system. Montfort (2007a) provides a detailed description of the potential narratology of IF and the formalization of Genette's system, along with a full description of Curveship and diagrams of the system's architecture.

The interactive fiction system Curveship was developed to allow for control over what I refer to as *narrative variation*. This is shorthand for narrating the same underlying content—the same events happening in a world with the same existents (Chatman 1978)—in different ways. There are, of course, other ways that a narrative can vary: it is possible to substitute one character for another, for instance, and then narrate the new story in the same style but with a different set of existents. This may be interesting to do, but changes of this sort are well supported by existing interactive fiction systems. The point of Curveship is, most generally, the opposite of this: to allow any events, given any set of existents, to be narrated automatically in many different ways.

It is hard to think of a narrative literary work that does not achieve some of its effect because of how it is narrated. Perhaps the clearest example of how narrating in different styles resonates in different ways is Raymond Queneau's *Exercices de style* (1947), translated by Barbara Wright as *Exercises in Style* (1958). Queneau tells the same rather uninteresting story in ninety-nine different ways. Matt Madden was prompted by Queneau's book to create a similar comic, published in 2005 as *99 Ways to Tell a Story: Exercises in Style*. While not all of Queneau's or Madden's variations are specific to narrative, several are. The two books provide a fascinating look at the power of stylistic variation across media.

Order, speed, and frequency are the topics of three of Genette's (1980, 1988) five chapters and major parts of his system. Figure 13 illustrates each of these by representing one particular change in narrative style— the same content (events 1 through 5) being told in two different ways. At the top, the five events are narrated chronologically, with one expression per event, as in "The king died. The queen grieved. The queen died. The clown usurped the throne. The jester laughed." At the bottom, the five events are narrated in a different way. There is no expression of event 2—it is simply elided, or, in Genette's terms, passed over with infinite speed. Events 1 and 3 are narrated together in a single expression. (This is a change in frequency, from singulative to iterative.) Also, the remaining two events are narrated out of order: First 5, then 4. This corresponds to "The king and queen died. The jester laughed after the clown usurped

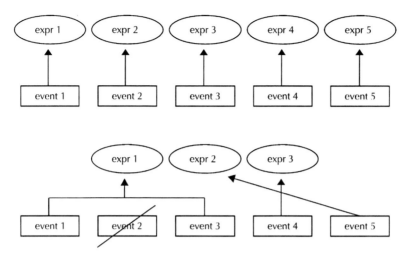

13. Narrative event told in two different ways. Created by Nick Montfort.

the throne." Other narrative factors beyond order, speed, and frequency are important to the basic functioning of Curveship. One is the focalization, which Genette discusses within the category mood, and another is the time of narrating, which he deals with as a quality of voice. Focalizing involves choosing a particular character, or no character, through which the information of the story world will be regulated. Time of narrating, in its simplest formulation, means that a narrator can speak simultaneously with the action (and thus in present tense) or from a standpoint before or after it. Finally, the roles of narrator (the narrative's "I") and narratee (the narrative's "you"), as discussed by Prince (1982), also need to be freely assignable to different entities in a flexible system for narrative variation.

Given a representation of the content layer (events and existents, which I call items) and given some author-created rules about how to express events, Curveship was developed to be able to automatically narrate by making changes in order, speed, frequency, mood (specifically, focalization), and voice (specifically, time of narrating). An example interactive fiction was also developed to compose some of these variations and effect a change in narrative distance. The style of narration can be changed during a session based on the user's progress through the simulated world, or based on user input, or based or many other factors.

For decades, interactive fiction has had the power to automatically change what happens in a simulated world. This has been central to the innovations that have been made in the form. It has not, however, had nearly as much capability for changing how events are told. This seems a significant omission, since so much of what makes stories interesting relates to the telling. The development system Curveship was created to address this issue and to facilitate narrative variation.

The Architecture of Curveship

The architecture of Curveship draws on well-established techniques for simulating an IF world and a standard pipeline architecture for natural language generation. It includes an additional set of worlds representing the perspectives of focalizers, a division between content (and simulating) and expression (and narrating), and a modularized way of carrying out other IF functions. In Curveship, representations of the world state, focalizer knowledge, and the discourse state are stored in models—namely, the IF World, the Concepts, and the Discourse Model. These are updated by modules—components of the program—some of which also handle input and produce output. The most important modules from a research standpoint are the Simulator and the Teller.

The IF World is the base, authoritative model within the interactive fiction, "actual" from the standpoint of interactive fiction actors, following the terminology of Ryan (1991). This IF World model is one of several world models, however; the models also include a Concept, based on perceptions and experiences, for each actor. Each Concept represents one actor's theory about the "reality" that the IF World encodes. The Simulator and IF World were developed to represent things such as the physical movement of objects and the configuration of a space in a flexible way, not to richly model emotional and mental qualities.

The IF World and Concepts each have their own tree of items, a hierarchical structure with the root representing the universe overall and each parent–child relationship signifying a type of containment—an apple being inside a lunch box, a chair being in a hallway, a newspaper being in a character's possession, and so on. Each also has its own lists of actions, connected by causality and marked as happening in time, with each action having preconditions, a template for generating its representation in text, and (in some cases) a postcondition. These can differ for several reasons, the most fundamental of which is that characters almost always have incomplete knowledge of what has happened in the IF World due to their limited perceptions.

Items are represented as *things, rooms, doors,* or *actors.* Inert objects such as the gold locket and the newspaper from *Anchorhead* would usually be represented as things. The vacant lot and other locations, whether interior or not, are best represented as rooms. Anything that can act on its own, including characters such as the old man from *Anchorhead,* are actors.

There are only four types of actions, and only two types actually change the state of the world: MODIFY alters the state of an object—a lunch box goes from being closed to being open, for instance, or a lamp from being off to being on—and CONFIGURE rearranges the tree of items, as when a character walks from one room to another or when a newspaper is put into a coat pocket. To walk into a kitchen, a character, say the emperor of ice cream, could first perform a BEHAVE action representing starting off in a certain direction and then CONFIGURE himself into the new location. A SENSE action (representing perception) will be automatically attempted after this, since people habitually look around when entering a new space.

Representing both events and items explicitly allows the narration of events to be accomplished as easily as are descriptions of places, people, and objects.

The Teller Module

The task of generating textual output is handled by Curveship's Teller module. While all interactive fiction systems accomplish some sort of simulation, none of the released systems have well-developed facilities for narrating. Typically, an interactive fiction system simply prints out strings of text that have been pre-written by the author or provided by libraries for developers. This happens as the simulation runs, event by event, so there is no easy way to accomplish something like an analepsis or any other reordering of events in the telling (that is, any sort of anachrony).

The Teller module has its own internal architecture. Its organization is based on a standard three-stage pipeline for natural language generation. The first stage is the reply planner, where the high-level arrangement of expressions is managed. The output of this stage is an ordered tree that, among other things, indicates the sequence in which these expressions will finally appear. In the next stage, the microplanner, the grammatical specifics corresponding to this structure, including tense, aspect, and number, are determined. Finally, the last stage, the realizer, produces the particular strings that will be formatted and output.

The narrator is capable of varying several aspects of the narrating. Among these are Genette's previously mentioned categories of variation in narrative tense: order, frequency, and speed. It is also possible to vary focalization (a type of narrative mood) and time of narrating (a type of narrative voice). In the remainder of this discussion, I describe the system's ability to vary order and the time of narrating—two types of variation that are actually closely linked from the standpoint of text generation. To have a computer generate narrative, it was necessary to define not just different sequences of events that fall into the categories described by Genette but also the particular processes that characteristically generate these sequences. In other words, formally defining an analepsis (or flashback) is not enough for narrative generation; it is also necessary to specify an algorithm that can generate an analepsis—preferably most or all analepses. That is, the task of generating narrative demands that we have not only formal models for *narrative* but also formal models for *narrating*. Characterizations of such formal models—specifically, algorithms for reordering events—follow.

Chronicle—Sort a set of events into chronological order. "Chronicle" may not specify a unique order, because some events may be simultaneous.

Retrograde—Sort a set of events into reverse chronological order.

Zigzag—This is the process of interleaving sections from period 1 (the "now") with those from period 2 (the "once") while narrating chronologically within each. A passage from Marcel Proust's *Jean Santeuil* provides an example (Genette 1980, 37–38). The "now" and "once" must be designated along with a rule for moving between sequences. This could be as simple as "narrate a single event before switching," or it could involve specifying that all the events in a single physical location are narrated in the "now," then the corresponding events in the "then," and then similarly with the next physical location.

Analepsis—Also called *flashback* or *retroversion*, this indicates an anachronism inserted into a main sequence that is presumably chronological to begin with. For this process to work, both a main sequence and the point of insertion of the analepsis need to be designated. From the standpoint of the analysis of narrative, measures such as Genette's (1980) *reach* and *extent* are useful, but when generating an analepsis, those measures, the difference in time and the overall duration of the analepsis, are not the most useful things to specify. It is better to specify what should be included in the analepsis based on features of events. For instance, "select the most salient event from the first time the focalizer encountered this character," or "select the most salient events that the focalizer has seen happen in this room in the past, up to three of them." Of course, to make the latter rule useful, a rule for determining the salience of events must also be precisely specified. Given the main sequence, the point of insertion, and a fully specified rule for selecting events from the past, the process of ordering events so as to include an analepsis is straightforward.

Prolepsis—To insert a prolepsis, also known as *flashforward* or *anticipation*, the same three inputs are needed: a main sequence, a point of insertion, and a rule for selecting events from the future. When some newly simulated events are being narrated for the first time, there will not be a supply of simulated events waiting in the future. However, there are still circumstances under which a prolepsis can occur. An IF author can prepare "inevitable" events with future time stamps, representing things like the sun going down or nuclear missiles arriving. Also, there will be plenty of times in which the main sequence of events being recounted is from the past, so that future events relative to that time span will be available.

Syllepsis—This is the organization of events into categories. Beyond the original set of events, only a sequence of categories seems essential for specifying sylleptic narrating. For instance, such a sequence might have these three categories of events in it: "the adventurer entering a new area," "the adventurer defeating a monster," and "the adventurer acquiring a treasure." If all events are in exactly one category, the categorization will be unique. The narrator can move through each of the categories and, within each category, can represent each of the events chronologically. There is no reason to restrict a sylleptic narration to chronological order within categories, though. Any principle for ordering based on time alone (chronicle, retrograde, achrony) can be specified for ordering the narrative within categories.

Achrony—Ordering events at random seems a suitable way to produce the type of order needed for achrony.

This describes how events can be rearranged from a chronological sequence into a narrative one that may not be chronological. Reordering has been characterized as producing a sequence, but there are problems with this view, because much structural information is lost in the flattened representation of the sequence. An analepsis, for instance, is not well represented by the sequence 3 4 5 1 2 6 7. The sequence of events that is in the past, relative to the main sequence—the 1 2, in this case—is actually embedded, but there is no evidence of this when seven numbers are presented in a row. The information about the embedding of "1 2" will usually be necessary to generate a narrative. When the main sequence is being told in the present tense, the 1 2 will almost certainly be told in the past. If the main sequence is already being told in the past tense, there will almost certainly be some cue that 1 2 occurs at a much earlier time: a phrase such as "before that," an explicit reference to the earlier date, some statement about habitual occurrences in the past, or a statement in the perfect tense leading into the analepsis. Without knowing that "1 2" is embedded, it is difficult to figure out how to shift the tense appropriately or add such a cue. Furthermore, using a simple sequence, there is no way to distinguish this analeptic case from an achronic jumble or from a sylleptic narration in which "3 4 5" are in the first category, "1 2" is in the second, and "6 7" is in the third. The representation used in Curveship does distinguish these three cases, as shown in figure 14.

Even without attempting to generate all of these sorts of transitions, there is clearly a need to designate more about the order of events than a simple sequence encodes. Such a representation should not force the tense of the analepsis to be different, but it should allow for this difference. It should also integrate the times at which events occurred into the decision about tense. Simply associating an arbitrary tense with the main sequence and another arbitrary tense with the analepsis would not accomplish this. The grammatical tense should be a result of the position of the simulated events in time and other essential parameters. To accomplish this, an ordered tree representation is used. For this particular analepsis, the tree will have a root node at the top level, 3, 4, 5, a special node, 6, and 7 at the level below, as children of the root, and then 1 and 2 at the lowest level, as children of the special, internal node. Such a tree is called a reply structure.

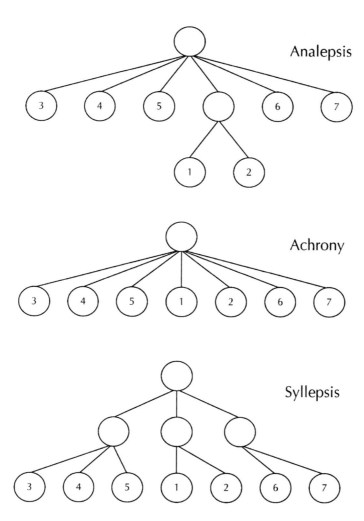

14. Chronology in Curveship. Created by Nick Montfort.

The temporal position of the narrating vis-à-vis the narrated has a special status: "I can very well tell a story without specifying the place where it happens, and whether this place is more or less distant than the place where I am telling it; nevertheless, it is almost impossible for me not to locate the story in time with respect to my narrating act, since I must necessarily tell my story in present, past, or future tense" (Genette 1980, 215). These tenses lead to the "three major possibilities" for the temporal position of the narrating relative to the narrated: posterior, anterior, and simultaneous narration (Prince 1982, 27). While Genette deals with this in his category *voice* rather than in *order*, from the standpoint of generating narrative and determining grammatical tense, the temporal relationship of the narrator to events is as important as the temporal relationship of events to one another. Both must be dealt with jointly.

The tense of a proposed expression is necessary for realization; fortunately, this tense can be determined from three points in time assigned to the proposed expression that are called E, R, and S. Furthermore, these points can be defined for each specific expression using general rules (specifically, FOLLOW, MAX, MIN, a numeric value, and HOLD) that reside in the reply structure on these special, internal nodes—they do not have to each be individually prepared by the author.

To allow the time stamps of the events and the temporal position of the narrator to participate in the determination of tense, an ordered tree of internal nodes and proposed expressions of events is used. This is the reply structure, a specification of what content to include, what order to include it in, and how to embed sequences. To realize a particular expression, there must be enough information to fully specify its syntax; in particular, this means that the system must be able to determine the tense.

Tense is determined using a theory that relates speech time (S), reference time (R), and event time (E) to grammatical tense (Reichenbach 1947, 287–98). Three times are necessary because in a sentence such as "Peter had gone," there are three relevant points of time that are needed to explain the tense: the time at which the sentence is spoken (S, the time of speech); the time at which Peter left (E, event time), and another time that is being referred to, in this case, a time after the event time and before the time of speech, by saying "had gone" rather than something else, such as "went" or "was going." This last time is R, the time of reference. Specifically, "the position of R relative to S [corresponds to] 'past,' 'present,' and 'future.' The position of E relative to R . . . 'anterior,' 'simple,' and 'posterior'" (Reichenbach 1947, 297).

Because all events in Curveship are simulated as happening at some specific time, Reichenbach's E (event time) is always available. The Teller would not be very helpful if it were then necessary for the author/programmer to write code to determine every value of R and S. Instead of requiring this, the reply planner uses the topology of the reply structure to assign R and S in a systematic way across each embedded sequence.

Each embedded sequence has a parent, an internal node. On each internal node, a rule for determining the R and S values for children is provided. For each of R and S, there are several rules available. One is FOLLOW, which sets the value of R or S to E so that reference time or speech time "follows" the events. Other rules include MAX, MIN, a number (to specify a fixed time), and HOLD (to keep the value from the level above). For example, consider a reply structure that consists of just a root (a single internal node) with one level of n proposed expressions beneath it, their event times indicated by $E_1 \ldots E_n$. Setting speech time to MAX and reference time to FOLLOW in this internal node will assign $S_1 \leftarrow$ MAX, $S_2 \leftarrow$ MAX $\ldots S_n \leftarrow$ MAX, and $R_1 \leftarrow E_1$, $R_2 \leftarrow E_2 \ldots R_n \leftarrow E_n$, so that throughout the sequence, $E = R > S$. This results in simple past-tense narration for the entire reply.

Setting both speech and reference time to FOLLOW will similarly mean that $S = R = E$ everywhere, producing simple present-tense narration. When narrating events and moving back in time to narrate previous events, in an analepsis the speech time can be held at the current point in the main sequence using HOLD while the reference time is set to FOLLOW, so $E = R > S$ for past-tense narration throughout the embedded sequence. This is the case shown in figure 15. Present-tense narration will be generated for the top level, while the expressions corresponding to 1 and 2 will be in the simple past. There are other options. For instance, in narrating some events that happened between time 500 and time 600, R can be set to 600 and S to MAX to generate representations of the events in the past perfect. A narrative sequence can be generated in any of Reichenbach's nine fundamental forms (<anterior, simple, posterior> ⊗ <past, present, future>) by specifying S and R in such ways.

Each proposed expression has its R and S values set in the reply planner using the rule from its parent. Once all the proposed expressions have been defined with specific values for E, R, and S, all the necessary information is in place for the next stage of the Teller to compute the tense using Reichenbach's formulas. The R and S rules on the internal nodes are general (they do not require that every R and S value be specified or computed by author-written code) but also flexible (they do not demand, for instance, that every analepsis is told in a different tense from the sequence in which it is embedded).

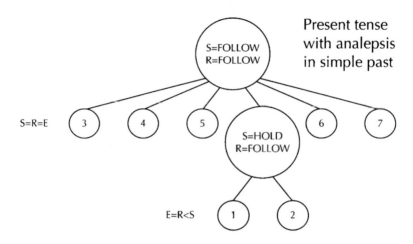

15. Present-tense narration. Created by Nick Montfort.

The Future of Automatic Narration

While interactive fiction seems a particularly interesting form for future work in digital narrative, there are certainly other forms, including non-fiction ones, which could be improved by providing capabilities for narrative variation.

The story generator is a particularly interesting digital form from the standpoint of automatic narrative variation. The first well-known system of this sort was James Meehan's 1976 Talespin, which created parable-like stories about animals. A more sophisticated model of the creative process was incorporated in Scott Turner's Minstrel from the late 1980s. The contemporary system Mexica by Rafael Pérez y Pérez develops stories about the ancient inhabitants of Mexico by finding unlikely events and using abductive reasoning to explain them. Story generation systems have traditionally focused on producing interesting content (at the story level) rather than interesting tellings (at the level of discourse, where narrative variation operates). Their representations of story are not entirely unlike the world model of an interactive fiction system, however. The Curveship Teller could be adapted as a second stage in a story-generating pipeline. It could also be integrated more deeply into such a system, so that the decisions about what is told and how it should be told can be made jointly.

This chapter has described the research system Curveship, a general interactive fiction system with new capabilities for altering the way narratives are told, and has discussed how variation in order and time of the narrating are accomplished. Efforts will be made to develop and refine the system further so that it can be released and used beyond the lab. The creative work that I hope will be done in Curveship, by myself and others, should nourish further development of the system and prompt additional theoretical work. Only when author/programmers begin to make serious use of the system, creating works in it and modifying it, will the effects of narrative variation on literary and gaming production, and the literary potential of such capabilities, really be seen. What happens as interactive fiction progresses will certainly be informed by past and current developments in narrative theory; it is hoped that experiments in interactive fiction will also, at times, outpace them.

References

Chatman, Seymour. 1978. *Story and Discourse: Narrative Structure in Fiction and Film.* Ithaca NY: Cornell University Press.

Genette, Gérard. 1980. *Narrative Discourse: An Essay in Method.* Trans. J. E. Lewin. Ithaca NY: Cornell University Press.

——. 1988. *Narrative Discourse Revisited.* Trans. J. E. Lewin. Ithaca NY: Cornell University Press.

Gentry, Michael. 1998. *Anchorhead.* Z-Machine program in Inform 6. Available at http://www.wurb.com/if/games/17 (accessed January 7, 2011).

Mathews, Harry, and Alistair Brotchie. 1998. *Oulipo Compendium.* London: Atlas Press.

Montfort, Nick. 2003. *Twisty Little Passages: An Approach to Interactive Fiction.* Cambridge MA: MIT Press.

——. 2007a. "Generating Narrative Variation in Interactive Fiction." PhD diss., University of Pennsylvania.

——. 2007b. "Riddle Machines: The History and Nature of Interactive Fiction." In *A Companion to Digital Literary Studies*, ed. Ray Siemens and Susan Schreibman, 267–82. Oxford: Basil Blackwell.

Prince, Gerald. 1982. *Narratology: The Form and Functioning of Narrative.* Berlin: Mouton.

Reichenbach, Hans. 1947. *Elements of Symbolic Logic.* New York: Macmillan.

Ryan, Marie-Laure. 1991. *Possible Worlds, Artificial Intelligence, and Narrative Theory.* Bloomington: Indiana University Press.

6

Digitized Corpora as
Theory-Building Resource

New Methods for Narrative Inquiry

ANDREW SALWAY AND DAVID HERMAN

Introduction: Key Questions and Core Concepts

Whereas previous work at the intersection of media studies and narrative theory has explored the impact of the digital media on processes of storytelling and on the interpretation (or experience) of storyworlds,[1] our chapter outlines a different approach, examining how computer-assisted analysis of digitized texts can provide new resources for developing a theory of narrative itself. The chapter derives from our collaborative work, which we have christened the Corpus Narratology Initiative (http://people.cohums.ohio-state.edu/herman145/CNI.html) and which centers on the following key question: will coming to terms with large narrative corpora—not single narratives or even groups of stories but rather multi-million-word collections of narratively organized texts—alter the foundational concepts of narrative theory? Or, to put the question in somewhat more specific terms, what methods for studying large amounts of textual data have been developed in other fields, such as corpus linguistics, and how might incorporation of those methods into narrative inquiry afford new foundations for the study of stories, and perhaps also new applications for narratological research? Thus, rather than trying to develop narratological tools to analyze the narratives now being conveyed or co-enacted in digital environments, we seek to show how understandings of what stories are and how they work may need to be rethought in light of concepts and methods used to study digitized corpora.[2]

To assess how corpus-analytic methods bear on the core concepts and explanatory aims of narrative inquiry, we examine two broad approaches: top-down or hypothesis-driven approaches, and bottom-up or data-driven approaches. Top-down methods have been used in stylistics-based research that begins with categories of structure proposed in advance by analysts and then seeks to (dis)confirm their existence—and study their patterns of distribution—in textual corpora. In the area of narrative research, the top-down approach has been exploited, as Wynne (2006) notes, by Semino and Short (2004); this work builds on earlier studies by Semino, Short, and Culpepper (1997) and Semino, Short, and Wynne (1999). Collectively, these researchers take the modes of speech and thought representation identified by Leech and Short 2007) as their starting point and then test the degree to which the initial hypothesis about the range of available modes (including direct, indirect, and free indirect modes) is borne out by distributional patterns found in an actual corpus of narrative texts—a corpus that in fact suggests the need to make scalar distinctions between modes that were cast as discretely different in the original model. More generally, corpus-enabled research methods of this kind fall into a first family of approaches that Adolphs (2006, 38–39) characterizes as *testing hypotheses*; Tognini-Bonelli (2001) terms this same family of approaches *corpus-based*. In our next section, to clarify the possibilities and limitations of such methods, we revisit as a case study an earlier research project by one of the authors (Herman 2005) that likewise draws on top-down or hypothesis-driven strategies for analysis. Focusing on the level of the story or fabula (= the "what" of the narrative) rather than the level of discourse or sjuzhet (= how that "what" is conveyed), this pilot study uses quantitative evidence to test hypotheses about genre-based preferences for representing actions and events. Our discussion below indicates how our collaborative work has yielded new perspectives on the problems as well as the potentials of this earlier research.

What is more, revisiting the earlier project allows us to throw into relief the scope and aims of the second broad family of methods for analyzing digitized corpora. This second category of studies, which Adolphs (2006) associates with *generating hypotheses* and which Tognini-Bonelli (2001) characterizes as *corpus-driven* methods, can be described as bottom-up in its general orientation. Corpus-enabled research of this second kind seeks to remain as much as possible at the surface level of the texts included in corpora, rather than assuming beforehand that some features will be more relevant than others for the analysis of those texts. Translated into the domain of research on narratively organized discourse, the bottom-up approach begins with textual features that are computationally tractable, aiming to work up from there to an account of the structures and functions of narrative. The end-goal is to develop a theory of narrative that emerges from what a computer can identify as statistically significant distributions of textual features. Illustrating the key concerns and representative methods of a corpus-driven approach to narrative corpora, our second case study focuses on a 1.3 million-word corpus consisting of ten sets of slave narratives recorded as part of the post–Great Depression Work Progress Administration (WPA) initiative in the United States and freely available through the digital textual archive at Project Gutenberg. As reported in more detail below, we used a freeware text-analysis software package to identify frequently occurring words and clusters of words and to measure their rate of occurrence against how often those words and clusters tend to occur in general language use—attempting to frame an account of core properties of narrative on the basis of these distributional patterns.

In what follows, we discuss some specific results of the analytic strategies used in our two case studies and suggest how, taken together, the top-down, hypothesis-driven and the bottom-up, corpus-driven approaches afford a range of productive new methods for narrative inquiry as well as a basis for reassessing foundational concepts of story. In this respect, we characterize the two broad approaches to corpus-narratological research as complementary initiatives. At the same time, however, we underscore gains that might be made through a more concerted use of the corpus-driven approach in particular. Specifically, we suggest that starting with computationally tractable features of narrative corpora may provide new strategies for addressing one of the root problems of narratology—namely, what constitutes *narrativity*, or the property or set of properties that makes stories interpretable as narratives to begin with. Our suggestion is that narrativity can be defined, at least in part, as a distinctive mode of information packaging, which contrasts with how lists, syllogisms, and other kinds of representations structure the information that they convey. Corpus-driven methods may prove especially useful for research on narrativity from an information-theoretic perspective of this sort.

Two Case Studies in Corpus Narratology

General Characteristics and Aims of Corpus-enabled Research

We view corpus narratology as a subdomain of the more general field of corpus-enabled research. Though we are currently developing corpus-analytic tools for the study of multimodal narratives that exploit visual as well as verbal information tracks, such as films and television shows, the two case studies discussed in the present chapter focus on verbal narratives. Thus, the primary context for our illustrative cases is corpus-linguistic research, which we seek to leverage for the study of narratively organized texts in particular.

Biber, Conrad, and Reppen (1998) identify the following distinguishing traits of corpus-enabled research on language:

- it is empirical, analyzing the actual patterns of use in natural texts;
- it utilizes a large and principled collection of natural texts, known as a "corpus," as the basis for analysis;
- it makes extensive use of computers for analysis, using both automatic and interactive techniques;
- it depends on both quantitative and qualitative analytic techniques[3]—e.g., measuring the rates of occurrence of features and then developing interpretations of what those distributional patterns suggest about the nature of the corpus being studied. (4)

As the authors go on to note, the corpus-enabled approach to language study allows researchers to identify and analyze complex "association patterns," that is, "the systematic ways in which linguistic features are used in association with other linguistic and non-linguistic features" (Biber, Conrad, and Reppen 1998, 5; cf. McEnery and Wilson 1996, 87–116; Knowles 1996).[4] A particular linguistic feature might be studied in relation to lexical patterns or grammatical constructions, on the one hand, or in relation to stages in the evolution of a language or a social variable such as age, regional background, or gender, on the other hand. Corpus-enabled analyses can also be used to study ways in which groups of linguistic features commonly *co-occur* in specific text-types or registers (Biber, Conrad, and

Reppen 1998, 7), that is, modes of discourse usage linked to situational or contextual parameters. Hence, there are collocation patterns specific to (and partly definitive of) the register of coaching, the register of academic debate, the register of public auctions, and so on. In this sense, a key issue raised by the second case study to be discussed below—namely, our bottom-up, corpus-driven analysis of the corpus of slave narratives— is whether collocation patterns specific to the narrative text type might be discovered, and used as a route of access to the core features associated with narrativity. At issue, again, is the property or set of properties that makes stories amenable to being construed as narratives.

First Case Study: Using Corpora to Test and
Refine Prior Models of Narrative Structure

Our first case study used a corpus-based, hypothesis-testing approach to study association patterns among verbs of motion and eight narrative genres. The overall aim of the project was to test one of the central research hypotheses proposed in previous, nonquantitative work on the role of spatial reference in narrative domains (Herman 2002, 263–99): namely, the hypothesis that modes of spatial reference, like other design principles bearing on the construction of mentally modeled storyworlds, take their character from how they are anchored in preference-based systems for "spatializing" such narrated worlds. The hypothesis further suggests that these systems of preferences for spatializing storyworlds in turn help constitute particular narrative genres as different *kinds* of stories. Examining verbs of motion across eight genres—including tales of the supernatural recorded during sociolinguistic interviews, nineteenth- and twentieth-century psychological novels, Holocaust testimonies, and other kinds of stories—the follow-up study deployed quantitative methods to test the hypothesized link between spatialization and genre by mapping out patterns in the use of motion verbs in a small pilot corpus consisting of approximately 212,000 words.[5] The corpus was untagged; that is, items (words, phrases, clauses, etc.) were not marked with symbols indicating the grammatical category of graphic tokens corresponding to data-points in the corpus. A freeware concordancing program was used to generate automatically a word concordance and index for each text in the corpus. Lemmas, or sets of words having the same stem and/or meaning and differing only in spelling or inflection (cf. *walk, walked, walking*), were tabulated for 132 different verbs of motion (for a full list, see http://www .narratology.net/narr5-appcs/). Further, because the corpus was untagged, interactive analytic techniques (e.g., manual checking of lists of verbal forms) had to be relied on to a greater degree than would have been necessary for a tagged corpus, which would have facilitated more fully automated frequency counts.

The corpus was then tested for several sorts of association patterns: Does the distribution of motion verbs in the corpus in fact reveal genre-based differences in spatialization processes? Which verbs of motion are the most common across all narrative text-types in the corpus? Conversely, which text-types feature the highest overall concentration of motion verbs, and which genres feature the greatest *variety* of motion verbs, that is, the largest number of different motion verbs? Within a particular narrative text, can fluctuations in the frequency of motion-verb usage be reliably mapped onto shifts between diegetic levels, such as a framing tale and the embedded narratives contained within it?

Three noteworthy association patterns emerged. First, with one exception (explainable perhaps by the small sample size, and hence the possibility that an individual author's style may have skewed the results of the analysis), the lowest overall frequency for motion-verb usage was found in nineteenth- and twentieth-century psychological fiction. This finding harmonizes with Herman's (2002) hypothesis that narrative genres can be correlated with preference-based systems favoring particular event-types over others (35–37); according to this model, psychological fiction in particular favors (interior) states and inchoative processes over accomplishments or achievements, to use Vendler's (1967) terms for analyzing verb semantics. In the storyworlds of psychological fiction, then, motion events (and the motion verbs encoding them) would be relatively dispreferred. Second, leaving aside the exception just mentioned, the two genres having the lowest overall frequency of motion-verb usage, nineteenth- and twentieth-century psychological fiction, also featured the two highest rankings for the number of different motion verbs. This finding, too, supports the hypothesis concerning genre-based preferences proposed in the original study: although psychological fictions disprefer motion events as such, favoring states and inchoative processes instead, when they do portray such events, narratives foregrounding characters' psychological experiences are likely to draw on a richer repertoire of verbs than would other narrative genres. A larger array of verbs is needed to encode how the events are being processed by the minds through whose conscious activity the events are being filtered. Third, the analysis revealed an association pattern between narrative levels and verb frequencies—though again, the small sample size may have skewed the results of the study. Analysis of part of the corpus that involved framed narration, or the insertion of an embedded story within a framing tale, revealed that more than 80 percent of the motion verbs were used in the framing, diegetic level versus the embedded, hypodiegetic level. Thus, different spatialization processes may be triggered by cues located at different narrative levels, while readers' discernment of shifts in diegetic levels may in turn derive from such (quantifiable) changes in frequency distributions.

As we have already begun to suggest in the foregoing synopsis, given that "a crucial part of the corpus-based approach is going beyond quantitative patterns to propose functional interpretations explaining why the patterns exist" (Biber, Conrad, and Reppen 1998, 9), the case study sought to leverage the association patterns initially revealed to develop additional interpretive heuristics that did not factor into the original hypothesis concerning the link between modes of spatial reference and narrative genres. In this sense, the process of using quantitative methods to test an intuition-based hypothesis itself led to new intuitions and generated new strategies for exploring their scope and validity; here top-down or hypothesis-driven research finds a point of overlap with bottom-up, corpus-driven methods.[6] Engaging with the distributional patterns found in the corpus generated new research questions like the following: How tight is the correlation between genres that seek to capture the effects of motion events on one or more observing consciousnesses in the storyworld and the use of a large number of different verbs of motion to trigger fine-grained spatialization strategies? In what ways, exactly, do mapping relationships between frequency distributions and shifts in diegetic levels bear on readers' ability to parse particular narrative texts into framing and embedded narratives? In other words, just how typical is it for framing and framed narratives to show such drastically different frequency rates for verbs of motion?

Although up to now we have been highlighting the potential of the hypothesis-driven approach adopted in our first case study, it is worth pointing up some of the limitations of the project as well. (Not all of these limitations are specifically related to the top-down approach used in the study.) One limitation has already been mentioned but bears repeating given its general importance for corpus-enabled studies of all kinds: the small size of the corpus. More texts need to be included in each generic category, to avoid conflation of individual authors' stylistic proclivities or text-specific patterns with broader, genre-based features and trends, and to provide a more reliable measure of the robustness of the association patterns that the pilot study suggested might obtain. Another limitation pertains to the counting methods used. As pointed out by Inderjeet Mani (personal communication, May 18, 2008), the corpus needs to be rechecked so that metaphorical extensions of verbs of motion to nonspatial motion senses (as in *reach for the stars* or *walk you through the process*) can be properly filtered out. Furthermore, our collaborative research, and in particular our efforts to develop corpus-driven methods of analysis, brought into focus a more salient limitation of the earlier study. Although the pilot study did roughly cross-compare the most common verbs of motion in the corpus against those in the Brown Corpus (see Francis and Kucera 1982), no attempt was made to determine the "keyness" of the distributional patterns discovered in the corpus—that is, how the frequency rates for particular items found in this target corpus compared with their rates of occurrence in general language use, as represented by a larger reference corpus. In consequence, the current setup for the study, though it affords a basis for cross-comparing patterns of spatial reference in different narrative genres, does not allow a key narratological question to be addressed. The question is this: to what extent are the processes of spatialization indexed to motion-verb usage in the corpus distinctly narrative in nature, and to what extent do those processes cut across a variety of text types or representational practices, nonnarrative as well as narrative? Insofar as narrative inquiry has as its proper object all and only those modes of representation that fall within the domain of stories, being able to address the previous question constitutes something of a litmus test for corpus-narratological research. And it may be that corpus-driven methods, rather than hypothesis-driven approaches, offer the best means to address this issue.

Indeed, the measure of keyness provides one of the cornerstones of our second case study. For this project, which we detail in our next subsection, rather than starting with any prior hypothesis about the corpus at issue, we instead worked to generate hypotheses from collocation patterns that became discernible after we performed frequency counts, that is, measured rates of occurrence for particular words and clusters of words and compared those rates with the rates characteristic of general language use.

Second Case Study: Using Corpora to Build
New Models of Narrative Structure

The purpose of our second case study is to investigate the extent to which a corpus-driven approach to the development of narrative theory may be possible. Here we seek to pilot an approach, inspired by the work of Zellig Harris and colleagues on science sublanguages (summarized in Harris 1988, 40–56), in which an automated formal linguistic analysis of a corpus of narrative texts reveals information structures rooted in how stories (as opposed to other types of discourse) are organized. In its ideal form, this approach would proceed with no prior assumptions concerning linguistic theory (e.g., about parts of speech, grammar, etc.). However, we see no way of escaping some contingencies of this sort, such as the prior classification of texts as narratives and the machine-level separation of words—which becomes more of an issue in some languages other than English. Through a manual analysis, Harris and colleagues showed how something like a *local grammar* (Gross 1997) could be induced from texts by analyzing the co-occurrences of words, and by studying how this structure reflected the structure of information in the scientific domain under consideration. With a view to developing an automated analysis over a much larger collection of texts, we are encouraged by results reported by Solan and his colleagues (2005) that showed how grammar could be induced from untagged text. The work reported below stops short of inducing a "grammar of narrative"; nonetheless, we believe that our results are extensible and capable of being refined through further research.

To assess the potential for a bottom-up, corpus-driven approach we discuss the analysis of a corpus consisting of slave narratives downloaded from Project Gutenberg (http://www.gutenberg.org/wiki/Main_Page) and containing more than 1.3 million untagged words of text. These narratives were originally collected as part of a WPA-sponsored project, in which interviews were conducted with former slaves from ten different states (Arkansas, Florida, Georgia, Indiana, Kansas, Kentucky, Maryland, Mississippi, Ohio, and South Carolina); the former slaves' accounts were tape-recorded and subsequently transcribed. To give a sense of the accounts that make up the corpus, we provide the following short excerpt from one of the accounts: "Wartrace was a very nice place to make our home. It was located on the Nashville and Chattanooga and St. Louis railroad, just fifty-one miles from Nashville not many miles from our old home. Mother found work and we got along very well but as soon as we children were old enough to work, she went back to her old home in Georgia where a few years later she died. I believe she lived to be seventy-five or seventy six years of age, but I never saw her after she went back to Georgia."

In order to direct our analysis toward word patterns (and hence information structures) that are characteristic of our corpus, we wished to compare frequency counts for items in this *target corpus* with frequency rates for those same items in a *reference corpus* that approximates patterns of general usage. Thus, we obtained the second release of the American National Corpus, or ANC2, which consists of around 22 million words of written as well as spoken American English. This reference corpus includes "texts of all genres and transcripts of spoken data produced from 1990 onward" (see http://americannationalcorpus.org/), and though many of the texts included in the corpus date from a period later than the slave narratives, we assumed that ANC2 would nonetheless provide a reasonably reliable baseline against which to measure the distributional patterns peculiar to our target corpus.[7]

The first step of our analysis was to identify the most frequently occurring words in our collection of slave narratives. The second step was to compare the frequencies of these words against their frequencies in general language usage, as per the ANC2. A ratio between these two frequencies affords a measure of "keyness," with items occurring relatively more often in a target corpus than in a reference corpus being judged higher in keyness. To calculate keyness values, and for later stages of our analysis, we used a freeware text-analysis software package called AntConc, developed by Laurence Anthony (see http://www.antlab.sci.waseda.ac.jp/). After calculating keyness values, we used AntConc to generate word clusters and concordances. The following describes more precisely the outputs generated by AntConc, used as bases for our analysis:

- Keyness—Keyness (computed by AntConc as "log likelihood")[8] is established statistically as a ratio between how frequently a form occurs in a corpus of interest and how frequently it tends to occur in general language, as measured in a large reference corpus such as the American National Corpus or British National Corpus.

- Word cluster—AntConc equates word clusters with n-grams, that is, sequences of n words (where *n* stands for a specified number); thus, a list of word clusters in AntConc is the frequency of n-grams with specified n's.
- Concordance—The concordance of a given word or word cluster comprises all instances of the word or cluster together with some surrounding words (as per the specified concordance width).

We selected out what AntConc identified as the two hundred most frequent words in the corpus that also had a keyness ranking of greater than one thousand (with reference to ANC2). We then created a list of clusters of three or more words that included at least one of those unusually frequent words and that occurred more than one hundred times in the target corpus. Finally, we created concordances for these clusters. These procedures were used in the service of our overall analytic goal for the project, which is to begin working up from what is computationally tractable (the surface forms of words and data about their occurrence and co-occurrence) to the larger structures of information in which those countable features participate—larger structures that may afford clues about the nature and scope of narrativity itself (see our concluding section below).

There was a total of 172 clusters obtained that matched our threshold criteria, and 21,489 concordance lines for these clusters were generated; some examples of clusters and their immediate contexts are provided below. From this point, the analysis turned from automation to the explanation of the observed phenomena through manual inspection of the concordances. In other words, we now asked why these particular clusters should be so frequent in the corpus at hand. The presence of some clusters can be explained by the subject matter of the texts, for example, "the Civil War"; some by the speakers' dialect, such as "a heap of"; and some by the manner in which these texts came to be (they were elicited through interviews), for instance, "interviewer: Miss Irene Robertson." However, a great many clusters are not explained by these factors, and so we proceeded on the assumption that they are unusually frequent because they are used to provide information crucial for the telling of this kind of narrative (and perhaps other kinds of narrative as well). Most of the remaining clusters were classified quite comfortably as giving information about Action, Time, Location, or Persons and their Attributes); a few others were categorized as Narrational, since they function as hedges by virtue of which tellers signal, during the process of narrative communication, uncertainty about the status of the information contained in a story. To save space, and more importantly to highlight signs of an emerging local grammar, we use the following notation where clusters have one or more words overlapping with one another. The use of brackets— ( ) — shows that the word contained may or may not be present. The use of a pipe between two words— | —shows that either word may be present. For example, the transcription "work(ed) in the (field|house)" captures the fact that the following clusters, among others, were observed: "work in the field," "worked in the field," "worked in the house."

Action clusters: "(I) (never) went to school," "went to the," "work(ed) in the (field|house)."
Example: when my mother did anything at all, she *worked in the field*

Time clusters: "in dem|them days," "in slavery time(s)," "the war was (on|going on|over)," "when he|she|I|it|they was," "when the war (ended|started)."
Example: I married *when I was* fifteen just fore *the war ended*

Person clusters: "mother and father," "(many|most) of the slaves," "my white folks"
Example: *Mother and father* had 12 children and we lived in a one-room log cabin

Person Attribute clusters: "was a good man|woman," "was born in," "she|he was a"
Example: Marse Lordnorth *was a good* man

Location clusters: "in de|the (big) house," "on the place|plantation," "to the house"
Example: They took him up *to the house* but he died

Narrational clusters: "I don't know (about|anything|exactly|how|if|just|much|what|why)"
Example: *I don't know* why they thought he wouldn't be whooped.

To gain a further impression of the patterning of information in our corpus, we took the hundred most frequently occurring clusters and tried to sort them into categories just listed. We eliminated a number of clusters that were ambiguous (that is, could fit in more than one category) or that seemed to us to reflect the specifics of the interview situation.[9] The result was the following distribution of clusters: Person Attribute (31 percent), Time (25 percent), Action (16 percent), Person (13 percent), Location (9 percent), and Narrational (6 percent). Although our classification is tentative and underscores the need to develop more sophisticated techniques for automating our analysis, it does at least suggest how corpus narratology might contribute to central debates in the field. For example, nearly half of the information encoded in the top one hundred clusters pertains to persons and person attributes; this is almost double the amount of information about time and triple the amount of information about action. A key question is how this finding bears on traditions of narrative study that foreground temporal sequence and plot structure as hallmarks of story, that is, as constitutive of narrativity.

In any case, our analysis relies on relatively simple corpus-analytic techniques to characterize a collection of narrative texts in terms of frequently occurring clusters, and to point out overlaps between clusters that would make these texts amenable, at least in part, to the automatic induction of a local grammar given more sophisticated methods of analysis. We would like to apply such techniques in the future to capture a more structured description of language use in a corpus. The ultimate success of such grammar induction lies in the extent to which patterns of words repeat and partially overlap: data about the occurrence and co-occurrence of words in similar contexts are what drive the kind of automatic grammar induction described by Solan and his coauthors (2005). We would expect a more complete grammar to be derived from texts that are more constrained; thus, we view the scientific sublanguage texts analyzed by Harris and colleagues to be optimally constrained in subject matter and register. This suggests that we must be careful not to expect too much for the induction of local grammars from most kinds of narrative texts; such texts will likely vary more in subject matter, register, and so forth than would instances of a sublanguage like that used for biology instruction, say.

Whatever results we may glean from automatic corpus analysis, however, we are still left with the issue of how they inform the development of narrative theory. In this case study, we sought to explain the phenomena observed via corpus analysis, that is, unusually frequent word clusters, by suggesting that they are frequent because they play a role in communicating information essential for this kind of narrative. This grounding assumption led us to postulate some broad categories of narrative-related information and to record some common realizations of these categories in narrative discourse. If this kind of analysis were to be done in more depth, on the basis of more structured descriptions of the language in corpora, and for corpora of multiple kinds of narratives, then we expect there would be additional evidence with which to (dis)confirm the robustness (or general validity across narrative genres) of the categories we have identified. That said, if narrative is defined as a text-type category, instances of which may be more or less prototypical (see below), then we should not expect to see all of these categories realized in the same way in all narratives.

Conclusions and Directions for Future Research

Though we are continuing to refine the goals and procedures of our corpus-narratological project, as well as our understanding of how it might contribute to the broader project of developing new approaches to language understanding in general and narrative understanding in particular, the present chapter outlines what we take to be a range of productive methods for inquiry. Indeed, we believe that these methods have the potential to reshape the field of narrative study. On the one hand, hypothesis-driven corpus research can be used to ascertain the scope and validity of generalizations about narrative structure based on individual analysts' intuitions about stories—intuitions that, once they have circulated sufficiently broadly among the community of narrative scholars, can take on the appearance of canonical truths or givens for the study of stories. On the other hand, corpus-driven research can be used to generate new research hypotheses concerning what features and patterns may be distinctively narrative in nature, and how they account for the structural and functional contrasts between stories and other kinds of representational practices.

In connection with corpus-driven methods in particular, we wish to point out what we take to be one especially salient implication of our research. The approach developed in our second case study suggests the productiveness of regarding narratively organized discourse as a distinctive mode of packaging information about actions, times, locations, persons, and other elements of the mental models or storyworlds evoked by narrative texts. From this perspective, stories can be described as a way of bundling information about represented situations, actions, and events that contrasts with the modes of information packaging that are the signatures of other discourse types (unordered lists, deductive arguments, ritualized exchanges of insults, etc.; cf. Harris 1988 for an information-theoretic approach to language study in general). In this respect, our corpus-enabled work harmonizes with other ongoing (independent) research that characterizes narratives as text-type category, specific instances of which differ more or less sharply from instances of other, neighboring text-type categories such as description and explanation (Herman 2008, 2009). In the present chapter, however, rather than drawing on theories of categorization processes and text-linguistic models to enrich narratological accounts of how stories relate to syllogisms, driving directions, or descriptions of the weather, our aim has been to suggest that automated analysis of surface features of texts might provide the basis for an account of narrative-specific modes of information packaging. Thus far, we have analyzed just one narrative genre—slave narratives—using the method piloted in our second case study; but in principle, cross-comparing analyses of multiple story genres (fictional narratives, biographies, children's stories, etc.) might afford a composite picture of the *range* of ways of packaging information encompassed by the text-type category "narrative," which is more inclusive than any particular kind of story. In turn, identifying the range of information-packaging strategies accommodated by narrative is tantamount to exploring the nature and scope of *narrativity*, or what makes a printed text, film, or other representation (interpretable as) a story.

More broadly, we believe that corpus-narratological research, of both the hypothesis-driven and the corpus-driven varieties, has implications for multiple fields, including not only narrative theory but also corpus and computational linguistics, semiotics, cognitive and social psychology, and artificial intelligence research, and can potentially inform the design of systems meant to emulate the experience of being immersed in storyworlds. Our chapter is thus an attempt to initiate more sustained dialogue among practitioners in these and other areas, whose combined expertise must be pooled if analysts are to come to terms with the richness and complexity of narrative as a means for structuring, comprehending, and representing human experience.

Notes

1. As we use the term here (cf. Herman 2002, 9–22), *storyworld* is consonant with a range of other concepts proposed by cognitive psychologists, discourse analysts, psycholinguists, philosophers of language, and others concerned with how people go about making sense of texts or discourses. Like *storyworld*, these other notions—including *deictic center, mental model, situation model, discourse model, contextual frame*, and *possible world*—are designed to explain how interpreters rely on inferences triggered by textual cues to build up representations of the overall situation or world evoked but not fully explicitly described in a text or discourse. Storyworlds, then, are worlds evoked by narratively organized discourse. See Herman (2009, chapter 5) for additional discussion of distinctively narrative ways of worldmaking—a discussion that stands to be informed in turn by the research findings reported in this chapter.

2. Ultimately, however, these two investigative routes may overlap, since narratives are increasingly "born digital"—with the result that users now expect to be able to edit and interact with stories in ways made possible by what might be characterized as machine understanding of narrative.

3. In Johnstone's (2000) account, quantitative methods address questions about *how* and *why* data have the particular character that they do; by contrast, quantitative methods address questions about *how much* (the degree to which) and *how often* (the frequency with which) those data display a given property or set of properties.

4. Semino, Short, and Wynne (1999), in their study of representations of hypothetical modes of speech, thought, and writing in narrative texts, catalog several advantages of the corpus-based approach over traditional, strictly qualitative, methods. For one thing, corpora are balanced according to preset criteria, thus discouraging the analyst from picking his or her favorite examples randomly. For another, a corpus-based approach compels analysts to face difficult or "messy" cases, and therefore instances that might constitute counter-examples to their basic research hypotheses. See Short (2001) for further discussion of relevant issues.

5. The ten most common verbs of motion across all eight genres were *go, take, come, get, leave, turn, bring, move, run*, and *reach*. See Herman (2005, 134–35) for more information about the principles of selection and counting methods used in the study.

6. For this reason, Adolphs's (2006) proposed distinction between hypothesis-testing and hypothesis-generating approaches to corpus research strikes us as being perhaps too starkly drawn. In testing prior models through corpus analysis, theorists may need to restructure those models in light of the data that thereby emerge—in effect generating new hypotheses as part of the very process of testing previous ones.

7. It should be noted that ANC2, like the general language use of which we take it to be representative, does consist in part of narratively organized discourse (e.g., about 3.5 million words taken from newspapers). But the inclusion of other genres in ANC2 (e.g., academic discourse, travel guides, technical writing, etc.) makes it appropriate as a reference corpus against which to compare frequency patterns specific to our target corpus, which consists exclusively of narrative texts.

8. For a good tutorial on log likelihood, see http://ucrel.lancs.ac.uk/llwizard.html.

9. For more information about the top one hundred clusters and how we categorized them, see http://people.cohums.ohio-state.edu/herman145/top100.html.

References

Adolphs, Svenja. 2006. *Introducing Electronic Text Analysis*. London: Routledge.

Biber, Douglas, Susan Conrad, and Randi Reppen. 1998. *Corpus Linguistics: Investigating Language Structure and Use*. Cambridge: Cambridge University Press.

Francis, W. Nelson, and Henry Kucera. 1982. *Frequency Analysis of English Usage: Lexicon and Grammar*. Boston: Houghton Mifflin.

Gross, Maurice. 1997. "The Construction of Local Grammars." In *Finite-State Language Processing*, ed. Emmanuel Roche and Yves Schabes, 329–54. Cambridge MA: MIT Press.

Harris, Zellig. 1988. *Language and Information*. New York: Columbia University Press.

Herman, David. 2002. *Story Logic: Problems and Possibilities of Narrative*. Lincoln: University of Nebraska Press.

———. 2005. "Quantitative Methods in Narratology: A Corpus-based Study of Motion Events in Stories." In *Narratology beyond Literary Criticism*, ed. Jan Christoph Meister (in cooperation with Tom Kindt, Wilhelm Schernus, and Malte Stein), 125–49. Berlin: de Gruyter.

———. 2008. "Description, Narrative, and Explanation: Text-type Categories and the Cognitive Foundations of Discourse Competence." *Poetics Today* 29, no. 3:437–72.

———. 2009. *Basic Elements of Narrative*. Oxford: Wiley-Blackwell.

Johnstone, Barbara. 2000. *Qualitative Methods in Sociolinguistics*. New York: Oxford University Press.

Knowles, Gerry. 1996. "Corpora, Databases and the Organization of Linguistic Data." In *Using Corpora for Language Research*, ed. Jenny Thomas and Michael Short, 36–53. London: Longman.

Leech, Geoffrey, and Michael Short. 2007. *Style in Fiction: A Linguistic Introduction to English Fictional Prose*. 2nd ed. Harlow: Pearson/Longman. (Orig. pub. 1981.)

McEnery, Tony, and Andrew Wilson. 1996. *Corpus Linguistics*. Edinburgh: Edinburgh University Press.

Semino, Elena, and Michael Short. 2004. *Corpus Stylistics: Speech, Writing, and Thought Presentation in a Corpus of English Narratives*. London: Routledge.

Semino, Elena, Michael Short, and Jonathan Culpeper. 1997. "Using a Corpus to Test a Model of Speech and Thought Presentation." *Poetics* 25:17–43.

Semino, Elena, Michael Short, and Martin Wynne. 1999. "Hypothetical Words and Thoughts in Contemporary British Narratives." *Narrative* 7:307–34.

Short, Michael. 2001. "Epilogue: Research Questions, Research Paradigms, and Research Methodologies in the Study of Narrative." In *New Perspectives on Narrative Perspective*, ed. Willie van Peer and Seymour Chatman, 339–55. Albany NY: SUNY Press.

Solan, Zach, David Horn, Eytan Ruppin, and Shimon Edelman. 2005. "Unsupervised Learning of Natural Languages." *Proceedings of the National Academy of Sciences* 102, no. 33:11629–34.

Tognini-Bonelli, Elena. 2001. *Corpus Linguistics at Work*. Amsterdam: John Benjamins.

Vendler, Zeno. 1967. *Linguistics in Philosophy*. Ithaca NY: Cornell University Press.

Wynne, Martin. 2006. "Stylistics: Corpus Approaches." In *Encyclopedia of Language and Linguistics*, ed. Keith Brown, 12:223–26. 2nd ed. Oxford: Elsevier.

7

From (W)reader to Breather

*Cybertextual De-intentionalization
and Kate Pullinger's* Breathing Wall

ASTRID ENSSLIN

Introduction

The aim of this chapter is to investigate and exemplify a recent phenomenon in the practice of digital narrative, which engages creatively with the
interplay between intentionality and corporeality in the reading process.
Drawing on Espen Aarseth's (1997) alternative communication model, I
introduce the concept of "cybertextual retro-intentionalization." This concept refers to a hitherto unforeseen kind of transmedial and multimodal
"reading" that is governed by corporeal processes operating in competition with mental forces.

I begin by discussing existing theories of philosophical and narrative
intentionality. This is then followed by an examination of Aarseth's (1997)
cybertextual "text machine," which places the encoded text (notably the
underlying software code) at the center of literary communication and
is therefore particularly suitable for the analysis of narratives that set out
to "de-intentionalize" the process of reception. The text machine reduces
the intentional powers of the receiving human operator and makes them
part of a text-driven digital "performance" (see Ensslin 2007). By the
same token, George Landow's (1997) hypertext-centered theory of the
empowered "(w)reader"—a reader who virtually coauthors the hypertext
by assembling and, thus, sequentializing text chunks provided and interlinked by the writer—is replaced by a concept that emphasizes the power
of the code and the resulting physical connection between the reader, the
text and the hypermedium.

Against this backdrop, I then go on to analyze Kate Pullinger, Stefan
Schemat, and babel's physio-cybertext *The Breathing Wall* (2004) and discuss the extent to which the text employs the concept of cybertextual de-
intentionalization. I conclude that the term *retro-intentionalization* more

appropriately describes the redirection of thought to the reader's physicality and the relative (im)possibility of controlling the body's subcortical functions—breathing, for example—during the act of reading while being part of an entextualized cybernetic feedback loop.

Of particular interest is the physicality of cybertextual perception. I therefore draw on recent developments in cybercultural theory, phenomenology, and the philosophy of mind. Most importantly, I shall be looking at the discourses of transcendence and of the *multiple* situatedness of the perceiving human body as put forward by cybertheorists (e.g., Martii Lahti), phenomenologists (e.g., Maurice Merleau-Ponty), and neurobiologists (e.g., Antonio Damásio).

The chapter is rounded off by a discussion of how far and by what means *The Breathing Wall* subverts the claim that digital fiction—especially hyperfiction—defies a reworking of the crime novel. I demonstrate what specific elements of the hypermedium and the software used in *The Breathing Wall* innovate the genre and reflect—as crime fiction typically does—a specific world picture: in this case the ontological, aesthetic, and epistemological implications of posthumanity.[1]

Intentionality and Physicality in Text Reception

Our bodies are spatially, temporally, socioculturally, and, not least, physiologically situated, that is, contingent on a variety of external and internal influences that have an impact on our mental disposition. In fact, the two cannot be separated. What this means to narratologists is a shift in focus from the primacy of readerly *intentionality* to the interplay of corporeal and psychological functions at work during the receptive process.

The notion of intentionality has been explored by leading scholars in philosophy, psychology, and narratology since the early 1970s. I want to make it clear that I do not wish to confuse "intentionality" with either the critical concept of "intention" (the writer's or text's assumed purpose, or the effect he, she, or it is aiming at; see Richards 1929; Hirsch 1967; de Beaugrande and Dressler 1981). Nor am I referring to intentionality as propagated by Speech Act Theory (e.g., Austin 1962; Searle 1969), which denotes the communicative intention of the speaker in performing an illocutionary act successfully, as well as the hearer's recognition of this intention. Likewise, despite my fascination with Peter Brooks's *Reading for the Plot: Design and Intention in Narrative* (1984), I do not share—in the present investigation—his specific idea of narrative intention, which, essentially, relates to the "motor forces" of plot, or rather "plotting," and, hence, narrative meaning. In fact, most of the aforementioned theories associate intention and intentionality with either the author-producer's side or the text itself as an abstract static or dynamic concept. Conversely, my main interest lies in the receiver's side and the degree to which we can uphold purpose-driven, goal-directed intentionality in a multimodal cybertextual experience.

With regard to the receptive focus, the term *intentionality* has two basic meanings, both of which are, in my view, relevant to the theory and analysis of cybertext fiction. The first, more common, meaning implies purpose-driven human action (including linguistic behavior and, more specifically, narrative reception). The second, far more technical, notion is "reference or aboutness or some similar relation" (Harman 1998, 602; see also Dennett 1971, 1987; cf. Diamond and Teichman 1979; Chisholm 1981) to a so-called Intentional object (what we see/hear/perceive; Searle 1983). Both meanings are examined and conflated by John Searle (1983) in his phenomenological monograph *Intentionality*. For Searle, a (physical) action has two components: the physical action itself (e.g., movement), which is—given a fully functioning, healthy body—intentional in the sense of deliberate (though not always conscious). The second component is his notion of experience, which he equates with directness, immediacy, and involuntariness, and which is "intentional" in the sense of directed at an Intentional object. According to Searle, experience forms a major component of perception in that its direction of fit is mind-to-world, while, at the same time, the Intentional object follows the direction of causation, which is world-to-mind. It is this second notion of intentionality—the sense of directedness to the Intentional object—that Searle shares with a school within analytical philosophy and cognitive science that, since the early 1970s, has focused on the intentionality of perception in terms of relating to objects including material units, the self (not unlike Descartes) and past events (e.g., Anscombe 1957; Dennett 1971, 1987; Chisholm 1981).

The term *intentionality* as I treat it in this chapter thus has two basic meanings. The first, unmarked meaning (with lower-case "i"), implies purpose-drivenness, such as in extracting meaning from a textual object. The second, philosophical notion (with upper-case "I") refers to aboutness (i.e., direction of attention to a thought, or Intentional object) and perspectivity (i.e., the beholder's point of view; Lyons 1995).

It is the first, "naïve," of the two meanings that ties in with significant receptive implications of Aarseth's (1997, 21) cybertextual "machine." This alternative model of textual communication has at its center the (programming) code, which interacts with the (human) "operator," the "[verbal] sign" (on page/screen) and the material "medium." These four elements engage in a complex interplay, resulting in a variety of different cybertextual subgenres. Aarseth aims to communicate a distinct sense of performativity, which renders the operator a constitutive yet potentially disempowered element of (cyber)textual performance.

Some new media writers have picked up on the idea of textual empowerment by creating what I refer to as "cybertexts proper" (e.g., Stuart Moulthrop's *Hegirascope* and Urs Schreiber's *Das Epos der Maschine*; cf. Ensslin 2007), that is, digital literature that "assumes power" over the reader by literally "writing themselves" rather than presenting themselves as an existing textual product. I cannot here discuss the sheer variety of manifestations this writerly agenda can produce but shall instead focus on one particular example that literally "embodies" the conflict between voluntary and involuntary respiratory and cognitive mechanisms at work within the cybernetic feedback loop.

Despite its strong emphasis on cognitive aspects of reading and textual procedurality, narrative criticism still lacks a significant degree of auto-physiological awareness. Due to the fact that "consciousness and Intentionality are as much part of human biology as digestion or the circulation of the blood" (Searle 1983, ix), I argue for a more comprehensive anthropological engagement, which will include the psychological *and* the physical nature of text reception, as well as their interaction with the text and its medium of representation and dissemination. To that end, I advocate turning to game theory, more specifically the "discourse of transcendence in writing about digital technology" (Dovey and Kennedy 2006, 106), that is, the transgression of the Cartesian body–mind dualism via the concept of bodily double-situatedness in new media environments. Arguing against cybercultural theories of "disembodiment" (Lister et al. 2003, 248; cf. Dery 1994), Marie Laure Ryan rightly asserts the "embodied nature of perception" (2001, 14; cf. Merleau-Ponty 1962). Martii Lahti

(2003, 169) adds, particularly in relation to video game reception, that "we remain flesh as we become machines." Furthermore, to give an example of contemporary science-informed philosophy, Antonio Damásio (2004) describes such allegedly "mental" phenomena as emotions as "a complex pattern of chemical neural responses," which, given certain stimuli, cause a "temporary change in the state of the body proper" (53).

Put differently, we need to distance ourselves from the traditional Cartesian separation of "text" and "reader." Instead, we might view the two elements as part of a procedural, material apparatus that includes the physicality of the reader to the same extent as that of the medium and the nexus between the two.

The double-situatedness of the body implies, on the one hand, that user-readers are "embodied" as direct receivers whose bodies interact with the hardware and software of a computer. On the other hand, user-readers are considered to be "reembodied" through feedback they experience in represented form, such as through visible or invisible avatars.

I would argue that we can transfer not only the first but, more interestingly, the second dimension of situatedness to the analysis of digital fiction. Clearly, digital fiction differs from games and virtual environments in that, as readers, we do not need a physical representation of our own subjectivity in the text world. That said, every narrative assumes an implied reader, and it is a major achievement of cyberfiction that this implied reader or "breather," as in our example, shares his or her phenomenological physicality with the narrator and/or hero of the story.

Based on the aforementioned notions of intentionality and physicality, I suggest a dual dialectic: firstly, the dialectic of corporeal double-situatedness in new media, which ultimately renders the dually embodied user part of a cybernetic feedback loop involving the text machine, the "implied cybertextual reader," and the actual reader. To this I would add, secondly, the dialectic of i/Intentionality, which refers, on the one hand, to purpose-driven readerly action, and to the receiver's experience of—in the sense of relation to—the Intentional object, on the other. As we shall see, the philosophical implications of "aboutness" and "perspectivity" intertwine so much with human perception and thinking in general, that, ironically, they run counter to the alleged disempowerment of the reader-user and the assumption of de-intentionalization evoked by the "naïve" meaning of intentionality. Rather, I contend that physio-cybertext, with its emphasis on body–machine amalgamation, refocuses on the relative possibility of cortical control and, thus, readerly agency over material-corporeal interaction with the text. I refer to this process, which entails the reader's subconscious and conscious engagement with subcortical (involuntary) physiological processes versus cortical control and manipulation as "retro-intentionalization."

The Latin term *retro* means "back" or "backwards." As a prefix, it is used to denote reversal and reaction as well as recursivity, retrospectivity, and reflexivity. My concept of retro-intentionalization involves all five of these notions: "reversal" because it reverses the direction of fit from the text back to the reading organism; "reaction" because the text requires perpetual reactive flexibility; "recursivity" because, by directing the reader's attention to the cybernetic feedback loop, textual understanding inevitably occurs at a metafictional, metamedial level; "retrospectivity" because the reader is permanently made to remember how to breathe appropriately in order to retrieve more textual information; and "reflexivity" because the process of retro-intentionalization triggers off more general processes of meta-theoretical, meta-phenomenological contemplation.

Cybertextual Retro-Intentionalization: *The Breathing Wall*

Along with other breath-driven new media texts and installations (e.g., Lewis LaCook's *Dirty Milk*, whisper[s]'s *exhale* project, and Char Davies's *Osmose*), *The Breathing Wall* aesthetically implements both the double-situatedness of the reading body and, in close connection to it, the partly involuntary interplay between the physiological and the psychological. First presented at trAce's 2004 Incubation Conference in Nottingham, it is a particularly interesting artifact in that the authors confront their readers with the entextualized threat of losing control of intention-driven textual decoding and inferencing, for the sake of a partly involuntary, cybernetically controlled process of information disclosure.

The Breathing Wall consists of two key components: a hypertext-based, largely sequential narrative, organized into five parts, or "daydreams," and a set of (nightly) "dreams," which reveal the protagonist Michael's nightly conversations with his late girlfriend, Lana. The story opens with Michael, who has been in prison for six months over allegations of having murdered Lana, a crime he did not commit, yet for which he cannot provide a satisfactory alibi. In fact, when her body was spotted in the park, a note he scribbled the day before was found and used as evidence against him. It reads as follows:

> I don't know what I'm going to do without you.
> Whatever happens—it's your fault. It's your responsibility.
> You shouldn't have broken up with me.

The daydreams reveal Michael's frustration over his hopeless situation. In those dreams, Lana speaks to him, giving him clues as to what really happened. She suggests that he should consult his sister Florence, her best friend, who, despite her suspicions, decides to help her brother. Florence finds out that Lana was killed by her own father in one of his psychopathic attacks. The last daydream is set after Michael's release, as he converses with Lana at the cemetery, under a cherry tree. Whereas the hypertext sequence serves to reveal the gist of the crime narrative, the essential detail of how the murder happened and was physically perceived by the victim can only be obtained from the night dreams.

Running on a specially designed software called "Hyper Trans Fiction Matrix,"[2] *The Breathing Wall* uses the reader's respiratory system as a driving force for revealing essential referential meaning, or, more precisely, "clues" to solving the "who-dunnit" or rather "how-did-it-happen" question. To "read" the text from CD-ROM or hard disk, a headset with attached microphone is required. Unusually, however, the microphone is placed under the reader's nose to measure his or her breathing rate. Depending on the rate and depth of inhaling and exhaling, the text (in the combined sense of program code and audio-visual, interactive user interface) will release either more or less information. In other words, the quality of reception depends largely on the reader's momentary physiological, psychological, and spatio-temporal situatedness and their ability to "control" their own breathing. This is particularly interesting considering the fact that neurologists disagree to what extent breathing is an involuntary process.

The Breathing Wall investigates creatively to what extent intentionality may be constrained through textual autonomy and the entextualized emphasis of the perceiving body. A fully fledged analysis of this augmented sense of corporeality involves a close examination of how semiotic resources are combined multimodally to form a multi*sensory* artifact that is more than the sum of its individual elements (see Ensslin 2010). Furthermore, and this will be the focus of the remainder of this section, we need to look at how the (cyber)text "'codes' the player into the [text] world" (Dovey and Kennedy 2006, 108), and how this multisensory feedback loop allows the thus "embodied"/"reembodied," implied reader to evolve and develop a mental image of the text world and, not least, his or her own corporeal, spatio-temporal subjectedness. *The Breathing Wall* purports to undermine the "normal" cybernetic accommodation process usually experienced in gameplay, where the particular technological idiosyncrasies of a game, in the sense of both hardware and software, are readily "adapted to and appropriated into our available repertoire of bodily behaviours and aptitudes" (Dovey and Kennedy 2006, 111). These appropriations, performed by the human body through repetitive use of the same "moves," are ultimately based on the workings of intentionality, in the sense of purposefulness and object-directedness, yet do not usually redirect the player's attention to the physical nature of the interaction. *The Breathing Wall*, however, does exactly that, by making the reader aware of the physical conditionality of text reception and the indispensable interplay of perceiving body and mind.

The text as a whole integrates audio recordings of speech, noise and music, flash animation, photography, and hypertextual interaction. With regard to "hypertext," coauthor/programmer Chris Joseph, alias babel (2004), admits that "for this project it meant, very loosely, moving from one chapter to another, or from one passage of text to the next, through (clickable) links or mouse movements." Evidently, the creative team soon realized that the crime mystery is, in its generic macrostructure, more contingent on linear perception than most other fictional genres and hence unsuitable for hypertextual representation in the Joycean or Landowian sense. Similarly, babel (2004) explains that "a cinematic (sit and watch) approach also contrasted well with Stefan[Schemat]'s software, and the unique physical interaction it requires. So the term hypertext was superseded by 'daydreams'—as opposed to Stefan's 'nightdreams.'"

The gothic feel to the story is evoked by the aforementioned nocturnal appearances of Lana's voice in Michael's dreams, as she speaks to him through the prison wall. In those "nightdreams," which the reader co-experiences by watching filmic sequences of mostly inanimate "backgrounds" (e.g., trees, pavement, fields, and clouds), Lana gives Michael—and the reader—clues as to what happened to her on the night of her murder. And although, even without "breathing" their way through those "nightdreams," readers will know by the end of the hypertextual "daydreams" who the killer was, they will not have been initiated in the exact phenomenological processes experienced by the victim. In fact, depending on the extent to which the actual reader succeeds in "controlling" his or her respiratory mechanisms along the lines of an "implied breather," Lana's death experience will be conveyed more or less completely through her ghostly analepses.

For example, in Dream 4, the climax of the story, Lana gives away core information about how she perceived the last moments of her life. Against a visual and aural background that evokes the multisensory image of the park where she was murdered, the successfully breathing reader hears—almost as in a cut scene from a computer game—Lana's whispering voice calling Michael's name intently, as if to wake him from his dreamless sleep. After another period of (appropriate) breathing, the thus activated software reveals the key sequence of text spoken by Lana, in which her anxious yet strangely calm voice reveals intermittently what she experienced in the park:

But Michael, what if there's someone behind you in the park? . . . And suddenly you feel his hands, but you can still see the trees around you; [. . .] but you can't speak, because this time the hand is over your mouth; [. . .] you can feel fear flooding through your body [. . .]: cold fear, cold, liquid fear. It should be easy to tell whose hand it is; . . . it's under your nose, . . . and you can smell it, you really can smell it [. . .]. In this moment, with the hand over my mouth, I heard myself scream, . . . as if my mouth was still open. But the scream was everywhere, the wind was screaming, the trees were screaming, [. . .] and then I felt that I was not made of flesh any more; I was made of thin air, [. . .] with these hands holding my head, like my head was in the mouth of a big animal, [. . .] shaking all the life out of my body. Then there was a sound, [. . .] the sound of dry wood cracking, snapping underfoot in the darkness, and with the silence came the light, [. . .] bright white light, no more screaming, no more fear, no more hands closing over my lips.

Clearly, by referring to the "hand over [her] mouth" and "under [her] nose," the text draws the "breather's" attention back to his or her own physicality and the technological "extension" (McLuhan 1964) that connects him or her cybernetically to the text world. Thus, by co-experiencing (with Michael) Lana's phenomenological death narrative, which merges her physical metamorphosis into "thin air" with the reader's breathing motor, the reader reaches a maximum level of psychosomatic "union" with the text machine and the characters within it. At the same time, however, the reader is again reminded of the fact that, without intentional interference in the sense of goal-directedness and perspectival focalization on the Intentional object, the body's unmonitored interaction with the software would not have yielded the same textual depth.

Against the Odds—Cybertextual Crime Fiction

Along with Bill Bly's *We Descend* (1997), M. D. Coverley's *Fibonacci's Daughter* (2000), and Frank Klötgen's *Spätwinterhitze* (2004), *The Breathing Wall* may be regarded as one of the few digital fictions defying the allegation that the detective story has never really entered the realm of "anti(mono)linear" storytelling (Ensslin 2007). As a matter of fact, we have seen that *The Breathing Wall* deviates from—and thereby reconfirms on a metageneric level—the rules of conventional crime fiction by leaving the solution of the mystery not merely to the reader's intention-driven, cognitive engagement with the plot but—to an equal if not greater degree—to his or her very physical condition both at the time of reading and, more generally, in comparison with the implied, "ideal" reader, or "breather."[3]

Especially in its narrowest and most pristine instantiation, the detective story, crime fiction per se represents the perhaps most rigid, traditional form of narrative (Krutch 1944; Auden 1962). It depends for its effects on a carefully composed, strictly linear plotline that, typically starting with a dead body, analytically reveals the gradual solution of a mystery. Contrarily, digital narrative in its primeval form, hypertext, seeks to subvert monolinearity by the roots.

The Breathing Wall offers a distinctly cybertextual solution to the dilemma of using a medium that by (hypertextual) definition seems to rule out a reworking of the crime fiction genre. First and foremost, it conforms with the basic generic requirements by presenting a problem, which then needs to be and finally is solved by an investigating agent through processes of logical deduction and reduction (cf. Symons 1992, 13–14). Furthermore, *The Breathing Wall* conscientiously obeys some of the "Ten Commandments of Detection" proposed by Ronald Knox (1928) in that, for instance, the criminal is mentioned fairly early on, the supernatural is ruled out in relation to the death of the victim, there is no more than one room or secret passage, and no hitherto undiscovered poisons are used.

That said, it is not long before the deviations set in. First, there is no detective. Instead, the implied reader assumes the role of both confidant and private eye of the protagonist. The reader-investigator, however, is exposed to the unfamiliarity of the technology—the microphone as a breathing meter and a software application that subverts the conventional, exclusively intentional rules of user interaction.

Readers' attempts at training their bodies to effectively use the Hyper Trans Fiction Matrix parallels their role as apprentice detective. Yet even more innovatively, as discussed earlier, the thus integrated reader is phenomenologically initiated into the physical sensations of the victim. We are hence dealing with a yet unforeseen narrative force that emerges with creative technological experimentalism.

Physical immersion in the narrative cybernetic matrix compensates for the frequently lamented lack of pleasure in reading digital narrative, thus situating *The Breathing Wall* in a fluid niche in between literature and computer game. In this respect, *The Breathing Wall* further reconfirms the ontological implications of the genre as mapped out by Stephen Knight (1980, 4–6), that form and content reflect and change with the specific worldviews they are seeking to convey and/or subvert.

The Breathing Wall mirrors, in its readerly and technological setup, a posthuman world picture that regards "the body as the original prosthesis we all learn to manipulate" and "configures human being so that it can be seamlessly articulated with intelligent machines" (Hayles 1999, 3). N. Katherine Hayles further asserts that "in the posthuman, there are no essential differences or absolute demarcations between bodily existence and computer simulation, cybernetic mechanism and biological organism, robot teleology and human goals" (1999, 3). I would argue that *The Breathing Wall* aesthetically implements the ontological and epistemological implications of this world picture, not least by adding to the physical a *meta*physical, gothic element, which drives forward the solution of the mystery as well as replacing the traditionally religious connotations of the restored sociopolitical order.

While the lack of a detective or inspector figure is not uncommon in crime fiction (Knight 1980, 8), the essential spiritual, social, and metaphysical function of the genre—to restore order in a world dominated by sociopolitical, psychological, and interhuman turmoil—is maintained. *The Breathing Wall* ends in Michael's release and the metaphysical union between the two lovers, although, of course, the sheer brutality of the murder remains looming in the reader's memory.

Finally, to come full circle, let me return to my point made above, that *The Breathing Wall* does not use hypertext in its traditional, multilinear sense. Nor does it subscribe to the lack of closure and the concomitant multiplicity of readings characteristic of early hypertext fiction. By contrast, the authors explicitly confine the boundaries of the text by stating the average length of reading on the CD blurb. As opposed to version 1.0, which features a menu of loosely arranged story parts (dreams and daydreams), version 2.0 further sequentializes the reading process by arranging the dreams and daydreams in the menu according to the order of perusal as intended by the authors.

Instead of subscribing to the potentially disengaging characteristics of multilinear plot construction, *The Breathing Wall* implements a contemporary array of appropriately thrilling multimodal techniques. It mixes them with quasi-ludic, bodily interactive elements that evoke an innovative narrative experience and, consequently, invite a new mode of anthropological, interdisciplinary criticism. I provisionally want to term this approach, which systematically integrates traditional narratological with physiological and cybernetic analyses, "cybersomatic."[4]

Conclusion

To summarize the major points made in this chapter, *The Breathing Wall* represents a rare hypermedia specimen of its thematic genre—crime fiction. It achieves its unique effects to a significant degree through *linearization* of modularized material, thus going against the major implications of "hypertext" proper. I have demonstrated how the text both conforms but also significantly deviates from the conventions of the genre that it purports to adapt to the digital medium. On the one hand, the solution of the mystery does not lie in the hands of an investigative agent who appears as the main character in the story. Instead, it is the reader who acts as the suspected murderer's advocate, and does so not merely by intention-driven, cognitive engagement with the text but chiefly by attempting to manipulate his or her own subcortical—respiratory—functions, both at the time of reading and, more generally, in comparison with the implied, "ideal" reader, or "breather." Simultaneously, the reader's "direction of fit" is made to work both ways, mind-to-world and world-to-mind. This makes for a process that I have referred to as "retro-intentionalization" as it ultimately reinforces the intentional nature of the reading process.

The implications of this analysis for narrative theory and criticism more generally include a stronger focus on the physicality of the reader on the one hand, and his or her embeddedness in the cybernetic feedback circuit on the other, which involves the interaction with electronic technology as much as with more "traditional" print narrative. With innovative forms of new media narrative proliferating and the boundaries between reading and gaming blurring, the significance of the reading body will increasingly move to the forefront of narrative reception and its analysis.

An archetypal object of the aforementioned cybersomatic approach, *The Breathing Wall* compellingly heightens the controversy surrounding the "discourse of transcendence." It confronts readers with the unconditional nature of their own physical situatedness and thus perceptive and cognitive contingency upon the full functionality of their body. One could argue, in fact, that the long-hailed Landowian (1997) "(w)reader" is transformed into a mere breathing apparatus, whose reading experience depends to a large degree on the spatio-temporal situatedness of their own metabolism. Nonetheless, the same insight seems to prove the plausibility of Cartesian dualism, as mind and body during the reception process do not seem to cooperate in such a way as to optimally facilitate text–reader interaction. By the same token, however, the possibility of a successful reading–breathing process intrinsically underscores the hegemony of the mind, that is, intentionality, over the body. After all, neither purpose-drivenness nor object-directedness or readerly perspective is ultimately undermined by the interfering physiological metric.

Finally, although it is probably too early to make predictions, I would conclude that it is in particular the convergence between semiotics, cybertheory, and narratology, with an emphasis on the narrated and perceiving body, to which future ("cyber-somatic") criticism—particularly in relation to "hyper-mediated" narrative—will have to turn its attention.

Notes

1. I would like to thank Kate Pullinger, Chris Joseph, Stefan Schemat, Alison Gibbons, Kerstin Paulsen, Jennifer Riddle Harding, and Roberto Simanowski for their advice and comments on earlier versions of this paper.

2. See the Breathing Wall website, at http://www.thebreathingwall.com (accessed January 4, 2011)

3. In an analogy to Wolfgang Iser's (1978) implied reader, the *breather* implied in the surface and source code of *The Breathing Wall* is a hypothetical receiver constructed by the text who is capable of adjusting his or her respiratory activities in such a way as to interact successfully with the Hyper Trans Fiction Matrix. Clearly, this implies an extension of Iser's concept, first, because it adds a second level of linguistic encoding—the program code—to the text's macrostructure, and, second, because it requires a degree of physiological awareness and aptitude in the reader that, when reading a standard print text, would not be necessary.

4. For a more detailed analysis of the term, see Ensslin n.d.

References

Aarseth, Espen. 1997. *Cybertext: Perspectives on Ergodic Literature*. Baltimore: Johns Hopkins University Press.

Anscombe, G. E. M. 1957. *Intention*. Oxford: Blackwell.

Auden, W. H. 1962. "The Guilty Vicarage: Notes on the Detective Story." In *The Dyer's Hand*, 146–58. New York: Random House.

Austin, J. L. 1962. *How to Do Things with Words*. Oxford: Oxford University Press.

babel. 2004. *The Breathing Wall: An Online Journal*. Available at http://tracearchive .ntu.ac.uk/studio/pullinger/bwone.html (accessed January 4, 2011).

Brooks, Peter. 1984. *Reading for the Plot: Design and Intention in Narrative*. Oxford: Clarendon Press.

Chisholm, Roderick. 1981. *The First Person: An Essay on Reference and Intentionality*. Brighton: Harvester Press.

Damásio, Antonio. 2004. *Looking for Spinoza*. London: Vintage.

de Beaugrande, Robert, and Wolfgang Dressler. 1981. *Introduction to Text Linguistics*. London: Longman.

Dennett, Daniel. 1971. "Intentional Systems." *Journal of Philosophy* 68:87–106.

———. 1987. *The Intentional Stance*. Cambridge MA: MIT Press.

Dery, Mark, ed. 1994. *Flame Wars*. Durham NC: Duke University Press.

Diamond, Cora, and Jenny Teichman, eds. 1979. *Intention and Intentionality: Essays in Honour of G. E. M. Anscombe*. Brighton: Harvester Press.

Dovey, Jon, and Helen Kennedy. 2006. *Game Cultures: Computer Games as New Media*. Maidenhead: Open University Press.

Ensslin, Astrid. 2007. *Canonizing Hypertext: Explorations and Constructions*. London: Continuum.

———. 2010. "Respiratory Narrative: Multimodality and Cybernetic Corporeality in 'Physio-cybertext.'" In *New Perspectives on Narrative and Multimodality*, ed. Ruth Page, 155–65. London: Routledge.

———. n.d. "From Revisi(tati)on to Retrointentionalism: Hermeneutics, Multimodality, and Corporeality in Hypertext, Hypermedia, and Cybertext." In *Reading Moving Letters: Digital Literature in Research and Teaching*, ed. Roberto Simanowski, Peter Gendolla, and Jürgen Schäfer, 145–62. In preparation.

Harman, Gilbert. 1998. "Intentionality." In *A Companion to Cognitive Science*, 602–10. Malden MA: Blackwell.

Hayles, N. Katherine. 1999. *How We Became Posthuman: Virtual Bodies in Cybernetics, Literature, and Informatics*. London: University of Chicago Press.

Hirsch, E. D. 1967. *Validity in Interpretation*. New Haven CT: Yale University Press.

Iser, Wolfgang. 1978. *The Implied Reader: Patterns of Communication in Prose Fiction from Bunyan to Beckett*. Baltimore: Johns Hopkins University Press.

Knight, Stephen. 1980. *Form and Ideology in Crime Fiction*. London: Macmillan.

Knox, Ronald. 1928. "Studies in the Literature of Sherlock Holmes." In *Essays in Satire*, 145–75. London: Sheed and Ward.

Krutch, Joseph Wood. 1944. "Only a Detective Story." *The Nation*, November 25, 1944.

Lahti, Martti. 2003. "As We Become Machines: Corporealized Pleasures in Video Games." In *The Video Game Theory Reader*, ed. M. J. P. Wolf and B. Perron, 157–70. London: Routledge.

Landow, George P. 1997. *Hypertext 2.0: The Convergence of Contemporary Critical Theory and Technology*. Baltimore: Johns Hopkins University Press.

Lister, Martin, Jon Dovey, Seth Giddings, Iain Grant, and Kieran Kelly. 2003. *New Media: A Critical Introduction*. London: Routledge.

Lyons, William. 1995. *Approaches to Intentionality*. Oxford: Clarendon Press.

McLuhan, Marshall. 1964. *Understanding Media: The Extensions of Man*. London: Routledge & Kegan Paul.

Merleau-Ponty, Maurice. 1962. *Phenomenology of Perception*. London: Routledge & Kegan Paul.

Pullinger, Kate, Stefan Schemat, and babel. 2004. *The Breathing Wall*. CD-ROM. London: Sayle Literary Agency.

Richards, I. A. 1929. *Practical Criticism*. London: Kegan Paul.

Ryan, Marie-Laure. 2001. *Narrative as Virtual Reality: Immersion and Interactivity in Literature and Electronic Media*. Baltimore: Johns Hopkins University Press.

Searle, John. 1969. *Speech Acts: An Essay in the Philosophy of Language*. Cambridge: Cambridge University Press.

———. 1983. *Intentionality: An Essay in the Philosophy of Mind*. Cambridge: Cambridge University Press.

Symons, Julian. 1992. *Bloody Murder*. Rev. ed. London: Pan Books.

8   Songlines in the Streets

Story Mapping with Itinerant Hypernarrative

BRIAN GREENSPAN

To understand the place of new narrative technologies, it is necessary to separate the stories we tell within digital spaces from those we tell about them. In *The Digital Sublime*, Vincent Mosco examines numerous myths surrounding cyberspace, including the belief that digital media herald "the death of distance" and the total redefinition of social space. According to this line of prediction, "[a] 'hard' city of facts, figures and determinate relations will be replaced by a 'soft city' of information, aspiration, imagination" (Mosco 2004, 111). Declarations of "the end of geography" are inevitably accompanied by the myth of "the end of politics," according to which national governments give way to a new post-urban, transnational era of virtual grassroots plebiscites, and social classes are replaced by "more loosely defined, shifting, transactional network-based affiliation[s]" of individuals, which exist only as long as their members stay connected (113).

These myths have found expression among hypertext theorists who celebrate the medium's apparent freedom from unilinearity and the confinement of the printed page as an implicitly progressive form of political deterritorialization. Readers are said to be released at long last from the tyranny of the author and invited to cocreate written narratives without deference to any inherited conventions, national traditions, or established communities of readers. But just as hypertext perhaps offers only the illusion of readerly freedom, so too digital networks do not entirely transcend national narratives or borders. On the contrary, there is growing evidence that cyberspace itself is not a global concept but one that is produced differently among users in diverse geographic regions. Even as cybertopians continue to celebrate the potential of networked technologies to produce social spaces that are nomadic, cooperative, and free of real-world constraints, new locative media are presenting techniques for linking virtual space to actual geophysical locations.

Location-aware technologies have already enabled geoblogging and digital graffiti, emergent practices for the engineering of imaginary and intentional communities unlike anything seen in traditional print culture. While political activists have embraced location technologies, the communities associated with these new practices are not necessarily progressive. In December 2005, Sydneysiders used text messaging as an ad hoc vigilante network to assemble a mob of thousands at Cronulla beach, one of the city's recreational suburbs, following an alleged attack by two Lebanese Australians against "Anglo-Celtic" lifeguards. It is not overly deterministic to say that text messaging enables certain kinds of social behavior—for instance, by inciting flash mobs through the peer-to-peer replication of jingoistic slogans—but conveying a considered narrative of social insight through this medium is a trickier matter.

At Carleton's Hypertext and Hypermedia Lab, we are developing new ways to transform ad hoc mobile networks into genuine communities of readers, by integrating textual interfaces with GPS and digital mapping tools for the delivery of site-specific information in narrative form. This chapter describes StoryTrek, our prototype system for *itinerant hypernarrative* currently under development. We are designing StoryTrek to add fine-grained locational functionality to our existing *live hypernarrative* system, an adaptive hypertext engine that builds stories on the fly from data mined in real time from the Internet (Greenspan et al. 2006). Any given page of the live hypernarrative contains both static text and dynamic Story Elements, or narrative placeholders that are conditional on practically any kind of data external to the hypertext itself: the time of day, the local weather, current news headlines, even regional dialects and expressions. These dynamic elements are retrieved in real time and integrated into the story page, which is displayed as a seamless narrative lexia. Like an improvised performance, a live hypernarrative changes depending on where and when it is accessed, and on what is happening in the world (and on the web) at any given time.

Building these syllepses into a narrative becomes a new aesthetic challenge for the hypertext author. If hypertext in general undermines our inherited notions of the stability, fixity, and authority of the printed text and reading subject, then live hypernarrative goes further still, allowing an author to create dynamic, time-sensitive stories that react to current events in real time. But what about real *space*? Live hypernarrative, while temporally aware, is spatially aware only in a limited sense, using domain name cues to determine the user's broad geographical location and adjusting the details of the story accordingly. For example, our prototype travel story, "Ice2Ice," draws data from actual airline schedules to construct different flight paths and travel times, depending on whether the reader is located in Toronto or Honolulu. Yet, the current system cannot integrate fine-grained geospatial information about the user's specific location in either city.

StoryTrek integrates textual interfaces with GPS and digital mapping tools, allowing an author to build geospatially sensitive data into the dynamic story elements for the delivery of site-specific information in narrative form. When completed, the new system will allow the production and dissemination of truly *itinerant hypernarratives* that integrate live material appropriate to the user's precise geospatial position, physical movement, and geographical context. We conceive it as a tool for enabling artistic and critical thinking about spatial environments, and articulating the relationship of imaginary maps to real social spaces.

From Songlines to StoryTreks

StoryTrek is not innovative, having been inspired by the most ancient hypertexts on the planet. In 2005 I was invited to the Royal Melbourne Institute of Technology to discuss a research initiative already underway within the Digital Songlines division of the Australasian Collaborative Research Centre for Interaction Design (ACID) Virtual Heritage program. The project's long-term goal is to develop next-generation "protocols, methodologies, and toolkits to facilitate the collection, education and sharing of indigenous cultural heritage knowledge" within Australia (Leavy et al. 2007, 261), including a digital interface for the presentation of traditional narratives, commonly known as *songlines*. Variously described as a mnemonic device, land map, or musical score, songlines can be understood as narrative guides to the terrain of the Australian continent that have traditionally helped Aboriginal families to survive as they ritually retrace vast ancestral "Dreaming tracks." Although songlines have no precise analog in Western culture, they can be understood as proprietary narratives linked to vast territories in an implicit geospatial organization, constituting a complex network of inherited knowledge about tribal lands and customs. Songlines are a nomadic people's narrative database, an archive of ancient stories that is accessed by traveling the land.

ACID's award-winning Digital Songlines project is a multifaceted application "that will protect, preserve and promote Indigenous cultural practices" (Digital Songlines 2005). The heart of the project is a database of natural and cultural features indexed to a virtual rendering of four hundred square kilometers of indigenous territories, and its developers have demonstrated both technological inventiveness and critical awareness of the issues involved in cross-cultural representation. Malcolm Pumpa and Theodor G. Wyeld (2006) recount their adaptation of a 3D game engine to encode the Aboriginal Dreamworld as an interactive storyworld, noting that Aboriginal knowledge can "amalgamate the power of database and narrative" (239), while emphasizing that the contextual, multidimensional, and nonrepresentational nature of Aboriginal knowledge needs to be considered at the basic levels of database architecture and interface design.

Unfortunately, the sophistication and cross-cultural sensitivity of their approach is belied by the larger project's promotional website, which, in emphasizing the experiential nature of the songlines, risks reducing them to a theme park. Users are told that "Digital Songlines *the experience* is a unique 3D simulation that engages the player in exploring the ancient Indigenous Australian landscape in quests for knowledge, food, weapons and items of cultural significance" (my emphasis). The site further claims that "Australians of all backgrounds will soon be able to experience an authentic Aboriginal dreaming, witnessing the landscape and its significance through indigenous eyes"; and that "[i]t's simply like being there, as an Indigenous person." From this splash screen, it would seem that indigenous cultures are to be preserved not as the lived relations of Aboriginal people to their land but as a technological spectacle. For all its rhetoric of experience, the Digital Songlines website emphasizes the natural features of the landscape but includes little or no reference to the lingering effects of colonial violence. The absence is especially glaring given such high-profile documents as *Bringing Them Home*, the 1997 Report of the National Inquiry into the separation of Aboriginal children from their families and communities, which contains over five hundred testimonials (Human Rights and Equal Opportunity Commission 1997). As Gillian Whitlock (2001) has shown, the act of bearing witness to these testimonials acquires added complexities in the economy of Aboriginal narrative exchange, preventing any simple identification with an indigenous perspective.

Yet, it would be hasty to conclude that information media have no place in representing traditional cultures. Australia's indigenous societies have always been information societies, as Eric Michaels points out in his influential report, *The Aboriginal Invention of Television*: "Secret and sacred knowledge is the major exchange item between Aboriginal people and communities. The result of this sharing . . . was the creation of a vast, dynamic network of linkages between all groups, similar to a broadcasting network" (1986, 4). Building on this network, Michaels helped the Warlpiri Media Association at Yuéndemu to establish television shows and an independent broadcast station. Over the last two decades, Warlpiri Aboriginals have "actively adopted" newer media, even while preserving their traditional languages through newsletters, radio broadcasts and CB radio networks, video production, and online services (Buchtmann 2000, 60; see also Ginsburg 1993).

Instead of emphasizing the immersive qualities of hypermedia, Barbara Glowczewski has explored their potential for interactively reproducing the "reticular" or nonlinear character of Aboriginal songlines. She conceived a multimedia database of audiovisual elements, including "images of rituals and landscape, photos of acrylic paintings, [and] sound recordings of myths and songs" (Glowczewski 2005, 5), and invited Aboriginal users to create hyperlinks between these elements. Through this adaptive linking process, Glowczewski explored and recorded the relationships perceived by the Warlpiri people between specific aspects of their land and culture—a cognitive map that would respect "the Warlpiri system of meaningful connections" (5). One can also point to artistic installations inspired by the songlines, like Teri Rueb's TRACE (1996), an environmental sound memorial database linked to the network of hiking trails in the Canadian Rockies. The project commemorates themes of personal loss and bereavement by exploring the "metaphoric relatedness of tombstones, fossils, cemeteries, databases, networks, computers and fossil beds" (Rueb 1996). TRACE exemplifies Gregory Ulmer's (2005) concept of "MEmorials," assemblages of image and text, of real and virtual spaces, hybrid sites of both individual and collective self-knowledge that constitute not just an "experience" or "attraction," but a "repulsion" as well, transforming the Internet into a "living monument" to human disasters. Even virtual reality technologies need not be implemented in a manner that sutures over the complications of intercultural identification. Lorne Leonard (2003) has used a computer-assisted virtual environment (CAVE) to create an immersive environment for teaching users about Aboriginal Dreamtime that is sensitive to the challenges of representing Aboriginal peoples and cultures. Significantly, Leonard perceives his installation as neither a record nor a representation of dreamtime narratives: "The virtual landscape design is not a replication of the contemporary or past Gabbe Darbal landscapes but rather, a design that encourages users to conceptualize these Dreamtime landscapes" (2003, 2).

Digital multimedia are especially well-suited to the emulation and archivization of songlines, and could potentially be used to record and communicate a fuller range of traditional Aboriginal storytelling and writing practices, which include oral narration and performance, hand signals, dance, message sticks, wooden carvings, sandwriting, petroglyphs, and body painting (Buchtmann 2000, 61–62). Of course, the technical capacities of digital media raise the broader issue that any representation borders on appropriation. Michaels points out that "in face-to-face transmission [of songlines], information access can distinguish differences between rights to *know* something, to *hear* something and the right to *speak* of it. Aboriginal society regulates these differences for oral information as well as for design and dance" (1986, 4). For this reason, the same story is often told differently depending on who's speaking and who's listening, and outsiders are not always granted access to all layers of meaning (Klapproth 2004, 43). But while universal-access broadcast media like radio and TV can't easily protect these distinctions, adaptive hypermedia systems can be designed to allow specific users access to only certain layers of information at certain times. Here is one instance where opponents of digital rights management protocols might need to reconsider the cross-cultural implications of full and open access.

The dynamic and scalable qualities of hypermedia also make them particularly amenable to the exploration of songlines. In her study of the oral narratives of the Pitjanjatjarra and Yankunytjatjarra people of Australia's Western Desert, Danièle Klapproth reports on "the practice of offering one's audience an . . . 'incomplete' story text. . . . [I]t is assumed that knowledge of the plot will be acquired gradually by the members of the culture through repeated exposure to various versions of the story over time" (2004, 75). Such narrative aporias are easily accommodated by the iterative linking structure of hypertexts, which can dynamically hide or reveal any scale of narrative detail (see Senbergs et al. 2005): hypertext, after all, is defined by its missing information, breakdowns, and broken links (Moulthrop 1997). Instead of thinking of digital media as a virtual system for rendering an absent culture present in its totality, then, we can instead work toward a "broken" model that emulates the elliptical and porous plots of the songlines, while opening out into their broader colonial history of irruption and occlusion.

Perhaps most importantly, songlines anticipate the collaborative aspects of digital media like blogs and wikis. As Stephen Muecke (1992, 48) explains, the "limited authority" of Aboriginal stories means that "no-one seeks to have total quality control, authority must always be deferred, to the old if you are young . . . , [or] to the people in the next community with whom one is linked by a story." Muecke has tried to capture this sense of collaboration by transcribing oral narratives from Broome, in Western Australia, using unconventional typographic layouts to great success; however, he admits that printed text can only approximate the geographical specificity of these narrative performances. Some Aboriginal narrators won't recount a story unless they can do so at the specific topographical site related to the story; in some cases, the storyteller sits with his back turned to his country, which also *situates* him in relation to his audience and a broad network of social formations (Muecke 1992, 89, 85). Moreover, the custodian of any given song is authorized to carry it only so far along a dreaming track (Klapproth 2004, 69), and completion of the story requires negotiation with the guardians of other sections of the Dreaming. To enable such negotiations is one of the chief functions of the Dreaming, and part of the dialogic structure of the stories themselves, which Muecke describes as a form of collective serial production. Even ACID's Digital Songlines experience, which employs Geographic Information System (GIS) software to situate a user's avatar in a virtual landscape that accurately locates images of natural features relative to one another within the virtual terrain, does not enact the complex deictic and geospatial dimensions of narrative collaboration that characterize the songlines.

The Itinerant Hypernarrative System

StoryTrek does not aim to record, reproduce, or otherwise represent Aboriginal territory or its features; instead, it builds on existing spatial hypertext research to emulate the close connection between narrative and landscape exemplified by the songlines, lending an enhanced spatial awareness to hypertext authoring. David Kolb's *Sprawling Places* project (2004) has explored spatial hypertext as a means of documenting contemporary regional and urban histories around the world but doesn't make use of location-aware technologies to gather geospatial user input. Others have experimented with various locative media for the delivery of site-specific audio information in urban environments. Sonic City (Maze and Jacobs 2005), Project MurMur (Parent, Spaccapietra, and Zimányi 2006), and 34N-118W (http://34n118w.net) all provide methods for the critical exploration of urban space using GPS units to access geotagged audio files. However fascinating, these systems all follow a landmark-and-graffiti model of geocaching; that is, if the user's GPS coordinates indicate that she is standing in front of Ground Zero in Manhattan, the interface can link to blog postings from survivors, or play an MP3 recording of 911 calls. Zhou et al. (2005) conclude that these types of applications "typically represent places quite simply, as a geographical point or a point plus radius. . . . [T]his simple representation is not expressive enough to represent the full range of people's everyday places" (886). Such systems are limited to the recognition of waypoints only, not travel vectors; they offer a tour, not a story. As Anthony Judge writes in his evaluation of the Internet's potential for representing songlines: "What's missing is any sense of the 'melody' which defines a succession of pathways, namely a line of sites through many different domains" (1998, 185).

StoryTrek is designed to provide just such a succession of pathways. By allowing any user to build fine-grained geospatial data into the story itself, our system will provide continuous feedback of live, richly contextual information in narrative form, matched to the user's route and location. Most spatial hypertext systems still depend on the standard WIMP GUI (Windows-Icons-Mouse-Pointer Graphic User Interface) for user input; by contrast, our system takes the user's actual geospatial position and physical movement as input. The user will carry a GPS- and wifi-enabled PDA or cellular phone that sends data about her current walking route (or *tracklog*) to a spatial parser, which selects and returns an appropriate *story segment*. She will be able to navigate a narrative by simply walking through an actual urban or natural environment, a practice that we call StoryTreking.

While all the components for itinerant hypernarrative already exist, they have not yet been integrated into a single narrative system. A Swiss team has proposed the creation of a "Kinetic User Interface" (KUI) for e-tourism and mobile blogging that would rely on signals from GPS units and embedded Radio Frequency Identification (RFID) networks to track a user's physical motion as a means of remote input (Pallotta et al. 2006). While their system would accept continuous input, it is designed to provide contextual information based only on landmarks and waypoints, not continuous feedback in narrative form. Frank Shipman has successfully integrated a spatial parser into his hypertext authoring tools, the Visual Knowledge Builder (VKB), but only for the management of user-generated content in a standard graphical user interface (Francisco-Revilla and Shipman 2005; Shipman et al. 2002). While it does allow the spatial organization of hypertext, Shipman's VKB system responds to mouse input, not to spatial input generated by the user's physical movements or location. Neither the VKB nor its successor, FLAPS, have the ability to generate narrative automatically or integrate live data mined dynamically from the Internet; its designers have, however, considered the special case of Geo-Spatial Hypermedia involving actual landscapes, which raises "the question of whether the [actual geospatial] background should be taken into consideration in the parsing process and how it could inform the parser" (Francisco-Revilla and Shipman 2005, 109).

With this question in mind, we are designing StoryTrek to parse the pattern of the user's physical movement at any moment, and match this pattern to a database of narrative *cases*, assembling coherent narratives on the fly that are relevant to the user's actual location. The system architecture uses case-based reasoning to match the user-generated trip segment with an appropriately patterned story segment consisting of textual lexia, images, audio-video files, dynamic Flash objects, or three-dimensional VRML data. Case-based reasoning has been used successfully for automatic story generation based on user interaction patterns in the MINSTREL (Turner 1992) and GEIST (Grasbon and Braun 2001) systems, though neither has the ability to link to real-world geospatial data. Like these earlier systems, StoryTrek will have a case database populated with narrative segments, but our method of segmentation will differ. Most story generators (Fairclough and Cunningham 2003; Gervás et al. 2004; Peinado and Gervás 2005) base their narrative segments on morphologies drawn from Vladimir Propp's classic (1968) formal analysis of the Russian folktale, building in an intrinsic bias toward heroic quests. By contrast, StoryTrek will match the user's movement pattern with narrative segments based on typical hypertext structural and navigational patterns, as anatomized by Mark Bernstein (2003): the *cycle*, the *tangle*, the *counterpoint*, and so on. Marie-Laure Ryan has further expanded the repertoire of hypertext patterns in her study of transmedial narratology to include such complex textual architectures as *track-switching* and *sea-anemone* (2006, 103–7), adding to the variety of potential hypertext patterns in our case database.

By leveraging the open-source Google Maps Application Programming Interface (API), we are designing the back-end StoryTrek authoring tool to allow users to drag icons representing narrative patterns onto actual street maps, linking individual story segments to specific city features. Once linked to geospatial coordinates, these story segments can then be accessed from the StoryTrek server using a portable GPS- and wifi-enabled browser. Walk around the block, and the StoryTrek server returns a *cyclical* or recursive narrative, or perhaps plays a looping audio or video track; move into the gridiron of laneways in central Melbourne, and the story likewise moves into a *sieve* pattern; backtrack down the same street, and the narrative backs into an historical *mirror world*, acting as a *dialectical interface* between past and present. Stand still and the system will know you are lingering, and take the opportunity to provide some background description of your actual location, including information about its history and architecture. Wherever you decide to stroll, the system will present you with a coherent but dynamically changing narrative cued to your specific location, walking speed, and direction. The city itself becomes an interface that accepts pedestrian motion as input, so that the explicit topography of the user's physical wanderings becomes a heuristic for exploring the implicit structure of the narrative.

Finally, StoryTrek will run each story segment through the live hyper-narrative layer, customizing it with up-to-the-minute data drawn from the web or open geospatial databases, such as Google Earth or Open-StreetMap. This dynamic customization ensures that the system will be both time- and space-sensitive, and will not output the same story repeatedly, even if the user retraces his or her steps. In practice, these operations need not be visible to the end-user, who can be presented with a technically seamless story that evolves continuously as she explores her urban environment. However, in keeping with the songlines metaphor, we continue to explore interface designs that will expose the limitations that proprietary rights and protocols impose upon universal access and transparent interoperability, in order to foreground the negotiation of access as an articulation of individual and community rights. Imagine a pedestrian in Melbourne who, instead of reading a printed translation of a songline, traces a dreaming track by navigating the shores of the Yarra River, meeting up there with other users at tribal boundaries to exchange the portions of the stories they guard. Unlike other forms of computer-mediated communication, such collective serial production allows users to reenact traditional patterns of collaborative narration in contemporary physical spaces.

Jorge Luis Borges dreamed of an infinite library (1964) and a fantastic map the size of the territory (1972); with our system, both fantasies converge in a library the size of the world.

Mapping Melbourne: Test Implementation and Critical Challenges

While the metropolis seems a long way from the songlines, that distance might only be an illusion of modern space-time. The traditional Aboriginal store of knowledge about the world sometimes referred to as the Dreaming, "although at one level mythologically related to a sacred reality of the past, is in an important way experienced simultaneously as eternally present and immediately relevant to the here and now of Aboriginal everyday life" (Klapproth 2004, 67). Jim Naureckas has elicited links between indigenous and modern urban spaces in his New York Songlines, an online schematic map of personal memories and oral lore about the city indexed to specific pedestrian pathways (Naureckas n.d.). Our own initial StoryTrek implementation will likewise take place not in the Outback but in an urban setting; again, our goal is not to represent songlines but to emulate their method of integrating stories, communities, and the real world. We intend to build a narrative interface for Melbourne, Australia, based on archival stories, photographs, video, and GPS tracklogs sampled from my own peregrinations during successive visits to the central business district. This particular StoryTrek will take a long historical view of songlines, exploring how antipodean urban development and waves of migration from Europe, China, and southeast Asia negatively affected Aboriginal populations in the period leading up to

Federation (1850–1901). The StoryTrek user will retrieve these peoples' stories of movement and migration, mined from the online archives of the State Library of Victoria—in effect turning the archive inside out in order to retrace Melbourne's pre-urban histories, and to recall the lost map of songlines paved over by modern development.

Our test implementation will link historical images and accounts of antipodean dissent and urban unrest to more recent cartographies of uprise. In February 2005, Sydney exploded in street riots over the death of two teenagers during a police chase in Macquarie Fields, a neighborhood characterized as predominantly white working class. Nearby Redfern was still calling for a renewed inquest from the riots that occurred a year earlier, when Thomas "TJ" Hickey, an Aboriginal youth, died during a police chase. Contrary to traditional representations of Australia as an idyllic bush community held together by the ideals of mateship and egalitarianism, Sydney and Melbourne are in fact striated by lines of power and privilege. Itinerant hypernarrative will make these divisions visible by providing continuous, collaborative, and context-specific narrative feedback about urban environments and populations, and by mapping alternative, more inclusive forms of collectivity onto actual city spaces in ways not possible in any other medium.

However, adding spatial awareness to our existing live hypernarrative prototype presents several technical challenges, most notably the establishment of interoperability between a real-time GPS motion tracker, an automatic plot generator, and library and geospatial databases. Merely maintaining a geospatial fix in an urban setting using consumer-grade GPS receivers can prove difficult, although StoryTrek emphasizes drifting patterns of movement as much as specific locations, requiring less overall precision in orienteering. In addition to these practical challenges, StoryTrek raises several key issues surrounding the spatial aspects of hypertext narrative generally, including user (dis)orientation, navigational aids, and the relationship between cognitive, textual, and virtual maps. During informal tests of our live hypernarrative engine, some users reported surprise when they realized how closely the time of the story matches the time of its telling, or that the story accurately described the current time of day and general weather conditions of the reader's actual location (Greenspan et al. 2006). In other words, the *liveness* of the narrative disrupted the reader's typical expectation regarding narrative temporality and referentiality. Similarly, itinerant hypernarrative will confound readerly assumptions about narrative space, such that narrative nodes presenting close correspondences between the space of the textual world and the spatial environment of the text could well prove to be highly disorienting. Writers using the StoryTrek authorware will need to respond to the usability issues arising from dissonance between a user's cognitive maps, his actual geospatial orientation, and the implicit spatial structure of the narrative, and learn to exploit artistically the various effects of dissonance, disjunction, and disorientation that arise as users slip between different represented spaces and spaces of representation.

On the other hand, itinerant hypertext could function to better orient the reader, at least in comparison with non-locative hypertext. Patricia Boechler (2001) has observed that users who navigate even non-adaptive hypertext perceive a variable spatial distance between nodes depending on the order in which they are accessed. She speculates that "in hypertext, as the user becomes more proficient the comparison between hyperspace and physical space may break down" (Boechler 2001, 29). By contrast, an itinerant hypernarrative that anchors textual topologies to real-world topographies could well limit both navigational options and the variability of the reading experience, while reinforcing the analogy between the physical space and hyperspace.

The effects of these mappings are unpredictable, given the relative positioning of represented spaces within fictional worlds generally, and the shifts in focalization demanded even by complex printed narratives. As Barbara Tversky notes in her study of spatial perspective, "when [printed] narratives described two observers in the same scene, . . . subjects seemed to adopt a neutral oblique perspective, rather than the viewpoints of either observer"; however, "when narratives described two observers in differen[t] scenes, subjects took the viewpoint of each observer in turn" (1996, 478). Ruth Ronen (1994, 184–91) likewise details how printed narratives shift regularly between internal and external focalizers, as well as between perceived and imagined spaces, to accommodate expansive or non-present spatial elements that would otherwise be unavailable to the limited perception of a given focalizing subject. To these complex but familiar shifts, itinerant hypernarrative adds an entirely new inventory of focalization effects, allowing the constantly changing background location of the reader's actual world to influence the arrangement of fictional spaces presented in the text. By dynamically layering narrative perspectives onto both the actual, ever-shifting space in which the user is situated and the mental maps he constructs while navigating them, StoryTrek further complicates the reader's orientation and perception of narrative space. It remains to be seen whether the itinerant reader will identify more readily with internal or external levels of focalization, and how navigation through the real world will affect the reader's perception of the topography of the narrative world.

Many questions remain regarding the interface and interaction design of such a system. Given that the songlines cover some half a million square kilometers, how can they be translated into a scale more suitable for urban explorers equipped with small-screened portable devices? And how much freedom will be granted the non-Aboriginal user to diverge from an ancestral dreaming track merely to pop into the local café? Perhaps most importantly, how will the system instill in its widely dispersed readers a sense of custodianship over the story, and respect for its traditional owners? While we do not expect easy answers, the fact that these very issues of navigation, knowledge transfer, access, and trust also arise in the context of online training sites, e-commerce interactions, pervasive games, and countless other applications of new media suggests that we still have much to learn from songlines.

References

Bernstein, M. 2003. "Patterns of Hypertext." Eastgate Systems. Available at http://www.eastgate.com/patterns/Patterns.html (accessed January 4, 2011).

Boechler, P. 2001. "How Spatial Is Hyperspace? Interacting with Hypertext Documents: Cognitive Processes and Poncepts." *CyberPsychology and Behavior* 4, no. 1:23–46.

Borges, Jorge Luis. 1964. "The Library of Babel." In *Labyrinths: Selected Stories and Other Writings*, ed. D. A. Yates and J. E. Irby, 51–58. New York: New Directions Pub. Corp.

———. 1972. "Of Exactitude in Science." In *A Universal History of Infamy*, trans. N. T. di Giovanni, 131. New York: Dutton.

Buchtmann, L. 2000. "The Use of Modern Communication Technology by an Aboriginal Community in Remote Australia." *Prometheus* 18, no. 1:59–74.

Digital Songlines: Virtual Dreamtime Comes to Life. 2005. Available at http://www.acid.net.au/indexad39.html?option=com_content&task=view&id=89&Itemid=153 (accessed January 22, 2007).

Fairclough, C., and P. Cunningham. 2003. "A Multiplayer Case Based Story Engine." In *4th International Conference on Intelligent Games and Simulation*, 41–46. Dublin: Trinity College Dublin Department of Computer Science, EUROSIS.

Francisco-Revilla, L., and F. Shipman. 2005. "Parsing and Interpreting Ambiguous Structures in Spatial Hypermedia." In *Hypertext '05*, 107–16. Salzburg, Austria: Association for Computing Machinery.

Gervás, P., B. Díaz-Agudo, F. Peinado, and R. Hervas. 2004. "Story Plot Generation Based on CBR." In *Proceedings of the 24th Annual International Conference of the British Computer Society's Specialist Group on Artificial Intelligence. Applications and Innovations in Intelligent Systems XXII*, ed. A. Macintosh, R. Ellis, and T. Allen. Cambridge: Springer.

Ginsburg, F. 1993. "Aboriginal Media and the Australian Imaginary." *Public Culture* 5, no. 3:557–78.

Glowczewski, B. 2005. "Lines and Criss-Crossings: Hyperlinks in Australian Indigenous Narratives." *Media International Australia Incorporating Culture and Policy* 116:24–35.

Grasbon, D., and N. Braun. 2001. "A Morphological Approach to Interactive Storytelling." Digital Storytelling Department, Computer Graphics Center, Darmstadt, Germany. Available at http://netzspannung.org/version1/extensions/cast 01-proceedings/pdf/by_name/Grasbon.pdf (accessed December 2, 2007).

Greenspan, B., C. Dormann, S. Caquard, C. Eaket, and R. Biddle. 2006. "Live Hypernarrative and Cybercartography: You Are Here, Now." *Cartographica* 41, no. 1:35–46.

Human Rights and Equal Opportunity Commission. 1997. *Bringing Them Home: The "Stolen Children" Report*. Available at http://www.humanrights.gov.au/social_justice/bth_report/index.html (accessed January 28, 2007).

Judge, A. J. N. 1998. "From Information Highways to Songlines of the Noosphere: Global Configuration of Hypertext Pathways as a Prerequisite for Meaningful Collective Transformation." *Futures* 30, nos. 2–3:181–87.

Klapproth, Danièle M. 2004. *Narrative as Social Practice: Anglo-Western and Australian Aboriginal Oral Traditions*. New York: Mouton de Gruyter.

Kolb, D. 2004. "Twin Media: Hypertext Structure under Pressure." In *Proceedings of the Fifteenth ACM Conference on Hypertext and Hypermedia*, 26–27. New York: Association for Computing Machinery.

Leavy, B., T. Wyeld, J. Hills, C. Barker, and S. Gard. 2007. "The Ethics of Indigenous Storytelling: Using the Torque Game Engine to Support Australian Aboriginal Cultural Heritage." *In Situated Play: Proceedings of the Digital Games Research Association*, 261–68. Tokyo: Digital Games Research Association.

Leonard, L. 2003. "Designing a Virtual Reality Nyungar Dreamtime Landscape Narrative." In *Proceedings at Anhalt University of Applied Sciences 2003*, ed. E. Buhmann and S. Ervin, 202–11. Heidelberg: Wichmann Verlag.

Maze, R., and M. Jacobs. 2005. "Sonic City: Prototyping a Wearable Experience."
In *Proceedings: Seventh IEEE International Symposium on Wearable Computers*,
160–63.

Michaels, Eric. 1986. *The Aboriginal Invention of Television*. Canberra: Australian
Institute of Aboriginal Studies.

Mosco, Vincent. 2004. *The Digital Sublime: Myth, Power, and Cyberspace*. Cambridge MA: MIT Press.

Moulthrop, S. 1997. "Pushing Back: Living and Writing in Broken Space." *Modern
Fiction Studies* 43, no. 3:651–74.

Muecke, S. 1992. *Textual Spaces: Aboriginality and Cultural Studies*. Sydney: New
South Wales University Press.

Naureckas, J. n.d. New York Songlines: Virtual Walking Tours of Manhattan Streets.
Available at http://www.nysonglines.com/ (accessed March 5, 2011).

Pallotta, V., A. Brocco, D. Guinard, P. Bruegger, and P. de Almeida. 2006. "Roam-
Blog: Outdoor and Indoor Geo-blogging Enhanced with Contextual Service
Provisioning for Mobile Internet Users." In *Distributed Agent-based Retrieval
Tools: The Future of Search Engines Technology*, ed. Alessandro Soro, Giuliano
Armano, and Gavino Paddeu, 103–21. Milan: Polimetrica.

Parent, C., S. Spaccapietra, and E. Zimányi. 2006. "The MurMur Project: Modeling
and Querying Multi-representation Spatio-temporal Database." *Information Systems* 31, no. 8:733–69.

Peinado, F., and P. Gervás. 2005. "A Generative and Case-based Implementation
of Proppian Morphology." In *Story Generators: Models and Approaches for the
Generation of Literary Artifacts. The 17th Joint International Conference of the
Association for Computers and the Humanities and the Association for Literary
and Linguistic Computing (ACH/ALLC)*, ed. B. Lönneker, J. C. Meister, P. Gervás,
F. Peinado, and M. Mateas, 129–31. Victoria BC: Humanities Computing and
Media Centre, University of Victoria.

Propp, Vladimir. 1968. *Morphology of the Folktale*. Trans. Laurence Scott. Austin:
University of Texas Press. (Orig. pub. 1928.)

Pumpa, M., and T. Wyeld. 2006. "Database and Narratological Representation of
Australian Aboriginal Knowledge as Information Visualization Using a Game
Engine." Paper presented at the Tenth International Conference of Information
Visualization (IV '06), July 5–7, London.

Ronen, Ruth. 1994. *Possible Worlds in Literary Theory*. Cambridge: Cambridge University Press.

Rueb, T. 1996. "TRACE: A Memorial Environmental Sound Installation." Available at
http://www.terirueb.net/old_www/trace/paper.html (accessed March 12, 2005).

Ryan, Marie-Laure. 2006. *Avatars of Story*. Electronic Mediations 17. Minneapolis:
University of Minnesota Press.

Senbergs, Z., W. E. Cartwright, M. Black, and B. Greenspan. 2005. "Geographical Storytelling." In *Proceedings of ssc 2005 Spatial Intelligence, Innovation and Praxis: The National Biennial Conference of the Spatial Sciences Institute*. Melbourne: Spatial Sciences Institute.

Shipman, F., J. M. Moore, P. Maloor, H. Hsieh, and R. Akkapeddi. 2002. "Semantics Happen: Knowledge Building in Spatial Hypertext." In *Proceedings of the ACM Conference on Hypertext*, ed. J. Blustein, 25–34. New York: Association for Computing Machinery.

Turner, S. R. 1992. "Minstrel: A Computer Model of Creativity and Storytelling." PhD diss., University of California, Los Angeles. Technical Report CSD-920057.

Tversky, B. 1996. "Spatial Perspective in Descriptions." In *Language and Space*, ed. P. Bloom, M. A. Peterson, L. Nadel, and M. F. Garrett, 463–91. Cambridge MA: MIT Press.

Ulmer, Gregory. 2005. *Electronic Monuments*. Minneapolis: University of Minnesota Press.

Whitlock, G. 2001. "In the Second Person: Narrative Transactions in Stolen Generations Testimony." *Biography* 24, no. 1:197–214.

Zhou, C., P. Ludford, D. Frankowski, and L. Terveen. 2005. "How Do People's Concepts of Place Relate to Physical Locations?" In *Lecture Notes in Computer Science*, ed. M. F. Costabile and F. Paterno, 3585:886–98. Heidelberg: IFIP. Available at http://www.springerlink.com/content/5xlbhldptfafw4h/.

9   Narrative Supplements

DVD and the Idea of the "Text"

PAUL COBLEY AND NICK HAEFFNER

The so-called DVD revolution is said to have brought about substantial change in films, change that also impinges directly on narrative. According to Barlow, the DVD is now "fundamentally changing the way we interact with movies," has taken films outside of "time" and into "boxes," and has created a new commodity or artifact in which the film's "original narrative" is not the sole feature (2005, xi). Of course, some claims made for the "revolutionary" aspect of DVD, particularly in respect of narrative, are open to challenge. In general, suggestions that the DVD newly empowers users in respect to their receptions of narrative need to be viewed critically. Cover, for example, is circumspect enough to speak of the matter in terms of "desire" rather than real change: "a desire for democratisation of the media process, by which I mean the desire or demand of audiences for co-participation in scheduling, timing, controlling, viewing and engaging with media and entertainment texts" (2005, 138). Similarly, he suggests that "DVD is a media audiovisual format and a media practice that not only invites, but often requires, the active engagement of the user," mainly in contrast to broadcast TV schedules and "within various author-given constraints" (139). In the last twenty years, especially in the climate of communication and media studies, the activity of audiences and fans has been to the fore, authority has been seen to be in decline, both in grand narratives and smaller ones, and successive entertainment technologies have been hailed as facilitating the liberation of the reader (see Cobley 2001, 183–200). It therefore makes sense to pause before jumping on the DVD bandwagon.

In the case of the DVD, it is worth considering how its innovations fall not just within existing narrative theory but also how it marks out new directions for understanding narrative. This essay will discuss some of the features of the aforementioned "DVD revolution," a revolution that, even now, may be seen to be merely the first wave with the establishment of new "sub"-technologies such as Blu-ray. It will ask how the mixed media facility of DVD contributes to narrative and how "add-ons" supplement or obliterate the notion of "text." Before this, however, and in order to be absolutely explicit, we should say exactly what DVD entails and give a couple of examples of the DVD experience.

The Medium and the Experience

The Digital Versatile Disc was developed in the mid-1990s as a portable and convenient format for the storage of multimedia data. The story of the massive adoption of DVD as a medium is well known, and it is usually assumed that all its features contribute to its popularity. The DVD format purports to provide more than other formats in which an audiovisual narrative might be offered. That is to say, the DVD has become synonymous with the "add-on" (see Brereton 2007). In the case of a film or television series, this might involve further content such as "official trailers," "making of" documentaries, interviews with auteurs and/or stars, outtakes, alternative endings that were shot, as well as material in non-audiovisual media such as photographic stills, facsimiles of scripts, storyboards, and so on. Although not visual, one of the most characteristic of add-ons for the DVD is the "audio commentary" offered by many DVDs, which consists of a running vocal account of the film or program's making, its content and form, given by directors or others involved in the production, and available to be switched on while the visuals and much reduced sound of the "main" narrative are playing. Even DVD presentations that do not contain a classical Hollywood narrative—for example, filmed performances of operas—invariably offer the same arrays of supplementary material. Often coupled with these "add-ons" are a series of further facilities that were previously unavailable to VHS video users: subtitles (in various languages), options for the viewing ratio on the screen, sound options (e.g., Dolby), and the opportunity to watch the film by choosing from a menu of "chapters" or discrete episodes.[1] Of course, it should be noted that the production of special DVD versions of narratives is an instance of the commodification that is visited on other products. Economically speaking, DVD special features render a previously cinematic or VHS narrative desirable by "adding value."

In spite of such commodification, the DVD experience of narrative is believed to be qualitatively different from the way that narratives, including other audiovisual narratives, are to be read in other media: "add-ons" seem to threaten to interrupt the linear direction attributed to narratives in other media. Although it is difficult to prove that narratives in other media are exclusively read in a linear fashion, Cover (2005, 139) argues that the selection of DVD special features are "made much as one selects from the database on a CD-ROM, computer hard-drive or website page." As far as narrative is concerned, the technological affinities of DVDs and CD-ROMs as new media technologies have one of two consequences. On the one hand, there are the analyses of Cover (2005), Hight (2005), and Bolter (2002), all of whom see a potential disruption of putative narrative sequencing (in practices such as watching a DVD narrative by random chapter, in reverse order, or just consuming the "add-ons" in general). This disruption is not too far removed from practices of narrative consumption witnessed in print media (such as jumping to the end of a detective novel to find out who committed the murder and then reading again from the front), although the technologies are obviously different. There is also the point that nonlinearity should not be overstated: unlike VHS, the entertainment form of the DVD-Video includes a framework called PUO (Prohibited User Operations), which allows the DVD author to determine and design the style of linear or nonlinear temporal flow and navigation that is possible at any point (see Lane 2006). Some parts of a DVD are designed so that they cannot be "skipped" by the user.

Cubitt's (2002) analysis, on the other hand, suggests that the relations within the new media have not been sufficiently explored owing to a bias toward entertainment media that invariably embody narrative. What has been downplayed, he argues, are all the workplace and labor-associated technologies such as spreadsheets and databases, which have no relation with linearity. In some of the new media, then, narrative is found to be marginal at best. It is a persuasive argument, and, despite our focus on an ineluctably entertainment medium, we need to take seriously the relation of some nonlinear aspects of DVD as medium to other new media where linearity is almost absent from their very conception.

Consider, then, the following preliminary experience of narrative offered by using DVDs, the DVD of Series 1 of the TV spy narrative *Spooks* (2002; *MI-5* in the United States). The cover of the DVD and the various inserts, as the DVD box opens out, use all the kinds of iconography—

logos, straplines, mock surveillance footage—employed in the television broadcast of the series itself as well as in the unprecedented publicity campaign that accompanied it (see Cobley 2009). Having inserted the first of the three DVDs in the box into the DVD player or computer, the copyright warning comes up, followed by the (unskippable) ident sequence of Contender Entertainment Group. The next sequence is in split screen and in surveillance-camera mode (both typical of the television broadcast of the series). It shows a masked intruder breaking into high tech offices (the offices of the fictional Thames House where the branch of MI5 featured in *Spooks* has its headquarters). The intruder is shown unlocking the alarm by means of a password on a computer; then there is an eternally looped sequence in which the intruder is among all the communications technology that have featured in close-ups during the earlier part of the intrusion sequence. As is commonly the case with DVD, this is one of those sequences that it is impossible to skip or, as one would say with the preceding media of VHS, "fast forward."

Yet, unless one has some sense of the connections of the images, there is also no possibility to proceed any further on the DVD. A repetitive beat from the *Spooks* theme plays on the soundtrack while the larger part of the screen showing a desk with technologies on it is split with two surveillance images of the intruder. It is only when one casts the mouse across various desk items or one presses the buttons on the DVD remote control that a cursor appears and it becomes clear that each item hides the route to a particular feature of the DVD. A random pile of cassettes on the desk at the left of the main picture play the episodes on the DVD with audio commentaries; the telephone with a large keypad just above the cassettes leads to the sound settings; the rolodex file beside the telephone leads to a featurette about the origins of *Spooks*; the pile of disks in a CD tower lead to the straightforward playing of each episode; and, finally, clicking on the closed file at the front of the desk or the file contents to its side lead to further "add-ons"—including fictional texts with stills purporting to be classified files on individual characters, filmed interviews with actors and directors, stills from the production, plus a DVD-ROM with wallpapers, scripts, and web links. This account of the interface for simply accessing the features of the DVD is actually a limited statement of what is offered and the steps that have to be taken to procure a narrative. Nevertheless, it should be said that many of the elements on the DVD that are accessed are, in fact, in narrative form, be it the series episodes themselves, the commentaries, the interviews, or the faux case files. Yet the interface itself (the masked intruder breaking into the offices) and many of the materials (for example, production stills) are not in narrative form or are only minimally so in the former case.

This particular DVD, one that is not untypical of the entertainment DVD in general, calls into question some aspects of the status of narrative while also asking a further question in relation to the status of the "text." This demands explicit consideration at some length.

The Myth of the "Text Itself"

What this example suggests is that there are at least two axes for narrative on DVD. There is the narrative that is provided by the presentation of the "original" film, television program, opera, and so forth (i.e., the narrative as it was presented in the cinema, television, or the theater, with only the most obvious changes to the viewing experience as a result of the transfer from one medium to another). Then there is the other narrative, sometimes conceived as an "anti-narrative" that is provided by the "original" narrative being embedded in a menu of supplements. The ability to access discrete chapters allows a degree of re-sequencing of the "original" narrative (although this could be done, albeit in a more cumbersome manner, in the old medium of VHS). Cover goes so far as to suggest that this device amounts to a "cocreation" of the narrative whose collaborative aspect is only further strengthened by the availability on some DVDs of "alternative endings" and "deleted scenes" (2005, 140). Brereton even goes beyond "cocreation" and suggests that "'control' appears to be a defining characteristic of DVD usage" (2007, 116).

Yet, there is a need to be careful that the ease of some of the features offered by new media does not lead to conclusions about the general nature of both texts and narratives. In drawing his classic distinction between "Work" and "Text," Barthes approached the matter from an "old media" literary perspective on narrative. Whereas the "work" was understood to be associated with traditional attributes of authorship and authority, the crucible of fixity for meaning, the "text," was rather *experienced only in an activity of production*" (Barthes 1977, 157). Lotman's (1982) similarly classic formulation of the text not only as embedding within itself a particular audience but also, in literary narratives, setting in motion a *game*, echoes Barthes's emphasis on the productivity of the audience. What Barthes concludes is that the text is bound to "*jouissance*"; the text "is that space where no language has a hold over any other, where languages circulate" (1977, 164). Put another way, the text is not restrained by the usual forces of time, place, situation, purpose, and specific addressee in the way that the work and standard dialogic utterances are (Lotman 1982, 81). Instead, it is the arena of pleasure, play, and production.

In addition to factoring the audience into textuality, it should be clear that texts, even while they are arenas of play, especially in the instance of narrative, are not discrete entities sealed from the world and from discourse. Furthermore, the fact that texts are bound to pleasure does not immunize them from the effects of fixity. In an approach to the text that has likewise become classic, Tony Bennett (1987) casts doubt on the idea of the "text itself," a core narrative that exists in pristine form at the center of any instance of textuality. He stresses the importance of a number of discursive practices that operate on readers before and simultaneously with what should be considered a "textual system" rather than an isolated text. These practices order the relations in a textual system in a definite way "such that [the text's] reading is always-already cued in specific directions that are not given by those 'texts themselves' as entities separable from such relations" (Bennett and Woollacott 1987, 64). Readers' knowledge of how texts are organized within a textual system can lead to the stabilization of readings through such factors as knowledge of authorship, knowledge of publicity in the textual system, knowledge of conditions of production and other above-the-line and below-the-line discourses which make up, in sum, a "reading formation" (cf. Cobley 2000, 15–54).

Following Bennett, then, it is clear that the reader's interaction in the textual system (as opposed to the "text itself") can be responsible for producing specific kinds of readings. Yet, while this has become a perfectly reasonable idea in communication, cultural, and media studies, as well as to a considerably lesser extent in narrative theory, Barthes's insistence on the text's pleasure deriving from the play within a textual system has been comparatively under-explored. It is probably for this reason that the narrative supplements that are part and parcel of the experience of narrative in the DVD medium have been treated with a degree of surprise and awe. They are so blatantly means of exercising pleasure, ludic propensities, production, and even creativity that they seem to constitute their own kind of textual system (in addition to being embedded in their own textual system of marketing, publicity, and word of mouth). Where previous considerations of narrative texts in different media may have sought to explicate pleasure in terms of the interaction of the "text itself" and the reader, DVD has made explicit the need to consider narrative pleasure as a matter of productivity within a textual system that includes numerous elements produced as part of cynical commercial imperatives. As Brereton notes (2007, 116), much add-on material on DVD appears to replicate electronic press kits or other public relations material issued by film and TV producers to encourage writing of reviews, although he also adds that DVD add-ons have become "much more expansive, even reflexive" to meet consumer demands (particularly fan demands—see Johnson 2005).

Pleasure, Affect, and Supplements

Clearly, the narrative supplements in the experience of DVD narrative need to be understood in relation to specific configurations of time in DVD use as well as in relation to the general affective motivation toward the use of a DVD's elements. The theoretical tools available from traditional narratology for understanding the former are simply inadequate. Genette's (1980) formulations regarding the operation of time in narrative—chiefly, analepsis and prolepsis—for example, are firmly rooted in the analysis of "original" narratives or the "text itself." Much the same could be said about other theoretical approaches to the status of time in the consumption of different narrative elements. Recent developments in cognitive science–orientated narrative analyses have addressed the issue of time and the reading process. In their concept of "resonances," Gerrig and Egidi (2003) attempt to identify and account for cues to "long-term" memory in narrative. In a not dissimilar fashion, Fauconnier and Turner (2002) explore the "double-scope" story, discovering and usefully conceptualizing in the process the phenomenon of "blending," in which large stories are habitually cut down to a conceptual human scale and where one or more stories can be "blended" for consumption simultaneously. The problem with Gerrig and Egidi's "resonances" concept is that it only considers the experience of connections in "story" and "discourse" or, to put it another way, in the text or "original narrative." In the case of Fauconnier and Turner, their idea of "blending" addresses the way in which the time of one or more narratives is collapsed into one; it does not consider how nonnarrative matters relate to, or become contained in, narrative. The relation between narrative and nonnarrative entities and between textual and extratextual entities is currently lacking at the very moment that the new media have made them imperative.

What is needed for the analysis of DVD narrative is a concept that begins to address the very affective dimension whose action induces seemingly disparate ingredients of a textual system to be invoked by readers and in such a way that time is not seen to be violated (for example, to the point where boredom induced by waiting may prevent the impulse to access "add-ons"). It would need to shed light both on the affective/pleasurable aspect of reading in a textual system as well as its productivity and creativity. A likely candidate for such a conception is Charles S. Peirce's notion of "abduction." Peirce's "abduction" is part of his logic (see, e.g., Peirce 1998) which augments classic models of logical inference, deduction, and induction. Whereas deduction is a mode of inference that deals with what, logically, *must be*, and induction is an inference of what is *likely*, abduction is a hypothesis—it is what is possible according to the knowledge available. As such, it is akin to "guessing" (Peirce 1929). It is a relational cognition, but unlike the other forms of inference that rely on available elements, abduction draws on the quality of immediate consciousness that can never be immediate to consciousness (Sheriff 1989, 89).

The status of abduction becomes clearer if we consider the broad forms of knowledge it comprises. To some extent, inference in deduction and induction relies on prior, stored knowledge (*logica docens*) as well as knowledge in use with immediate materials (*logica utens*) (see Sebeok and Umiker-Sebeok 1980). However, it predominantly relies on the latter rather than the former. Abduction, on the other hand, relies heavily on the former: stored knowledge, expertise, experience—knowledge that is buried deep in consciousness but which is usually called up through an affective connection and therefore bears the character of a "guess." Human awareness of the implications of nonverbal communication, arguably more acute during infancy, may be reawakened in the process of an abduction to make an inference (guess) that is quite accurate without the subject knowing what determined the inference. Where abduction differs in the most marked fashion from deduction and inference, then, is that it does not arise simply as logical procedure based on available predicates but is triggered by some component of feeling—broadly, pain or pleasure, mental phenomena that are "the least understood in biological or specifically neurological terms" (Damasio 2003, 3). Although it is difficult to identify what determines feelings, Damasio (2003) demonstrates that they are closely associated with emotions, with feelings being played out in the mind, and emotions, such as sadness, often being played out in the body. Emotions, then, for Damasio, are externalities that have had an evolutionary role in provoking (internal) feelings (2003, 27–30). The relation of external phenomena promoting internal phenomena fits abduction well and, in turn, this concept would seem useful for approaching the creativity and productivity involved in the use and negotiation of narrative supplements on DVD.

Let us take first the example of the "audio commentary" as an add-on to the "original" narrative on a DVD and observe some of the affective components of its constitution. Barlow notes that commentaries can have considerable potential. However, even in the best commentaries, much is left unfulfilled until the reader's productivity is brought to bear. He suggests that "the DVD audio commentary has become the sign of class in a DVD presentation" (Barlow 2005, 110), an affective rather than a traditionally and strictly rational aspect of what the DVD narrative supposedly has to offer. Yet Barlow does not leave the matter there. Note the prevarication in the following quotation, but also the adjective in the first sentence and the general attempt to avoid the lure of "reading too much" into the "original" narrative:

> At the oilier end of the spectrum is the academic analysis of each scene. Though these can show care and real attention to detail, they can also contradict the very spirit of the movie, sometimes even making it seem more of a deliberate crafting than might be the case. In the audio commentary for *The Day the Earth Stood Still* (Robert Wise, 1951), Nicolas Meyer gently quizzes Wise about Biblical parallels to the events in the movie. Though he is clearly not satisfied that Wise's memory that he had not thought at all about such parallels during the shooting is accurate, Meyer notes, "This really bears out my theory that oftentimes artists have very little idea, or very imperfect or very incomplete notions of what it is they've done." Many academic audio commentaries assume the contrary—that is, the filmmakers knew exactly what they were doing. (2005, 111)

Although the quotation features Barlow's resistance to interpretation of narratives rather than defined reference to add-ons, it is telling because not only is Barlow a commentator who touts the DVD's creative possibilities, but the wavering between disdain for reading too much into one film in "add-ons" and disregard for superficiality is palpable. Effectively, in the quotation about Meyer and Wise there is a playing out of abduction: Wise, according to Meyer, has, buried deep, some motivation for the connections he makes in his narrative, but they are not on the logical surface. Barlow muses in an adversarial way that there may have been a plan in the production but it is not clear where it came from. In each instance, the commentary and Barlow's observations are caught up in the play of the textual system: it is no clearer what the "original" narrative is "really about" after hearing the commentary and after seeing Barlow's comments. This exemplifies a problem with tracking the mechanics of abduction: the process seems superficial, but the train of thought and affect that produces it can be complex and convoluted, a fact illustrated in Sherlock Holmes's elucidation of his thought processes and his ambiguous declaration that he never guesses (see Sebeok and Umiker-Sebeok 1980).

DVD Narrative and Depth Analysis

Unraveling abduction necessitates "depth analysis," a general procedure that has a considerable heritage in the theory of narrative. Depth analyses, however, pose particular problems for the understanding of the status of narrative on DVD. On the one hand, DVD "add-ons" are supposed to offer many more opportunities for interaction and interpretation of narrative, as in the instance of fan reading. On the other, as an entertainment medium, the immediacy of choices in DVD viewing seems to some to eschew academic readings as unreasonable. Scholarly interpretations, such as so-called screen theory and its derivatives, often posit that the mainstream filmic narrative tries to conceal social and psychic contradictions (such as those in capitalism, patriarchy, the American dream, or heteronormativity). Certainly, the manufacturers of mainstream DVDs have shown little interest in airing such readings as extras on their products. Nevertheless, there has been some persistence of "screen theory" in relation to the discussion of the DVD as a narrative technology.

Mulvey (2006) suggests that the capacity of video and DVDs to provide slow motion, repetition, and, especially, freeze frame, offers the possibility of new engagements with even the most conservative mainstream narrative. Her contention is that the DVD specifically has the capacity to break up narrative, amounting to a potential to demystify. She asserts that "the process of delaying a film inevitably highlights its aesthetics and the illusion of movement" (2006, 185), asserting that "a moment of stillness within the moving image and its narrative creates a pensive spectator" (186). Mulvey does not say that devices such as the freeze-frame facility on a DVD player *might* give rise to a more thoughtful and politically progressive relationship with the feature film but simply that they *do*, that such technologies allow "the aesthetic of the film" to become feminized (2006, 165). Later, however, she quotes Annette Michelson, who writes of "the heady delights of the editing table," that is, the "making" of narrative by the audience, as "the thrill of power . . . grounded in that deep gratification of a fantasy of infantile omnipotence" (Mulvey 2006, 193). Of course, this view of new media's appeal that explains its strong lure to males with infantile control fantasies apparently contradicts Mulvey's earlier suggestion that disruptions to the filmic narrative such as freeze frame feminize the viewing experience.

What these conflicting takes on DVD narrative seem to suggest is a need for a mode of expression for affective relationships with narrative (and nonnarrative) that is scholarly but not reductive. To a great extent, this will require coming to terms with the fact that narrative is not reducible to psychoanalytic motifs but is an extension, in McLuhan's sense, or a technology, as well as a specifically human entity, and that both are embedded in a web of social relations, thus making neither susceptible to reduction. Bruce Clarke (2008, 19) has recently indicated the "coemergence of technological systems and the roles they have always played as mediating structures connecting psychic and social systems" adding, "Writing and narrative belong here, along with cell phones and airplanes." As a technology, narrative inhabits the DVD in the way that it has inhabited other media and, as such, facilitates connections with signs "outside" itself, with nonnarrative and with narrative signs.

With regard to "add-ons," the issue amounts to what can be discerned regarding the reader's operation within the textual system. In short, it would appear that links between elements in a DVD have major qualitative bearings rather than strictly linear narrative virtues of plot, narration and story. Rather than logical relations in the "original" narrative, DVD supplements encourage the use of affective connections and creative linking to make inferences. That is, DVD technology enables viewers to act upon their feelings immediately, before they dissipate with the flow of the narrative. It allows readers to attempt spontaneously to find out (where add-ons promise an answer) what motivated a feature of the narrative being viewed, dwelling or skipping according to affective (rather than strictly linear) preferences and re-experiencing qualia in parts or the whole of a narrative. Yet, emphasis on the affective qualities of the "textual system" facilitated by the technology should not be where the analysis of abduction ends. Revisiting the crucial connections in the television narrative of *Spooks*, adumbrated above, it is clear that the DVD, as well as the original television series, is caught up in a larger textual system of narratives and nonnarratives.

Spooks was embedded in a specific reading formation when its first series was shown on British television in May 2002 and when the DVD was released in September of the same year. It was launched with a wave of publicity, including a well-circulated press release, a press pack filled with references to the hidden nature of MI5's operations, and quotes designed to demonstrate the verisimilitude of *Spooks*'s scenarios (in terms of the world of espionage in general and in terms of the immediate post–September 11 West in particular); an official BBC website with semiserious competitions and other spin-offs; and a massive billboard campaign in London and the British regions, featuring the series' main slogan "MI5 not 9 to 5." On the back of this publicity, the first episode gained a 41 percent audience share, an exceptional figure for a new show.

Yet, arguably, the part of the reading formation for *Spooks* that really matters is the phenomenon of anxiety abroad in the social formation of the time, an affective disposition that is palpable in the media coverage of the series (see Cobley 2009). An awareness of the myriad social discourses surrounding or suffusing a narrative would seem to be the most obvious way of avoiding reductionism in evaluating narrative. Stated differently, this is an awareness of the relationship of specific narratives to history and other sign systems outside itself or the textual system of which it is a part. Where DVD narrative is concerned, the technology involved in entertainment DVDs is (merely?) an extension of the way that narrative in general invokes the process of abduction. That is to say, the DVD is a technology-enhanced extension of the way in which narrative connections are abductively made: the forging of a "rational" narrative through "affective" dispositions that bring together narrative and nonnarrative entities and textual and extratextual entities for narrative's users. The iconography of espionage and surveillance, so evident in the *Spooks* narrative as a whole, spreads out across the DVD package, as witnessed in the DVD intro presented above. The DVD clearly renders a dominant affective connection between anxiety and the desire to know that serves to link a range of elements in its textual system. That is to say, not only may the reading formation be characterized as a climate of anxiety, but the DVD's narrative can potentially open out onto that climate almost seamlessly. As a result, it is increasingly difficult to conceive DVDs as constituted by mere add-ons or supplements.

Conclusion

The DVD revolution as it concerns narrative is largely predicated on the supplements to the "original" narrative that entertainment DVDs offer. Yet, as we have seen, DVD technology is actually an extension of some features of the technology of narrative itself. The supplements to narrative that DVDs offer have, for some, signaled the end for linearity in narrative. While this conclusion is found to be somewhat hyperbolic, "add-ons" do force a reconsideration of the ways in which a narrative is constituted, what readers might bring to narratives and the way that they inferentially link up narrative elements. The DVD as a medium, in short, brings into question the myth of the "text itself." What DVD technology seems to offer is the possibility of renewing understanding of narrative processes, particularly in respect of the emotional coordinates by which narrative is negotiated, allowing "nonlinear" and "nonnarrative" features to be inculcated into narrative, a seemingly linear form.

Notes

1. It would be easy to forget that VHS video had begun to offer "add-ons" at the peak of its sales: the winter 1990 release of *Total Recall*, for example, offered the film in a "special edition" double VHS tape in which the second videocassette contained all the kinds of typical supplementary narratives—"making of" documentaries and so forth—which characterize contemporary DVDs.

References

Barlow, Aaron. 2005. *The DVD Revolution: Movies, Culture, and Technology*. Westport CT: Greenwood Press.

Barthes, Roland. 1977. "From Work to Text." In *Image—Music—Text*, trans. Stephen Heath. London: Fontana.

Bennett, Tony. 1987. "Texts, Readers, Reading Formations." In *Post-structuralism and the Question of History*, ed. Derek Attridge, Geoff Bennington, and Robert Young, 63–81. Cambridge: Cambridge University Press.

Bennett, Tony, and Janet Woollacott. 1987. *Bond and Beyond: The Political Career of a Popular Hero*. London: Macmillan.

Bolter, Jay David. 2002. "Formal Analysis and Cultural Critique in Digital Media Culture." *Convergence* 8, no. 4:77–88.

Brereton, Pat. 2007. "The Consumption and Use of DVDs and Their Add-Ons." *Convergence* 13, no. 2:115–17.

Clarke, Bruce. 2008. *Posthuman Metamorphosis: Narrative and Systems*. New York: Fordham University Press.

Cobley, Paul. 2000. *The American Thriller: Generic Innovation and Social Change in the 1970s*. London: Palgrave.

———. 2001. *Narrative*. London: Routledge.

———. 2009. "'It's a Fine Line between Safety and Terror': Crime and Society Redrawn in Spooks." *Film International* 7, no. 2:36–45.

Cover, Rob. 2005. "DVD Time: Temporality, Audience Engagement and the New TV Culture of Digital Video." *Media International Australia Incorporating Culture and Policy* 117:137–47.

Cubitt, Sean. 2002. "Spreadsheets, Site Maps and Search Engines: Why Narrative Is Marginal to Multimedia and Networked Communication, and Why Marginality Is More Vital Than Universality." In *New Screen Media: Cinema/Art/Narrative*, ed. Martin Rieser and Andrea Zapp, 3–13. London: BFI.

Damasio, Antonio. 2003. *Looking for Spinoza: Joy, Sorrow, and the Feeling Brain*. New York: Harcourt.

Fauconnier, Gilles, and Mark Turner. 2002. *The Way We Think*. New York: Basic Books.

Genette, Gérard. 1980. *Narrative Discourse: An Essay in Method*. Trans. Jane Lewin. Ithaca NY: Cornell University Press.

Gerrig, Richard J., and Giovanna Egidi. 2003. "Cognitive Psychological Foundations of Narrative Experiences." In *Narrative Theory and the Cognitive Sciences*, ed. David Herman, 33–55. Stanford CA: CSLI.

Hight, Craig. 2005. "Making-of Documentaries on DVD: The *Lord of the Rings* Trilogy and Special Editions." *Velvet Light Trap* 56:4–17.

Johnson, Derek. 2005. "*Star Wars Fans*, DVD, and Cultural Ownership: An Interview with Will Brooker." *Velvet Light Trap* 56:36–44.

Lane, Chris. 2006. "Close Reading the DVD—From the Male Gaze to Peer to Peer File Sharing: An Examination of Gender, Consumption, and Power in Film and New Media." *International Journal of Technology, Knowledge and Society* 2, no. 7:149–66.

Lotman, Yuri M. 1982. "The Text and the Structure of Its Audience." *New Literary History* 14, no. 1:81–87.

Mulvey, Laura. 2006. *Death 24x a Second: Stillness and the Moving Image*. London: Reaktion Books.

Peirce, Charles S. 1929. "Guessing." *Hound and Horn* 2, no. 3:267–82.

——. 1998. "Deduction, Induction, and Hypothesis." In *Chance, Love, and Logic: Philosophical Essays*, ed. Morris Cohen, 131–55. Lincoln: University of Nebraska Press.

Sebeok, Thomas A., and Jean Umiker-Sebeok. 1980. *"You Know My Method": A Juxtaposition of Charles S. Peirce and Sherlock Holmes*. Bloomington, IN: Gaslight Publications.

Sheriff, John K. 1989. *The Fate of Meaning: Charles Peirce, Structuralism and Literature*. Princeton NJ: Princeton University Press.

PART 3 : *New Practices*

10 : All Together Now
Hypertext, Collective Narratives, and
Online Collective Knowledge Communities

SCOTT RETTBERG

Collaboration and Literary Culture

Printed books are almost always products of collaboration, not necessarily in the sense of multiple authors writing together but in the less-considered sense of multiple people working together to produce an edited, designed, bound, printed, and distributed artifact. Yet literary culture operates in a manner that makes the contributions of those involved in the production and distribution of books, other than the author, less visible. Asked to name their favorite authors, almost any reader could rattle off a list of writers. Ask the same readers who their favorite book designer, typesetter, or editor is, and you're likely to draw a blank stare. As Rob Wittig suggests in *Invisible Rendezvous* (1994), there are historical reasons for the rise of the author, which can be boiled down to accountability, marketing, information management, combating piracy, and the "genius model" that explains quality writing as the product of extraordinary minds. The myth of the solitary author, toiling in isolation on the great work, is largely a convenience to simplify the complex collaboration involved in making and distributing books; the idea of authorship is driven more fundamentally by legal and market concerns than by artistic ones.

In the domain of electronic literature, the collaborative effort involved in creating, publishing, and distributing works is more clearly evident because, aside from hypertext publisher Eastgate Systems and a few other small operations, there is effectively no electronic literature publishing industry. The roles of contributors such as designers, artists, and editors are typically more clearly acknowledged, because without assistance, authors are compelled to do everything by themselves. There are few traditional publishers of electronic literature, so there is no apparatus in place to keep the labor of producing and distributing the work invisible.

If literary culture has centered on the cult of authorship, collectively written works of literature are not unknown. Both the Judeo-Christian Bible and the works of Homer, for example, could be considered as collective texts. The writing of the Old and New Testaments took place over about two thousand years and involved at least forty different writers, some of whom were adapting elements of an oral tradition. The processes of editing, canonizing, and translating the Bible are also collective endeavors, which will likely continue to be practiced by different sects for the foreseeable future. And while we assign the "authorship" of the *Iliad* and the *Odyssey* to one figure, "Homer," almost nothing is definitely known about Homer as a historical figure. Someone living between the twelfth and eighth centuries BC gathered, synthesized, and wrote down pieces of an oral tradition of poetry originally passed from generation to generation. While the individual or group who aggregated, edited, and inscribed the *Odyssey* was instrumental in the fact that we are now able to translate, read and enjoy the epic today, Homer is best understood not as an author of the solitary genius model but as a function in a social system of collective authorship.

Hypertext and Collective Knowledge

The idea of hypertext itself is based on harnessing collective knowledge. Even the Memex, the stand-alone device imagined by Vannevar Bush in his 1946 essay "As We May Think," was based on the idea of making collective knowledge available to individuals in new associative ways. The operator of the Memex would record the trails of associations he constructed over the course of his research. These trails would then become the foundation of further research by others.

Ted Nelson, who coined the term *hypertext*, conceptualized Xanadu, his vision of an ideal hypertext system. Nelson describes a hypertext system based on the idea that each field has a "literature," a "*system of interconnected writings*," persistent but open to constant expansion: "In our Western cultural tradition, writings in principle remain continuously available—both as recently quoted, and in their inviolable incarnations—in a great precession" (Nelson 2003, 446).

Nelson asserts that individual researchers always have their own thought trail of associative links through a given body of material. He notes that a field's collective view of its own past is furthermore subject to constant reinterpretation. Nelson bases the file system of Xanadu on the idea that an ideal literature would remain continuously accessible and that any given item could be linked to any other item in the database according to any criteria.

Nelson considers the absent link, the lacuna, to be as important as those already forged: "Within bodies of writing, everywhere, there are linkages we tend not to see. The individual document, at hand, is what we deal with; we do not see the total linked collection of them all at once. But they are there, the documents not present as well as those that are, and the grand cat's cradle among them all" (Nelson 2003, 446). Nelson emphasized the importance of the ability to introduce new material, and of new methods of organizing material that could coexist simultaneously with extant systems. Xanadu would not only preserve existing connections between bodies of writing, it would also allow for new ways of connecting the material according to the values of future readers.

Constructive Hypertext

In considering not merely organized aggregations of collective knowledge but, in particular, collective narratives, it is useful to note the distinction that hypertext author Michael Joyce made between "exploratory" and "constructive" hypertexts. He says, "Scriptors use constructive hypertexts to develop a body of information which they map according to their needs, their interests, and the transformations they discover as they invent, gather, and act upon that information. Moreso than with exploratory hypertexts, constructive hypertexts require a capability to act: to create, to change, and to recover particular encounters within the developing body of knowledge" (Joyce 2003, 616). What Joyce terms "exploratory" hypertexts are more in line with the idea of finished "works" we are familiar with from book culture. Exploratory hypertexts are stable editions. The work itself is understood as a separate entity from the reader's interaction with it. Thus, in the hypertext system Joyce discusses, the reader may explore, mark, and make annotations to an exploratory hypertext, but in doing so the reader is not modifying the work itself. In a constructive hypertext, neither the structure of the work nor its contents are yet fixed. All exploratory hypertexts were first constructive hypertexts. The pleasure of a constructive hypertext is not received narrative but the process of constructing a narrative topology. Constructive hypertexts can be individually written, in which case the author/reader is interacting with her own creation, or written collectively, in which case a community of reader/writers are actively interacting with, forging connections, expanding upon, and reacting to the work of others. A constructive hypertext can then be as productively understood as a participatory writing performance, an "event" as well as a "work." Both constructive and exploratory forms of hypertext literature have been written and published, though there are considerably more notable examples of exploratory hypertext literature published in both Storyspace and web formats than there are of constructive literary hypertext, perhaps because exploratory hypertexts are much more easily understood as fixed artifacts—works—than those of the vagarious constructive type.

Types of Constructive Collaborations

Most classic Storyspace hypertexts, including Joyce's *afternoon, a story* (1990) and Shelley Jackson's *Patchwork Girl* (1995), are purely exploratory. Deena Larsen's *Marble Springs* (1993), the story of the people of a Colorado mining town, enabled readers to contribute to the story by adding scenes and character biographies to the work's HyperCard stacks. While published as an exploratory work, Cathy Marshall and Judy Malloy's *Forward Anywhere* (1995) wore its constructiveness on its sleeve more explicitly than other early hypertexts, by virtue of the self-consciously collaborative process through which it was written.

The World Wide Web is not simply a global library of individual texts but offers the potential for new types of collective authorship. Early experiments in collective narrative on the web included "chain stories," in which participant readers would build on the contributions of previous authors in order to further develop a sequential narrative. Even concepts as rudimentary as *The World's First Collaborative Sentence* (Davis et al., 1994), to which readers were encouraged to contribute a phrase, flirted with the promise of literature authored by no single person but by the collective effort of many people. Roberto Simanowski (2001) has described "Beim Bäcker," a German chain story initiated by Carola Heine in 1996. Heine began the story with the introduction of a woman buying lollipops for three girls short on change in a bakery. A male contributor then responded to the first section. He wrote from a different perspective and changed the character in a way that the first author did not appreciate. The initial author then responded in the next section, attempting to correct the second author's contribution while integrating it into her portrayal. Other authors who introduced further characters with their own trajectories then continued the experiment. Simanowski describes this type of collaborative writing in terms of confrontation—as one author after another subverted the work of those who wrote before them. The principal limitation of a linear collaborative narrative of this sort is that it relies on an intimate and successful relationship between any given chapter and those that precede it.

Putting voice and style aside, the success of the story depends on continuity and causality, and on implicit contracts between the various contributing writers to respect the ontology presented in the early chapters in producing the later chapters. Simanowski reports that this lack of agreement caused problems for the project: "In the end, we realize that a new author hardly takes into account the legacy left by his predecessors" (Simanowski 2001). Without any explicit agreements between authors or editorial oversight, chain stories often succumb to incoherence.

Robert Coover's early electronic writing workshops at Brown University experimented with a collective constructive hypertext, the *Hypertext Hotel* (Coover et al., 1996). Loosely based on George Perec's *Life, a User's Manual* (1978), the hotel offered a spatial metaphor for a collaborative writing event: "In addition to the individual fictions, which are more or less protected from tampering in the old proprietary way, we in the workshop have also played freely and often quite anarchically in a group fiction space called 'Hotel.' Here, writers are free to check in, to open up new rooms, new corridors, new intrigues, to unlink texts or create new links, to intrude upon or subvert the texts of others, to alter plot trajectories, manipulate time and space, to engage in dialogue through invented characters, then kill off one another's characters or even to sabotage the hotel's plumbing" (Coover 2003, 708). As Coover described it, the *Hypertext Hotel* was never a fixed edition, not a work, but a writing process of subversion and play. Although some fragments of the *Hypertext Hotel* can still be found online, if one were to assess the hotel as a finished work, one would find it in disrepair. The *Hypertext Hotel* was always a writing event, anarchic in nature, never intended to conclude.

The relatively early hypertext experiment (1993–96) of the *Hypertext Hotel* was similar in structure to the type of collective storytelling employed in MOOs and MUDs, in that its primary organizing principle was the description of imaginary spaces. In these virtual environments, setting exists on a different diegetic level from plot and character. While rooms and objects can possess both descriptions and behaviors, MUDs exist only as potential narrative until fulfilled by participant readers. The players become architects of their own rooms, contributing to a collective textual geography. While a great deal goes into the writing of descriptions of rooms, objects, and personal descriptions in MOOs and MUDs, at least one and preferably several player-characters are necessary in order for the potential narrative to be realized. The unfolding interactions between the characters are typically what would be retold as "stories" from the MOO. There are examples of MOOs built with "story-disclosing objects" (Malloy 1999) and even time-based dramas that unfold as the reader enters a particular room, but the majority of the collaborative storytelling involved is either descriptive or takes place in the course of an active interaction with another character. Like a work of interactive fiction, a MOO is only a potential story until readers respond to and perform within the text. Unlike most interactive fiction, MOOs are typically cosmopolitan in the sense that the architecture of the virtual space is written collectively, and the dialogue is primarily dependent on multiple human intelligences interacting simultaneously in the same textual space.

Writing Process of *The Unknown*

Like the *Hypertext Hotel* or a MOO, the collaborative hypertext novel *The Unknown* (Gillespie et al. 1998) was, for a period of about four years (1998–2002), a constructive hypertext undergoing expansion and revision. New episodes were added to the work, links were added and removed, and the general structure of the hypertext changed. William Gillespie, Dirk Stratton, and I are the primary authors of *The Unknown*, although other writers and artists played some hand in its construction. *The Unknown* was not a completely open collective narrative but the product of ongoing and shifting relationships between authors who knew each other well.

We began with a general scenario (we would write a satirical hypertext about a book tour), but beyond that there was little conscious agreement about how the plot(s) might proceed, how the characters might develop, the general themes of the work, or how the work was to be structured. There was nonetheless a certain general social contract in effect: if we agreed to nothing else, we agreed to read the scenes that the others had written, to link to and from them when appropriate, and to allow those previously written scenes to provide a context for the scenes that we would subsequently write.

Because it was an extensively multilinear hypertext novel with many associative links through different scenes, we realized early in the writing process that the novel couldn't be dependent on any type of traditional narrative arc or sense of closure. The majority of our readers would read only fragments of the hypertext, which would have to function individually. We began talking about *The Unknown* as a picaresque, scattered across a vast territory of time and space. This allowed us some degree of flexibility in terms of the ontological continuity of the story. Certain tropes, character tics, and obsessions recur across scenes and serve as connective tissue, but the characters of *The Unknown* cannot be said to "develop" in the traditional sense. There are plenty of character developments in many different scenes, but they follow no overall arc toward epiphany or catharsis.

As we were writing *The Unknown*, we experimented with a wide variety of collaborative writing processes, ranging from in-person get-togethers where we would literally take turns at the keyboard, to collective expeditions, when we would haul a laptop to a location and write a scene set there. Occasionally we would invite others—friends and traveling companions—to sit in for a session or two. In addition to this form of "live" collaboration, we also wrote scenes and some linear sequences individually.

To the extent that *The Unknown* succeeded as an experiment in writing a collaborative hypertext novel, its success was dependent on the fellowship of its authors. While we had very few explicit agreements, along the way we had many conversations about the general direction of the project and the structure of the resulting "work." While *The Unknown* was certainly a writing event, a kind of performance, it was also always intended to result in an end product. *The Unknown* is an example of a type of collaboration directed by play, negotiation, confrontation, and compromise. Its authors understood each other both as people and as writers. Without these preexisting relationships and ongoing negotiations about the shape of the story, the project would not have come to pass.

Scott Rettberg   193

The Use of Constraints

Successful collaboration is always built upon constraints, whether the creators of the collective work explicitly agree upon the constraints or they are simply built into the system used to create the work. Unlike individually authored works, collaborations are both the work itself and the series of negotiations between collaborators that govern the work's creation.

Harry Mathews addresses the question of why one would want to write under constraints in his *ebr* essay, "Translation and the Oulipo: The Case of the Persevering Maltese." He says, "The Oulipo supplies writers with hard games to play. . . . [T]he games have demanding rules that we must never forget (well, hardly ever), and these rules are moreover active ones: satisfying them keeps us too busy to worry about being reasonable. Of course our object of desire, like the flag to be captured, remains present to us. Thanks to the impossible rules, we find ourselves doing and saying things we would never have imagined otherwise, things that often turn out to be exactly what we need to reach our goal" (Mathews 1996). The forms of constrained literature range from the very complex, for example the constraint to "write a 2002 word story that is also a letter palindrome," followed by Nick Montfort and William Gillespie in producing their *2002* (2002), or "write a novel without using the letter E," followed by Georges Perec in his *A Void* (1995), to the more mundane, such as "write only interior descriptions," or "write episodes no longer than 500 words in length." Even Mad Libs, those juvenile writing games wherein the reader fills in random adjectives, proper nouns, names of places, types of animal, and so forth to construct a zany story, are a rudimentary form of constrained literature. A constraint is simply a rule that a participating writer agrees to follow in the process of producing writing. The constraint itself need not be evident to the reader; indeed, it is typically not revealed. The overall narrative structure into which a piece of constrained writing might fit also needn't be evident to the contributing writer.

Regardless of how one feels about the application of structuralist theory to works of literature generally, structuralist ways of thinking can be useful in the context of developing a collective storytelling system, or for that matter a storytelling "engine" of any kind. In designing the interactive drama *Façade*, for instance, Michael Mateas and Andrew Stern designed the engine to track an Aristotelian dramatic arc, based on a system of "beats" described in Robert McKee's guide, *Story: Substance, Structure, Style, and the Principles of Screenwriting* (Mateas and Stern 2002). If truly collective web narratives, open to contributions from anyone on the network, are to be successful as stories, they either need to be edited and structured by some subset of the contributors, or need to be structured by the system used to create the work. The larger the scale of the collaboration, the more important it is that contributors' roles in the writing of the project are clearly defined, as are the constraints under which individual contributions should be written.

Writing Process on a Large-Scale Collective Narrative: *Invisible Seattle*

One of the most successful experiments in collective narrative took place well before the widespread adoption of the Internet. Invisible Seattle was a writing group, first formed in 1979, that gathered regularly in the basement of Eliot Bay bookstore to present its members with a variety of collaborative, psychogeographic, and Oulipan (constraint-driven) writing games. The group's first project was the *Map of Invisible Seattle*, a project loosely based on Italo Calvino's *Invisible Cities* (1974). The project's intention was to recreate the city of Seattle, substituting draconian modernist structures with "architectural visitors" and imaginary spaces, such as replacing the Space Needle with the Eiffel Tower, and the Kingdome with the Coliseum of Rome.

During the summer of 1983, the invisibles launched a multifaceted data-gathering project throughout the city of Seattle, the goal of which was to produce a novel authored by the city itself. The methodologies employed in the construction of *Invisible Seattle* are useful to consider as we contemplate contemporary network-based collective narratives. Different strategies were deployed to collect writing for the collaborative novel, including "roving safaris" conducted by "literary workers" who would roam the city with questionnaires asking questions of passers-by. Other ways the group gathered material included Mad Libs–style fill-in-the-blanks; clip-out-and-return coupons encouraging readers to contribute photos along with descriptions of settings and major plot developments; data such as overheard conversations and descriptions of quotidian life gathered via a call-in radio show; and finally by having anonymous participants type segments of narrative into a fantastical word processor, "Sheherazade II—

the first of a new generation of literary computers," at the Bumbershoot arts festival. The novel experiment of *Invisible Seattle* involved thirty active 'literary workers' who spent a summer combing Seattle "in search of novelistic fodder" (Wittig 1994, 37).

The writing process of *Invisible Seattle* was idiosyncratic. Some of the writing methodologies were highly structured, such as a set of seventeen instructions intended to elicit a thorough description of exterior and interior settings, while others elicited anonymous one-line suggestions for major plot turns in the novel, such as "What happened to Proteus?" (the main character of the novel) and "What was Proteus' mission in Seattle?" The architects of *Invisible Seattle* were inviting both macro- and micro-level input. Even before the project involved a computer of any kind, the invisibles had "begun calling text 'data' and spoke of gathering contributions in 'data files'" (Wittig 1994, 69). In the process of assembling a collective narrative, the invisibles thought of themselves less as authors than as functions of a cybernetic text machine.

After this summer of engaging Seattle writ large in a variety of constrained writing assignments, the invisibles found their larders stocked with more storytelling material than one novel could reasonably contain. A group of invisibles culled and remixed several different selections of the material into versions of a novel. The most widely distributed version, *Invisible Seattle: The Novel of Seattle by Seattle* (version 7.1 published by Function Industries Press) was, according to Wittig, "a flagrant, multigenre collision involving the nouveau roman, a Dos Passos/Joycean catalog of particulars, the pulp detective/thriller genre, careful historiography, and a full load of what one kind commentator termed '*je ne sais* the fuck *quoi*'" (Wittig 1994, 76). The nature of the material that ended up in the novel was to some extent determined by the constraints that governed the nature of the data gathered. A writing process guided by different constraints would have generated different types of material from the same group of writers.

A collective narrative project such as *Invisible Seattle* cannot be described solely on the basis of the published work or works that proceed from it. *Invisible Seattle* was both the published versions of the novel and all of the other versions that could have been derived from the same larger pool of story material the invisibles gathered. It was also all of the events and interventions through which the texts were gathered. Any type of collective narrative must be understood not only in terms of a resulting "work," but also as a performance.

The editorial process of constructing the versions of the novel of Seattle is not described in great detail in *Invisible Rendezvous* (Wittig 1994), though it appears that the procedures that guided this task were improvised, and not aspects of a preconceived system. In retrospect, we can certainly imagine enhancements to the *Invisible Seattle* project. Twenty years after the writing event, readers can consult only accounts of the project and the various printed editions of the novel. If all of the text involved in the project had been archived electronically, one could conceive of the project as a Nelsonian hypertext, which would include both the end product—the finished versions of the novel—and all of the texts that preceded the final versions. The collectivity of the endeavor could also extend to the editorial process. Given access to all of the source texts, and a system to rearrange the fragments, every reader could conceivably remix their own version of the collective narrative.

Conscious, Contributory, and Unwitting Participation

If we view networked literature not only as literary "works" in the traditional book culture sense but also as literary systems functioning within other systems, then we need to reconsider the connection between authorship and agency. Collective narratives are collective to varying degrees, dependent upon the distribution of agency both to distributed authors and to aspects of the system itself. Collective literary and artistic production in new media ranges from works in which principal authors are equally conscious participants in all aspects of the work's production, to those in which the contributors are not at all conscious that their activity is resulting in artistic production. We can distinguish three types of participation a contributor might have in a collective narrative project: conscious, contributory, and unwitting.

> Conscious participation: Contributors are fully conscious of explicit constraints, of the nature of the project, and of how their contribution to it might be utilized.

Contributory participation: Contributors may not be aware of how their contribution fits into the overall architecture of the project, or even of the nature of the project itself, but they do take conscious steps to make their contribution available to the project.

Unwitting participation: Texts utilized in the collective narrative are gathered by the text machine itself, and contributors have no conscious involvement in the process of gathering the material.

These three levels of participation are not mutually exclusive, in the sense that one collective narrative project could utilize contributions on all three levels. For instance, in the case of *The Unknown*, the three principal authors were fully conscious participants in all aspects of the project. Certain coauthors were asked to contribute in a limited way, such as contributing to a group writing in a New York bar. While Joseph Tabbi and Nick Montfort were aware that *The Unknown* existed and that we were "writing an Unknown scene," they had no conception of how their contributions might be linked into the hypertext as a whole—they were contributory participants. Finally, certain scenes in *The Unknown* were over-writings of other texts, such as a typing test used to gauge the typing speed of temporary employees of a Chicago law office, or a scene from Thomas Kinsella's translation of *The Tain* (1969). While the resulting texts were without a doubt collaborative, neither the author of the typing test nor Thomas Kinsella was consulted; they were unwitting participants.

The data-gathering safaris described in the production of *Invisible Seattle* provide a good example of contributory participation. Simply by filling out a questionnaire, members of the public were contributing to a collective novel, whether or not they understood how the constraints of the particular set of questions they were answering fit into the evolution of the project as a whole.

Projects based on aleatory elements typically make use of unwitting participants. *The Impermanence Agent* by Noah Wardrip-Fruin et al. (2000), for instance, began with a story of loss by Wardrip-Fruin that was then "customized" by material gathered from the browsing patterns of each participating reader. Wardrip-Fruin and his coauthors were conscious participants by virtue of designing the system and writing the original story, while the users of the agent were contributory participants as their process of browsing the web selected the material the agent would then integrate into the story, and the authors of the websites that the agent sampled were unwitting participants, having no knowledge that their work was being repurposed in this way.

Architectures of Participation

Collectively written constructive hypertext has become everyday practice on the web. Wikipedia is one prominent example of a constructive hypertext built on open source software and user-contributed content, which every reader has the capability to modify. Tim O'Reilly has described systems like Wikipedia as "architectures of participation," systems in which "a grassroots user base creates a self-regulating collaborative network" (O'Reilly 2004). The example of Wikipedia may offer some insight into the potential ramifications of the next generation of web applications and sharing methodologies on the development of narratives produced by collective activity.

In only four years, Wikipedia expanded from one entry to 1.5 million articles in ninety-two active language editions ("Wikipedia" 2005). Wikipedia forked from two antecedent projects, Nupedia, which lasted from 2000 until 2003, and GNUpedia, which was conceived by Richard Stallman in 1999 and launched in January 2001 but which fizzled shortly thereafter. The difference between Wikipedia and its immediate predecessor Nupedia offers one compelling secret to Wikipedia's phenomenal success: "Nupedia was characterized by an extensive peer review process designed to make its articles of a quality comparable to professional encyclopedias. Nupedia wanted scholars to volunteer content for free. Before it ceased operating, Nupedia produced 24 articles that completed its review process" ("Nupedia" 2005). While Nupedia shared the same idealistic central mission as Wikipedia, to build the best possible free encyclopedia on the Internet, it failed to trust the collective intelligence of the network. The developers of Nupedia wanted all of the articles on the site to go through a rigorous peer review process. A PhD, volunteering his or her time and expertise, would ideally have vetted each article. One reason that Stallman and others launched the GNUpedia project was that they thought Nupedia's methodology contrary to open-source ideology. Open source methodologies posit everything as a draft, a work in progress, open to revision. A centralized authority does not approve projects before they are launched, but rather decentralized authority improves them constantly. When Larry Sanger proposed that Wikipedia be launched as a wiki-based mechanism to begin articles that would later undergo the peer-review process, they almost immediately found an active and engaged community willing to contribute and more than willing to critique and review, and furthermore actively revise articles that they find inaccurate or incomplete.

Wikis have anarchic power structures, and before Wikipedia, many feared that such a project would be prone to amateurism, hucksterism, and vandalism. The logic ran that given a system that anyone could access, write to, and furthermore overwrite, would quickly devolve to graffiti. While Wikipedia is susceptible to vandalism, and is in fact mostly written by amateurs, it turns out that a large enough group of amateurs, passionate about the topics they know and care about, tends to trump both inaccuracy and vandalism over time.

One of the strengths of Wikipedia is that it has a clearly defined central mission, and that the principal functions that the Wikipedia community plays in fulfilling that mission are also clearly defined. The Wikipedia page "Wikipedia Community" explains:

> The community's role, as some kind of nebulous science-fiction super-entity, is to:
> - Organize and edit individual pages
> - Structure navigation between pages
> - Resolve conflict between individual members
> - Re-engineer itself—creating rules and patterns of behavior ("Wikipedia Sociology" 2005)

Wikipedia offers the collective a great deal more responsibility than virtually any other historical reference project. By making the distribution of power clear, by establishing collective responsibility, and by empowering literally anyone to not only opine but act in the formation of the knowledge base, Wikipedia has managed to avoid the bureaucratic bottlenecks that have plagued similar endeavors in the past.

The success of Wikipedia suggests that large-scale collectives with a clearly defined central mission, clearly defined roles for contributors, and an active and fervently deliberative community structure can develop more useful resources than traditional hierarchical approaches to managing knowledge. In the case of Wikipedia, the technology of the wiki enables this knowledge community to flourish by empowering every individual reader to act on behalf of the collective in a structured way.

Architectures for Collective Narrative

After they had completed the *Invisible Seattle*, in 1987 the invisibles laid out *The Plan for Invisible America*. They imagined expanding upon the vision of *Invisible Seattle* and, taking advantage of network computers, conducting a collective narrative experiment on much larger scale. The plan was epic in scope:

> First, it presents three years' worth of diverse activities and events—research, writing, programming, publicity, performance—as equal parts of the same project. There is a book in the mix, but it is only a small element. Then it shows how the project interacts with different sectors of the audience in different ways encouraging them to be authors, game players, and spectators.
>
> Finally, it sketches the outlines of a graphic "playing field" in which the game/novel grows through the contributions of both authors and players. (Wittig 1994, 117)

Invisible America never got past the conceptual stage, and a large-scale narrative of such scope, at least one with a literary outcome, has never been attempted. At the time, the project as laid out in *The Plan for Invisible America* would have required a great deal of funding to pull off. Existing computer and network technologies were furthermore extremely rudimentary in comparison to contemporary technologies.

In a longer version of this essay available online I discuss more recent attempts at creating collective narratives online.[1] Barbara Campbell's *1001 Nights Cast* (2005–8) used a frame tale and a constraint-driven participatory writing process to bring together short narratives written by many authors, and likewise *Mr. Beller's Neighborhood* (2002–present) uses a map of New York to bind together many different narratives into a collective online anthology. Most recently, *A Million Penguins* (Ettinghausen et al. 2007) was an attempt spearheaded by Penguin UK and faculty from De Montfort University for hundreds of contributors to collectively write a novel on a wiki. The project had mixed results. Although a novel-length work of writing was composed, as Jeremy Ettinghausen, one of the project's organizers, notes in a blog post, "we had vandals, pornographers, spammers and any number of people who had such differing ideas about what would make a good novel that a real sense of cohesiveness was always going to be hard to achieve" (Ettinghausen 2007).

This chapter has to a great extent been inspired by the thought experiment of *Invisible America*. What may have seemed outlandish in the 1980s is merely an extrapolation of existing technologies and methodologies today. One can imagine a writing community with the robustness of Wikipedia, dedicated to a collective vision of writing a novel that is in effect many novels with interchangeable parts, written according to sets of specific constraints to ensure a degree of formal unity, and tagged with metadata that would make it possible to easily remix novels in thousands of structured configurations. Such a project would be performance, game, and literature. What we do today with our collective references and photographs we could soon do, together, in collective narrative. We may not be there yet, but it is well within our reach.

Notes

1. A lengthier version of this essay, including discussion of recent examples of collective narratives and a discussion of the participatory structures of the online photo community Flickr, can be found online at http://retts.net/documents/cnarrativeDAC.pdf.

References

Beller, Thomas, et al. 2002–present. *Mr. Beller's Neighborhood.* Available at http://www.mrbellersneighborhood.com/ (accessed January 7, 2011).

Calvino, Italo. 1974. *Invisible Cities.* New York: Harvest/HBJ.

Campbell, Babara, et al. 2005–8. *1001 Nights Cast.* Available at http://1001.net.au/ (accessed January 7, 2011).

Coover, Robert. 2003. "The End of Books." In *The New Media Reader,* ed. N. Wardip-Fruin and N. Monfort, 705–9. Cambridge MA: MIT Press.

Coover, Robert, et al. 1996. *The Hypertext Hotel.* Available at http://www.hyperdis.de/hyphotel/ (accessed January 7, 2011).

Davis, Douglas, et al. 1994. *The World's First Collaborative Sentence.* Available at http://artport.whitney.org/collection/index.shtml (accessed January 7, 2011).

Ettinghausen, Jeremy. 2007. "A Million Thanks." Available at http://amillion
    penguins.com/blog/?p=28 (accessed March 1, 2010).

Ettinghausen, Jeremy, et al., eds. 2007. *A Million Penguins.* Available at http://www
    .amillionpenguins.com (accessed March 1, 2020).

Gillespie, William, and Nick Montfort. 2002. *2002.* Urbana IL: Spineless Books.
    Available at http://www.spinelessbooks.com/2002/palindrome/ (accessed January 7, 2011).

Gillespie, William, Scott Rettberg, Dirk Stratton, and Frank Marquardt. 1998. *The
    Unknown.* Available at http://unknownhypertext.com (accessed January 7, 2011).

Invisible Seattle: The Novel of Seattle. 1987. Seattle: Function Industries Press.

Jackson, Shelley. 1995. *Patchwork Girl.* Watertown MA: Eastgate Systems.

Joyce, Michael. 1990. *afternoon, a story.* Watertown MA: Eastgate Systems.

———. 2003. "Siren Shapes: Exploratory and Constructive Hypertexts." In *The New
    Media Reader*, ed. N. Wardip-Fruin and N. Monfort, 613–24. Cambridge MA:
    MIT Press.

Kinsella, Thomas, trans. 1969. *The Tain: Translated from the Irish Epic Tain Bo
    Cuailnge.* Oxford: Oxford University Press.

Larsen, Deena. 1993. *Marble Springs.* Watertown MA: Eastgate Systems.

Malloy, Judy. 1999. *Public Literature: Narratives and Narrative Structures in
    LambdaMOO.* Available at http://www.well.com/user/jmalloy/moopap.html
    (accessed January 7, 2011).

Malloy, Judy, and Cathy Marshall. 1995. *Forward Anywhere.* Watertown MA: Eastgate Systems.

Mateas, Michael, and Andrew Stern. 2002. "*Façade*: An Experiment in Building a
    Fully-Realized Interactive Drama." Available at http://www.interactivestory.net/
    papers/MateasSternGDC03.pdf (accessed January 7, 2011).

Mathews, Harry. 1996. "Translation and the Oulipo: The Case of the Persevering
    Maltese." *Electronic Book Review.* Available at http://www.altx.com/ebr/ebr5/
    mathews.htm (accessed January 7, 2011).

Nelson, Theodore H. 2003. "Proposal for a Universal Electronic Publishing System
    and Archive." In *The New Media Reader*, ed. N. Wardip-Fruin and N. Monfort,
    441–61. Cambridge MA: MIT Press.

"Nupedia." 2005. Available at http://en.Wikipedia.org/wiki/Nupedia (accessed January 7, 2011).

O'Reilly, Tim. 2004. "The Architecture of Participation." Available at http://www
    .oreillynet.com/pub/a/oreilly/tim/articles/architecture_of_participation.html
    (accessed January 7, 2011).

Perec, George. 1978. *Life: A User's Manual.* Boston: David R. Godine.

———. 1995. A Void. New York: HarperCollins.

Simanowski, Roberto. 2001. "The Reader as Author as Figure as Text." Available at
    http://www.poesis.net/poetics/symposion2001/full_simanowski.html (accessed
    January 7, 2011).

Wardrip-Fruin, Noah, Adam Chapman, Brion Moss, and Duane Whitehurst. 2000. *The Impermanence Agent.* Available at http://impermanenceagent.com (accessed January 7, 2011).

"Wikipedia." 2005. Available at http://en.Wikipedia.org/wiki/Wikipedia (accessed January 7, 2011).

"Wikipedia Sociology." 2005. Available at http://meta.wikimedia.org/wiki/Wikipedia_sociology (accessed January 7, 2011).

Wittig, Rob. 1994. *Invisible Rendezvous: Connection and Collaboration in the New Landscape of Electronic Writing.* Middletown CT: Wesleyan University Press.

"Update Soon!"

Harry Potter Fanfiction and
Narrative as a Participatory Process

BRONWEN THOMAS

Fanfiction: Some Preliminaries

Fanfiction may be defined as prose fiction of any length, style, genre, and narrative technique, produced by fans of a wide range of cultural products including TV shows, movies, video games, Japanese manga, and "classic" literature. This kind of "imaginative expansion" (Brewer 2005, 2) is said to have been with us since antiquity. But the advent of the World Wide Web has been responsible for a phenomenal growth in the scale and scope of these fan communities, while the technology has made it possible for fans to communicate and share content on message boards and forums, to organize stories according to genre and preference, and even to influence the production and evolution of the stories they read. Moreover, whereas scholars such as Brewer have bemoaned the paucity of evidence existing in the past for interactions between creative artists and their readers, fanfiction sites ensure that this process is much more open and available for inspection.

Online fanfiction has excited a great deal of critical interest, coalescing mainly around the subversive nature of fan cultures (Jenkins 1992) and the democratic potential of the form (Pugh 2005). Aligning themselves with the fandoms they describe, the emphasis in these approaches is on charting and validating the activities involved in participation, rather than on analyzing or critiquing the kind of writing and reading practices produced. This means that questions of access, design, and aesthetic evaluation are either completely ignored or elided. More significantly, the absence of any kind of close examination of the creative processes involved means that the features that make them distinctive and even unique may be overlooked. In this chapter, I will be focusing on two specific aspects of fanfiction, namely the ongoing interaction that takes place between authors and readers that is publicly accessible to any user of the website, and the continual process of updating and revising stories that often follows from these discussions. I will argue that these sites offer precisely the kind of new modes of user involvement for online narratives anticipated by Ryan (2004), meaning that we cannot analyze *what* is produced without paying just as much attention to *how* it is produced and made available to others.

Harry Potter Fanfiction

The analysis will focus on Harry Potter fanfiction, produced by one of the largest and highest profile of fandoms online. Examples will be taken from the Harry Potter section on www.fanfiction.net (by far the most populous in the Book category), and on two sites exclusively featuring Harry Potter fanfiction, www.mugglenet.com and www.sugarquill.net. By focusing on "literary" or book-based fandoms, I can explore how far such communities set out to challenge the boundaries between authors and readers and disrupt the stability and sanctity of the "text." This is true even of fanfiction based on "classic" texts written by long-dead authors. But the so-called Harry Potter Phenomenon is highly pertinent because of the specific publication history of these novels. J. K. Rowling announced from the outset that she would write seven novels in the series, and the launches of each of the novels have produced scenes of increasing excitement and even hysteria. The gaps between publication, and the use of continuing plotlines and enigmas have helped to fuel this sense of anticipation, while Rowling's declared interest in the fanfiction produced by her readers has led to all sorts of rumors about the extent to which the direction of the series may have been influenced by ideas generated on these sites.[1] Harry Potter fanfiction also illustrates how intrinsically intertextual and transmedial this kind of narrative is, as in addition to the novels the stories frequently draw on the film adaptations, interviews with Rowling, and other fanfics, making it difficult if not impossible to identify any single "source text."

Navigating Online Fanfiction

In terms of how it uses the technology at its disposal, it would seem that fanfiction could never be described as radically experimental in the way that hypertext fiction often is. No attempt is made to incorporate or play with multimodal affordances, but instead, the written word is placed at the forefront of every activity (with the exception of the much less popular "fan art"). Indeed, in many respects online fanfiction is barely distinguishable from print versions. Nevertheless, fanfiction cannot be understood in isolation from the "network culture" (Bolter 2001) that the World Wide Web has helped to generate. Thus just as with earlier communities of fans, such as the eighteenth-century readers studied by Brewer (2005), it is vital to try to understand the specific historical and social conditions that produce them. Busse (2006) argues that while individual fanfics may not make full use of the technological resources at their disposal, the creation, dissemination, and reception of the stories does. Moreover, Busse contends that we can only ever understand and evaluate the fan text in relation to the community that produces it, such that the traditional evaluative criteria of the literary critical apparatus cannot unproblematically be imported across to writing where repetition, familiarity, and faithfulness to the "canon" are highly prized.[2]

In their chapter in this volume, Simons and Newman contend that new media consumption is defined by patterns of accumulation and archiving, and these are readily observable within online fan communities. On a site such as www.fanfiction.net, the user is offered menus and hyperlinks to help her navigate and make selections from the categories offered, and which present a range of options in terms of what she may want to do on the site (e.g., read a story or enter an online forum), what she may want to read (e.g., book-based or anime fanfiction), what genre of story she is interested in (romance, angst, hurt/comfort, parody), and the rating of the story (e.g., whether it contains adult themes and/or language). Lev Manovich (2001) has argued that such designs can contribute to the idea of the user as a kind of coauthor, and that this is symptomatic of the logic of advanced and postindustrial societies where every act seems to involve choosing from a menu, catalog, or database. We may question the extent to which such choices are either as extensive or as free as they first appear, but nevertheless, they help to foster the idea that users can have some degree of control over how they make use of and engage with the site and its content.

With fanfiction sites, though stories are categorized and presented as separate, closed-off entities, the design facilitates browsing and "zapping" between stories in virtually any order or sequence. In this respect, fanfiction is not so far removed from hypertext fiction's dependence on a "rhetoric of spatiality" (Bukatman 1994, 13, cited by Ensslin 2007, 38). Thus while individual stories rarely if ever eschew linearity, patterns of reading will typically see fans reading across stories and moving freely between them, as evidenced by the habit of serial reviewing that is so common on these sites. The design of fanfiction sites caters to all kinds of narrative appetites, as stories can range from the more concise "drabble" or "one-shot,"[3] to volumes extending to multiple chapters and tens of thousands of words. Each time the site is accessed, stories will be ordered differently as new stories are posted or updated, and the user must rely on story titles, summaries, or keyword searches if a more specialized or directed search is required. We can no more understand fanfiction without reference to these wider processes of production and consumption than we can under- stand the individual narratives without reference to their many intertexts.

Fanfiction as a Participatory Process

All websites work against closure by constantly referring users outwards to other sites, and they also help to redefine the notion of the page (and hence the text) as something that is dynamic rather than static (Bolter 2001). Users are familiar with the idea of web pages being constantly refreshed and revised, and increasingly expect to be able to comment on and even revise content found online (as with wikis,[4] for example). Web- based texts are therefore not inert objects but sites of performativity. Users expect to be able to interact with the producers of websites, and expect that their comments, and the replies they may in turn elicit, will be pub- licly displayed. On fanfiction sites, I shall argue, such expectations feed into the creative process as authors review one another's work, review- ers refer outwards to other stories posted on the same or other sites, and authors frequently reply directly to the comments posted by their read- ers, their replies sometimes appearing alongside the original comment. Such relationships can develop over time, with the conversations between reviewers and authors providing an invaluable insight into the creative process and how the narrative has evolved. According to Henry Jenkins (1992), fans in effect translate the reception process into a kind of social interaction whereby relationships between users are built up around their discussions of one another's stories.

Of course, there is nothing new in the idea of authors revising their work in the light of readers' comments, and the practice of "process criticism" (Calonne 2006, 171) concerns itself with uncovering evidence of how and where this takes place. Calonne cites the creative collaborations between Pound and Eliot, and Anaïs Nin and Henry Miller, while the history of the publication and public performances of many of Dickens's novels is repeatedly held up as a prime example of a writer responding to feedback from his readers. Revision is also a feature of many media texts: for example, the responses of film audiences to pre-release screenings commonly lead to significant changes, particularly to the endings of these narratives. As suggested earlier, computer technologies have further facilitated dialogues and collaborations between authors and readers, with many authors such as J. K. Rowling now having websites that invite feedback and discussion of their work. But for Busse (2007) the kind of ongoing dialogue that takes place between fanfic writers and their readers, and the degree of intertextuality that characterizes this type of writing, means that it becomes impossible to keep separate the fan "text" from the myriad influences and creative interactions with which it becomes caught up.

Fanfiction's Review Culture

Fanfiction sites have built-in mechanisms facilitating systematic and ongoing reviews that help to generate a "review culture" among fans, whereby the roles of authors and readers become virtually interchangeable (Chatelain 2002). On these sites, social interaction is, in theory at least, the by-product of a process whereby some kind of aesthetic critique of the stories is to be offered, and where departures from the "canon" may be highlighted and debated. Before publication, authors are able to draw on the services of so-called Betareaders who may do anything from correcting errors of spelling and punctuation to offering advice on plotting and characterization. Betareaders are typically experienced writers who may also be involved in the running and administration of the site. Occasionally, users are referred to dedicated Betareading sites (e.g., www.perfect imagination.co.uk) where services and specializations are advertised.

While Betareaders fulfill an editorial role, and usually have to be selected or trained to do so, anybody registered on the sites can post reviews of published stories. Nevertheless, fanfiction sites typically carry advice or explicit guidelines about posting reviews. For example, www.sugarquill.net asks that users "put a bit of thought into your review before posting," and discourages negativity and netspeak in its "Posting Guidelines." Advice is also given to authors, to "ignore the needlessly cruel remarks" they may encounter. On www.mugglenet.com the "Review Policy" prohibits abusive comments or "flaming," while on www.fanfiction.net guidance is more gentle: "It is extremely helpful to use this opportunity to comment on an aspect of the story that can be improved. A well-rounded critique is often the most rewarding tool for the writer." Beyond this, little explicit advice as to the format or content of reviews is offered. However, Chatelain (2002) found that reviews tend to be short and to the point, so that users effectively generate their own sets of conventions and expectations. Moreover, users tend to police and regulate content themselves, responding to unfair or offensive comments and correcting any inaccuracies in other people's reviews.

The "Reviews Lounge" on www.fanfiction.net has been formed by a "community of authors" who set out to draw attention to what they consider to be underreviewed stories on the site. Once the stories achieve the required number of reviews, they are moved to another section. The implication is clearly that the sheer number of reviews received is somehow an indication of the quality or merit of the story. This is also evident from the way in which some authors actively solicit reviews, as with "spleefmistress" on www.fanfiction.net, who openly refers to herself as a "review whore." But the existence of the Reviews Lounge also exposes the extent to which cliques emerge on these sites, so that stories written by newcomers, or those outside of a particular clique, may be neglected or overlooked. This might suggest that access to, and participation in, fanfiction sites may not always be as open and fair as enthusiasts would have us believe. There is also evidence to suggest that would-be participants recognize that they may have to work to be accepted within the fan community. The reviewing process is commonly perceived as a way in to becoming a writer, whereby the reviewer is able to get a sense of the standard of writing required, and of the potential audience, but also to make her- or himself known to the fan community, and hopefully become accepted. For example, "mock_turtle's" biography on www.mugglenet.com reveals that she is "currently trying to work up the nerve to write a fic of my own," having posted a review of *Life in the Shadows* by "DaniDM."

Reviews generally provide approbation or encouragement for authors, a "complicit audience" (Pugh 2005) where most of the reviewers are themselves authors of stories, often but not always from within the same category or fandom. As authorship and reviewing overlap, authorship is (re)constructed to incorporate the activity of responding to comments and advice, while readers are (re)constructed as active participants in the creative process. Criticism is usually mild or highly apologetic. In his study of eighteenth century readers, Brewer (2005, 21) claimed that "a public can suspend its social differences while still showcasing its interpretative differences." Everything from the design of fanfiction sites to their mission statements militates against overt hierarchies or social distinctions of any kind, as stories are not ranked in terms of any kind of order of merit, and users can reveal as much or as little about their backgrounds as they choose. But it is far from evident that "interpretative differences" can be kept distinct from the social in the way Brewer suggests, because of the public nature of the reviewing process, and the fact that the sites are used as much for social networking as they are for the expression and sharing of aesthetic evaluations.

The language of the reviews generally works against foregrounding "differences" of any kind. Politeness rules, and the need to protect the face wants of users (Brown and Levinson 1978), ensure a supportive atmosphere but can threaten to undermine the whole concept of "reviewing" if genuine criticisms and creative disagreements are dispreferred. In her study of responses posted to blogs in this volume, Page finds some evidence to suggest a correlation between the gender of the blogger and the gender of those leaving comments on the site, and it is possible that such patterns might also be detectable in relation to the reviewing process on fanfiction sites. The language used by reviewers, and whether they offer support or give advice, might also be usefully mapped according to the gender of participants.

On dedicated sites such as www.mugglenet.com and www.sugarquill. net, it is obviously much more likely that the reviewer is another Harry Potter fanfic author, but even here, reviewers may only be interested (or even tolerant of) certain character pairings, meaning that they may restrict themselves to particular categories. Thus, the commonly expressed antipathy to stories pairing Ron and Hermione is likely to mean that some readers actively avoid reading stories from the Romance category. On www.fanfiction.net a reviewer of Harry Potter stories may be primarily a fan of other prose fiction, or a TV show or movie. For example, the

Harry Potter story "How to Deal?" posted by "mcdreamy1992" (accessed December 3, 2007), attracted reviews from fans of the TV shows *Grey's Anatomy* and *Doctor Who*, as well as from other Harry Potter authors. Such reviewers may not be as concerned with issues of canonicity, and may draw interesting comparisons and parallels across texts, which can in turn generate new kinds of crossover fiction, where characters from one fictional universe are "crossed" with those from another.[5] The reviewing process thus contributes to the generation of new stories and new possibilities, both implicitly, in the discussions that take place between reviewers and authors, and explicitly, where challenges are laid down by website managers, or by fanfic writers and readers, for stories involving specific pairings, "crosses," or plotlines.

Although the number of reviews a story elicits may vary considerably, the reviewing process is usually speedy and fervent and is perceived as an ongoing activity and responsibility. Even where criticism may be voiced, reviewers seem to feel obliged to monitor the progress of the story so that the same names keep cropping up: regular reviewers for "A Little More Time" by "Jess Pallas" on www.fanfiction.net include "creamteaanyone," "stupidpenname," and "Lady of the dungeon." Nearly all of the reviewers of "How to Deal?" on the same site posted more than one message, and "allyg1990"'s own Harry Potter story had in turn been reviewed by "mcdreamy1992" one day earlier, demonstrating the practice of returning the compliment that is typical within fan communities. Occasionally, reviewers explicitly respond to other comments, contributing to the impression that a debate is being generated. For example, reviews of "Life in the Shadows" on www.mugglenet.com focus on the time jumps in the story, express support for one another ("radcliffe4eva": "I agree with mock_turtle"), and even comment on the quality of the reviews, "riderof dragons" remarking that "I won't even try and compete with some of the reviews left on here."

Regular reviewers can gain a reputation within the fan community, and www.mugglenet.com carries lists of the ten most prolific reviewers along with a list of the ten most reviewed stories and awards for the best reviews. Reviewers may wield considerable power, therefore, although this is usually accompanied by awareness of the responsibilities of the role and the need to be seen to be fair and evenhanded. Criticism, where it occurs, is apologetic, and comes only after praise or expressions of support. Thus, "amber-chick" starts her review of "A Little More Time" on www.fanfic tion.net by calling it a "brilliant story," and appears reluctant ("though I have to say") to go on in her second paragraph to challenge the author's characterization and plotting. Instead of overt criticism, questions are often asked about the direction in which the story is going, especially if the post is a "chapter" forming part of an as-yet incomplete whole. Quotations from the story may be used where issues of style emerge, for example if a reviewer takes issue with a line of dialogue that is felt to be out of keeping with the kind of language used for a character in the "canon." Departures from "canon" produce the most adverse criticism, so that instead of friendly advice, the reviewer may take it upon herself to correct or challenge the author's interpretation of an event or a character. For example, "Lady of the dungeon"'s review of "A Little More Time" launches into a direct attack on the author's characterization of Remus ("I just can not believe he is just so stupid!"). As is so often the case, the review links criticism of this specific story with a more general complaint ("I just hate it when I read about this Remus who keeps sacrificing himself"), demonstrating how reviewers constantly make connections across stories, and between the stories and the canon.

Uptake and Updating: Responding to Reviews

Page's research on blogs suggests that the interaction between bloggers and those posting comments may actually help to shape the stories being produced. In contrast, Pugh's research (2005) found that fanfic writers hardly ever changed their stories in the light of readers' comments, and it remains relatively rare to find fanfiction authors explicitly collaborating on specific stories. Indeed, the process of updating consists more of adding material in the form of new chapters, rather than necessarily revising already existing material. In this respect, the process has clear parallels with the serialization of novels in the nineteenth century, or contemporary televised soap operas, where anticipation and discussion of coming plotlines and developments are intrinsic to the narrative experience.

Nevertheless, the very fact of updating, and the fact that authors so frequently acknowledge the influence and support of others, suggests that a degree of mutual influence or dependency exists. Moreover, as Pugh (2005) points out, fanfiction is itself the product of a consumer culture that fosters the belief that "I could do that," and where readers (and writers) by definition are never sated but constantly seek out new interpretations and versions of the tales and characters to which they are so devoted. Cross-referencing between stories is fairly common, and biographical information about authors on www.fanfiction.net includes references to favorite stories and favorite authors, as well as acknowledgments to friends and readers who have contributed to the creative process. Meanwhile, menu pages carry information about the number of reviews a story has attracted, and authors sometimes actively solicit reviews, demonstrating once again the extent to which they are seen as a mark of popularity and even quality.

The concept of updating is one that is intrinsic to many if not all new media texts. Users are familiar with the notion of web pages being updated and refreshed, particularly as new software and interfaces become available. Similarly, hypertext fictions are often available in different versions, although it is by no means a given that later versions of these texts are always going to be perceived as "better" than their earlier, less sophisticated manifestations. In one sense, every fanfiction is an update of some kind, given that it is responding to a preexisting story, assumed to be known by all users. Nevertheless, the design of fanfiction sites can have a significant impact on the way the author/reader relationship is constructed in relationship to the development and exchange of story ideas. On www.mugglenet.com, authors' responses appear alongside reviews, creating a sense of ongoing dialogue. For example, the author of "Where Light and Shadow Meet" responds to every review that is posted. This varies from detailed replies to specific points, to simple acknowledgment and thanks for support ("Glad you liked it!"). The tone is polite, and even where it may be felt a reader has misinterpreted the story, gratitude is expressed for the opportunity to clarify and explain what was intended ("I value your opinion very highly").

Updating and Narrative as Process

Intrinsic to the whole concept of updating is the idea of the work in progress, or "processurality" (Ensslin 2007, 37). In part, this reflects the fact that most writers of fanfiction see themselves as novices, often prefacing their stories with apologies and disclaimers, and actively encouraging advice and suggestions for improvement. Pugh's (2005) research showed that whereas some writers wait until they have completed their stories before posting them, others post unfinished stories, and this may be clearly indicated in the menu, where stories are ranked as Completed/Uncompleted. Yet the ubiquity and centrality of the updating process means that it is much more complex than simply providing a safety net for those who lack confidence in their writing. For fans, updating helps to fulfill both the "desire for the inexhaustible story" (Douglas 2001), and the "enactment of [the] denial of death" (Murray 1997). The vehemence of the fans' exhortations to authors to keep updating is testament to this, and most reviews actually consist primarily of exhortations to "keep going" or to "update soon," usually accompanied by the inevitable excess of expressive punctuation.

Henry Jenkins (2007) describes fans as having an encyclopedic impulse to seek out new material, which he sees as being in direct opposition to the need for closure, central to many models and theories of narrative. Fanfiction may therefore provide a kind of endless deferment of closure similar to the soap opera (Fiske 1987). Like soap opera, fanfiction is easily dismissed as feeding an addictive craving that is completely lacking in any discernment. Feminist critics (Modleski 1982; Warhol 2003) have contested these metaphors of addiction and the castigation of these narrative forms as perpetuating a denigration and repression of female pleasures. In contrast, Pugh (2005) draws a distinction between fanfiction that provides "more of" what the fans crave and find appealing, and those that offer "more from" the source texts, though she stops short of suggesting that the one is any more worthy or rewarding than the other.

To some extent, the design and structure of fanfiction sites helps to perpetuate the idea that fans have an insatiable appetite for "more of" these stories. As mentioned earlier, fanfiction sites generally provide the user with information about the number of stories existing for each category, the number of reviews posted and so on, conveying at a glance the sheer quantity of material that is available, as though that is some kind of guarantor of its quality. Recency and being "of the moment" also seem to be highly valued. The site www.mugglenet.com has a "Most Recent" category, while the default option on www.fanfiction.net takes the reader to the most recently updated stories. Moreover, the fact that dates and times of postings and updates are published seems to encourage a sense of anticipation and even impatience for ever-more content. Nevertheless, it would be unfair to characterize such a process as undiscriminating, as the sites also provide users with archives for accessing past stories, and menus to help them to narrow down their search options.

For authors, updating helps offset the sense of anticlimax and deflation that writers may feel on completing their story: J. K. Rowling herself has said she felt both "euphoric and devastated" having completed the last novel in the Harry Potter series (Borland 2007). At the same time, the enthusiasm for the process of updating is testament to the pleasures of rewriting and reengaging with the creative process. For fanfiction authors, updating facilitates an ongoing engagement with readers of their work, and an opportunity to take on board not only comments and suggestions on their own stories but also ideas and responses generated by other stories appearing on the fansites.

The process of updating is visible and traceable. Information is provided about the date of first publication, and the date of the most recent update. Where revisions are made to existing content, although it is not possible to access previous versions of the stories, reviewers' comments make it possible to draw some conclusions about the kinds of changes that may have been made and when, while authors themselves sometimes explicitly refer to revisions made, often in response to a specific reviewer's suggestions. Thus updating stories usually consists of changes or expansions to plotlines and aspects of characterization, or responses to criticisms based on departures from the "canon." In some instances, updates may more explicitly respond to the unearthing of some new fact or interpretation of the canon. In Harry Potter fandoms, J. K. Rowling's revelation that she had always thought of Dumbledore as being gay led to a number of new and revised fictions exploring the implications of this.

Conclusion

The closely related processes of reviewing and updating are fundamental to the whole ethos of online fanfiction, and to its potential significance as a "new narrative." While respect is paid to the creative rights of authors, and plagiarism is frowned upon, every aspect of what an author writes is up for debate, and equally important is the right of every fan to contribute stories but also comment on the efforts of others. A palpable sense of control and power may develop within a fan community, and mythologies emerge concerning the extent to which the creative processes generated by these sites feed back into and influence the source texts. The concept of "fanon" that has arisen within fan cultures consolidates this idea that fans can contribute to and help shape the "canon," closely corresponding to Brewer's (2005) notion of the "social canon" that exists both alongside and in opposition to its socially sanctioned and hierarchical "official" counterpart.

Thus, although fanfiction rarely engages in the pyrotechnics of other web-based narratives, the stance taken toward the source text is key to its potential for subversion and innovation. While fans are hugely protective of the canon, and often reverential toward the authors of the source texts, the very concept of fanfiction displaces the idea of the text as somehow being in the ownership of any individual or beholden to any specific set of aesthetic ideals. Moreover, fanfiction constantly contests the notion of the text as something that is stable and finished, as readers never know how long a particular version of a fanfic will remain on a site.

The transparency of the processes of reviewing and updating mean that fanfiction shares with hypertext fiction subversion both of "the Romantic notion of the author as a godlike creator of reality" (Ensslin 2007, 31), and of the idea that creative artistry must be the product of effortless inspiration (Bolter 2001). Individual stories, and even the source texts themselves, are conceived as being subject to constant modification and expansion. Authors, however much they may be revered, are conceived of as participants in an ongoing conversation, their creativity and handling of narrative technique seen as something to engage with rather than be admired from afar. Finally, reading pleasure is not understood as being contained either within or by the single text, or as something that is exhaustible. Instead, pleasure is dispersed across texts, categories, and genres, and thereby allows for all manner of sites of access, enjoyment, and participation that are unique to and limitless for each potential user.

As with so many of the chapters in this volume, narrative theory's tried and tested toolkit has proved invaluable for analyzing the structures and design of online fanfiction. But this chapter also demonstrates the challenge to some of these existing terms and categories posed by new narratives. Moreover, it highlights the need for post-classical narratology to move beyond formalist concerns to engage more fully with the processes of production and consumption that are so intrinsic to the understanding of new narratives.

Notes

1. J. K. Rowling's website (http://www.jkrowling.com) has links to many fan sites, and she declares herself a "huge fan" of "Leaky" or The Leaky Cauldron (http://www.the-leaky-cauldron.org). She has also given interviews to fan sites (e.g., to The Leaky Cauldron on July 16, 2005).

2. The term *canon* is used to refer to any kind of information that is verifiable from the source material (such as movie, book, or video game) on which the fanfiction is based, for example the color of a character's hair, where they went to school, and so forth. The term *fanon* has emerged to refer to information regarding the fictional universe that has become accepted over time within the fan community but is not necessarily verifiable by reference to the source material alone. For a fuller discussion of canons and fanons, see Thomas 2007.

3. A drabble is a short piece of fiction usually defined as consisting of exactly one hundred words. A one-shot refers to a stand-alone, self-contained work of fiction—that is, not an installment from a longer piece.

4. A wiki is "software that allows users to create, edit, and link web pages easily. Wikis are often used to create collaborative websites and to power community websites" ("Wiki," Wikipedia, available at http://en.wikipedia.org/wiki/Wiki [accessed January 7, 2011]).

5. Examples of crossover fiction found on www.fanfiction.net include stories where Harry Potter is crossed with the *Lord of the Rings*, with Pokemon, and with the TV shows *Buffy the Vampire Slayer* and *Monty Python's Flying Circus*.

References

Bolter, Jay David. 2001. *Writing Space: Computers, Hypertext and the Remediation of Print*. 2nd ed. London: Lawrence Erlbaum Associates.

Borland, Sophie. 2007. "JK Rowling Howling at End of Harry Potter." *Daily Telegraph*, July 6. Available at http://www.telegraph.co.uk/news/main.jhtml?xml=/news/2007/07/06/nrowling106.xml (accessed December 28, 2007).

Brewer, David. 2005. *The Afterlife of Character 1726–1825*. Philadelphia: University of Pennsylvania Press.

Brown, Penelope, and Stephen Levinson. 1978. "Universals in Language Use: Politeness Phenomena." In *Questions and Politeness: Strategies in Social Interaction*, ed. Esther N. Goody, 56–311. Cambridge: Cambridge University Press.

Busse, Kristina. 2006. "Will the Real Ending Please Stand Up? Experimental Multimedia Narratives and Fan Fiction." Paper presented at Console-ing Passions Conference, University of Wisconsin–Milwaukee. Available at http://www.kristinabusse.com/cr/research/cp06.html (accessed January 13, 2011).

Calonne, David S. 2006. "Creative Writers and Revision." In *Revision: History, Theory and Practice*, ed. Alice Horning and Anne Becker. Anderson sc: Parlor Press. Available at http://wac.colostate.edu/books/horning_revision/chapter 9.pdf (accessed December 28, 2007).

Chatelain, Julianne. 2002. "Learning From the Review Culture of Fan Fiction." *Journal of Digital Information* 3, no. 1. Available at http://jodi.ecs.soton.ac.uk/Articles/v03/i03-old/chatelain/fanfic.html (accessed March 3, 2007).

Douglas, Jane Yellowlees. 2001. *The End of Books—or Books without End? Reading Interactive Narratives*. Ann Arbor: University of Michigan Press.

Ensslin, Astrid. 2007. *Canonizing Hypertext: Explorations and Constructions*. London: Continuum.

Fiske, John. 1987. *Television Culture*. London: Routledge.

Jenkins, Henry. 1992. *Textual Poachers: Television Fans and Participatory Culture*. London: Routledge.

———. 2007. "Transmedia Storytelling 101." Available at http://www.henryjenkins .org/2007/03/transmedia_storytelling_101.html (accessed June 9, 2008).

Manovich, Lev. 2001. *The Language of New Media*. Cambridge ma: mit Press.

Modleski, Tania. 1982. *Loving with a Vengeance: Mass-Produced Fantasies for Women*. London: Methuen.

Murray, Janet. 1997. *Hamlet on the Holodeck: The Future of Narrative in Cyberspace*. Cambridge ma: mit Press.

Pugh, Sheenagh. 2005. *The Democratic Genre: Fan Fiction in a Literary Context*. Bridgend: Seren Books.

Ryan, Marie-Laure. 2004. *Narrative across Media: The Languages of Storytelling*. Lincoln: University of Nebraska Press.

Thomas, Bronwen. 2007. "Canons and Fanons: Literary Fiction Online." *dichtung-digital* 37. Available at http://www.dichtung-digital.org/2007/thomas.htm (accessed March 6, 2011).

Warhol, Robyn. 2003. *Having a Good Cry: Effeminate Feelings and Pop-Culture Forms*. Columbus: Ohio State University Press.

12   Blogging on the Body

Gender and Narrative

RUTH PAGE

Web Logs: Definition and History

Blogs (also known as web logs) are frequently modified web pages in which the dated entries appear in reverse chronological order, so that the reader views the most recently written entries first. Blogs emerged as a web genre in the late 1990s, and since then blogging activity has increased exponentially. It is perhaps unsurprising that the term *blog* masks considerable variation, for blogs may be written about diverse subjects and for many different purposes. Herring, Scheidt, Bonus, and Wright put forward the most important categorization, resulting in a three-way division of Filter, Knowledge logs, and Personal Journals. They note that by far the most common (but overlooked) subcategory is that of personal journals (2004, 6). In turn, personal blogs are best characterized as a highly varied and hybrid genre, influenced by online forms of communication such as e-mail and personal web pages along with offline genres, particularly diary writing and autobiography.

Most research to date has not yet considered the narrative potential of blogs. However, as one of the fastest growing online platforms for personal storytelling, blogs have much to offer narratology. Feminist narratology might find personal blogs of particular interest. The demographics of bloggers and the offline antecedents of diary writing associate personal blogs with female writers (Nowson and Oberlander 2006) and feminine practice (Sorapure 2003). However, Herring, Kouper, Scheidt, and Wright (2004) argue that blogs have been discursively constructed so as to downplay the contribution of young women. From its outset, feminist narratology has cautioned those formulating narrative theory not to ignore the texts authored by women (Lanser 1986, 343). As new media shapes contemporary narrative studies, it is vital that we bear Lanser's imperative in mind and give due attention to personal blogs as a rich resource that might reshape our understanding of narrative theory and practice. In particular, personal blogs offer fresh material against which feminist narratology might test one of its central yet contentious questions: whether women and men use different storytelling styles.

Previous studies exploring the relationship between a speaker's gender and narrative style present a wide-ranging and complex picture. At one extreme, researchers working in a literary critical tradition of autobiography have claimed online journaling as a new discursive tradition for women (Bowen 2004). At the other end of the spectrum, corpus-based studies have examined correlations between linguistic choice and the author's gender in blogs (Herring and Paolillo 2006), finding more points of cross-category similarity than difference. While sociolinguistic accounts rightly refute a binary and universalized contrast between women's and men's conversational storytelling, there is some evidence to suggest that gendered values do bear on narrative style. Typically, these differences reinforce hegemonic masculinity and femininity, whereby women's stories are seen to promote solidarity through affective emphases and self disclosure (Coates 1996), while men's stories tend to be factually oriented and present the protagonist in a heroic light, or in isolation from others (Eggins and Slade 1997). Tracing the extent to which patterns of offline gendered interaction carry over into online personal storytelling is, as yet, relatively uncharted territory. My study is a small step in this direction, looking at a very specific set of narratives told on personal blogs: narratives of illness.

Data Sample

The blogs considered here concern their authors' experiences of being diagnosed with and treated for cancer.[1] As narratives of personal experience (Labov 1972) and more specifically narratives of illness (Frank 1994; Rimmon-Kenan 2002), the reported events have the potential to involve transformation in time and a projected teleological focus, both of which might invoke narrativity more readily than would a random selection of personal blog entries. Clearly, the sample deals with a specific narrative subgenre, and is by no means universally representative of personal storytelling, or of all writing on personal blogs. As such, the results reported here must be understood within the limits of their localized context, and any findings concerning the gendered nature of storytelling taken as tentative suggestions rather than universal absolutes.

The primary data sample consists of slightly more than two hundred blog posts, taken from twenty-one cancer blogs. Ten blogs were authored by women; eleven were authored by men. Eighteen of the cancer blog authors were American, two were British, one Spanish (but writing in English). All the women wrote about experiences with breast cancer, whereas the men's blogs covered a range of cancers. A smaller sample of travel blog entries was examined as a secondary point of comparison. The second sample contains thirty travel blog entries, authored in equal quantity by women and men. A summary of the data sample is given in Table 1.

A first glance at the size of the data sample suggests variation in the length of blog post that correlates with both the blogger's gender and the blog topic. Within this sample, men wrote markedly longer travel blog posts than did the women. Conversely, the women's posts about experiences with cancer were twice as long as the men's. The variation in the length of the men's posts in particular is remarkable. While this could be skewed by the size of the data sample, it would seem that men write much more on personal blogs when the topic is externally focused and stereotypically masculine (Coates 2003). There is much less variation in the length of the women's posts, but the smaller difference suggests the opposite to be true: women write more on personal blogs when the topic is personally centered on the self rather than on external events or objects. Although these results cannot tell us anything about the quality of the storytelling on blogs, they do suggest that gender does make a difference to participation in the blogosphere, and that narrative analysis cannot divorce form and content.

TABLE 1. Data sample in detail

Topic	Author	No. of blogs	No. of posts	No. of words	Average words/post
Cancer	Women	10	100	54,155	541.6
	Men	11	97	23,411	241.4
Travel	Women	15	15	7,050	470
	Men	15	15	30,037	2,002
Total		51	227	114,653	

Storytelling in an Online Community

Unlike the private world of offline diaries or autobiography, blogging is not a solitary occupation but takes place within a community of web users. It is the interactive potential of the blog that distinguishes it above all from its offline counterparts (Sorapure 2003, 5). Defining types of interactivity, however, is a complex business. Narratological approaches emphasize the formal properties of digital interaction. Thus, Walker (2003) positions users as external or internal to the story, and Ryan (2006) distinguishes between exploratory and ontological interaction. Control of the text and influence on narrative content lie at the heart of these distinctions, implying a contrast between users who are positioned outside the text, who may navigate but not change narrative content (exploratory interaction) and users who can create or alter the content, even participating as characters within the story world itself.

A formal analysis of the blog's interactive facilities locates the reader as external to the story (they do not participate as characters in the events being reported) and typifies the interaction as exploratory (they do not alter the events being told). The blog readers would seem to have little influence on the content of the blog, which remains under its author's control. However, this belies the significance of the community in which the blog is situated, for as McLellan puts it, "the most remarkable feature of the electronic narrative is its connection with an audience" (1997, 99). Indeed, sociolinguistic approaches characterize narrative interaction as interpersonally motivated and dynamically shaped by its social context. A pragmatic reorientation of digital interaction might then be a useful complement to formal typologies, elucidating the critical role that interaction plays in refashioning narratives of illness in the blogosphere. This is of particular interest from a feminist perspective, given that gendered patterns of verbal interaction have been seen to shape storytelling styles in the offline world of conversational storytelling.

Blogger and Audience Interaction: Commenting

The importance of the audience is signaled clearly by nearly all the authors of the cancer blogs, who regardless of gender tell their stories explicitly with the purpose of connecting with a community of users:

I decided to deliver my story in real time, as it happens, in this journal. This is my therapy, and my way of sharing the story in its raw, unedited form. It is my hope that other people who encounter difficulties can read this and gain strength from knowing that they are not alone.

    Sylvie (August 8, 2006)

Here are my random thoughts as I get a grip on having cancer at 42 (now 44) years old. I would like to inspire hope in all of you and in myself as well as to provide a place for you to keep track of me through this ordeal.

    David E. (homepage)

The blogger's awareness of his or her audience is evident throughout their writing, and it shapes the blog posts in various ways. Many bloggers directly invite comments, encouraging the members of the audience to make themselves known:

If you have comments please leave them because they do help us.
    PLEASE add yourself to our *Frappr map* as we would LOVE to know where our readers are from.

    Dan (Homepage)

The quotation from Dan's homepage suggests the dialogic relationship between audience and blogger. Indeed, the primary function of the comments on the cancer blogs is to provide or seek support in the form of shared experience, advice, and encouragement. The interaction appears intended to influence the blogger and his or her life experiences, not to respond to a textual segment alone. Examples of support include the following:

Hi Sylvie,
    We don't know each other, but I do know what you're going through. What you're doing is called "participating in life"—it's what keeps you alive, keeps you going during this tumultuous time. What you need to know is that this is a special time . . . a you time.

    (Comment on Sylvie's blog)

In turn, the support from the audience is acknowledged in the blog posts, and shapes the events that are reported.

> A few of you wanted me to let you know how things went today, on my first day of chemo. I appreciate your support more than I can explain. I thought I'd let you know how things are going.
> David Hahn (July 29, 2005)

Clearly, the interaction between the blogger and audience influences not only what gets written in the posts but the blogger's experiences in the offline world. Pragmatically, the comments seem to have a co-constructive influence on the narrative development that goes beyond the limitations of their formal involvement. The mismatch between the formal categories (exploratory or ontological) and the pragmatic impact of blogging interaction occurs in part because the evolution of the blog takes place over time. Readers do not comment on the blog as a completed artifact, as they might a literary hypertext or simulation, but rather in episodic fashion as the blog unfolds. In addition, the blogs are assumed to be authentic accounts of personal experience, not fictional worlds in which the audience may participate as virtual role-play. The evolving and "real world" influence of these blog comments pushes their narrative potential up against the formalist boundaries that distinguish between external and internal reader positions. While formal categories remain intact, their limitations are exposed by the interpersonal dynamics of storytelling revealed here. Indeed, the blog's capacity to reach and interact with a hitherto unknown audience is the central contribution that critically reshapes narratives of illness told online.

The invitation to comment directly on an individual post is the most prominent means by which the audience can interact with a blog. An empirical analysis of the cancer blog comments provides a more detailed profile of the interaction between the bloggers and at least a portion of their audience.[2] Comments were categorized according to the gender of the blogger and the commenter. There was considerable variation in the number of comments generated by posts, ranging from posts that provoked no comment at all to posts that gained up to 191 responses (although such a high response was unusual). In light of this extreme variation, the aggregate figures must be taken as suggestive tendencies

TABLE 2. Average number of comments per post for cancer and travel blogs

	Male blogger	Female blogger
Cancer blogs	2.6	12.7
Travel blogs	5.3	4.6

only, not a consistent picture of this sector of the blogosphere. The gender of the commenters includes an "anonymous" category for individuals who did not disclose their gender identity online. Several observations are prompted by these results. First, it is notable that the cancer blogs written by women attracted on average more than double the number of comments than any other blog subgroup. Second, women tended to post over twice as many comments in total as the men did (59 percent compared with 25 percent). However, it is too simplistic to suggest that gender alone can be used as a bottom-line explanation for patterns of interaction. Instead, the tendency for a commenter to respond to a blogger of the same sex merits further consideration.

One explanation is that the interaction occurs primarily between users with a common experience. As some types of cancer are gender-specific (e.g., prostate cancer) and readers comment on blogs relevant to the illness of interest to them, this gives rise to a gendered correlation between commenter and blogger, especially as within this sample the women bloggers all had the same type of cancer while the men did not. Thus, it would seem that it is the appeal to a shared experience that primarily determines these interactive patterns, not the gender of the user in an abstract sense. Nonetheless, there is evidence that the concept of shared experience can

TABLE 3. Percentage of comments made by women and men on cancer blogs

	Male commenter	Female commenter	Anonymous
Male blogger	46	39	16
Female blogger	18	66	16
Overall totals	25	59	16

be put to gendered uses, and is of particular importance in women's story-telling as a means of establishing friendship and solidarity (Coates 1996). The gendered value of shared experience, here aligned with constructions of hegemonic femininity, might then explain why commenting is done mostly by women in response to blogs written by women, functioning as an online means of promoting solidarity.

Hyperlinks

The hyperlinks within a blog have a different interactive potential, manipulating the reader's movement in the blog, not the blog itself. Indeed, hyperlinks are primarily intertextual, connecting web pages rather than blog users. However, hyperlinks have a social dimension and may indicate what the blog is perceived to be "good for" (Beaulieu 2005, 183), both through the hyperlink's point of reference and its position within the blog. Hyperlinks may be found both on the sidebar of the blog homepage and within individual entries. Links on the homepage are deemed more significant due to their permanent presence (once individual posts are archived, they disappear from view) and their function as identifying the social network to which a blogger belongs (Nilsson 2007, 8). They are the focus of analysis here. In addition, the distinction Herring, Scheidt, et al. (2004) make between personal blogs and knowledge logs suggests a contrast between hyperlinks that emphasize sources of information (an online form of annotation), and those that promote a user (through their own personal blogs). Examples of both types are given below:

> After some discussion it is decided to do a Tru-Cut <u>biopsy</u>.
>   Kelly (May 11, 2006)

> Please, I implore you, even if you are a complete stranger or a lurker, please in the spirit of Christmas, reach out and give <u>Minerva</u> some love.
>   Jeanette (December 23, 2006)

The links in each blog were analyzed for their point of reference, and the results summarized in Table 4. These results prompt several observations. First, women's blogs contain more hyperlinks than the men's. Superficially, the high number of links might have some alignment with the

TABLE 4. Average number of sidebar hyperlinks per blog (cancer blogs)

	Information	Personal blog	Total
Male blogger	3	3	6
Female blogger	3.9	8.3	12.6
Total	6.9	11.3	18.6

theoretical description of women's writing as open-ended (Cixous 1989), as the greater number of hyperlinks provides more points of navigation beyond the text for the reader. However, this fails to explain the function of the links within this particular context, or what the blog is being deemed "good for." On closer examination, it is notable that the women's homepages contain more than double the number of links to personal blogs on average than do the men's. It would seem that the women use these links to identify themselves within a community of personal bloggers to a greater extent than do the men, presenting their blogs as personal writing rather than a source of medical knowledge, for instance. Moreover, the women's cancer blogs were more frequently linked *to* from other personal blogs than were the cancer blogs written by men. Calculated on the basis of searches taken from Technorati, on average, 133 blogs linked to each of the women's blogs, while 61 blogs linked to each of the men's. The hypertextual profile of the blog sidebars thus presents a clear picture of women's cancer blogs that align themselves with personal blogs, emphasizing their densely connected positions within a network of users.

Evaluation and Story Genres: Reflective Anecdotes

The interactive nature of blogging is not limited to its digital resources—it also influences the linguistic choices made by narrators. The narrative framework employed to explore this here is that developed by Labov (1972, 1997), with a special interest in evaluation devices. According to Labov, evaluation is the resource a speaker uses to make her or his narrative "tellable," vivid, and of perceived relevance to their audience. Although not criterial to narrative, evaluation serves important structural, semantic, and interpersonal functions. The identification of the evaluative highpoint, usually coinciding with "the most reportable event," both demarcates the transition between Complication and Resolution and functions to engage the audience, warding off the withering question, "so what?" (Labov 1972, 366). As such, the evaluation may be used to ascertain the structural profile of personal stories in this context, and one means by which the relationship between audience and blogger is managed.

Previous research has indicated that men and women use evaluation in their stories in differing ways (Eggins and Slade 1997): women use more evaluation devices than men, in line with a more affective style of storytelling. An analysis of the evaluation in the blogs supports this trend. For both cancer and travel blogs, the women used more evaluative devices than men, with the cancer blogs being slightly more densely evaluated than the travel blogs (summarized in Table 5). The distribution and function of the evaluation devices is of particular interest here. Labov predicted that evaluation would typically cluster at the climactic high point of a fully formed narrative, but it could also be dispersed throughout the narrative (1972, 369). As might be expected, the cancer blogs by both women and men contained a wealth of evaluation devices, but these are distributed in a complex manner, not concentrated around a single turning point in the narrative sequence that marks a definitive move toward closure. A partial explanation for this is that although cancer blogs certainly contain stories of personal experience, they are much lengthier and more complex than the minimal narratives considered by Labov. Even while narratives of illness embrace notions of mortality, they deal with a range of experiences, many of which do not offer the teleological release of resolution or closure realized by a narrative climax and resolution.

A fuller analysis draws on Martin and Plum's (1997) typology of story genres. They position the classic Labovian model as one of four story genres, which also include Anecdotes and Recounts. These story genres are categorized pragmatically (according to their social purpose) and structurally (dependent on the position of evaluation in the narrative

TABLE 5. Average number of evaluative devices per one hundred words

	Travel blogs	Cancer blogs
Male blogger	5.3	5.5
Female blogger	6.4	6.9

sequence). Thus Recounts are a temporal sequence of events where the evaluation is less prevalent and ongoing rather than found in a concentrated climax (Eggins and Slade 1997, 269). A typical example is as follows, with evaluation underlined for ease of reference:

> The chemo is done for today. I've had fluids, anti-nausea medication and the chemo drugs and now I'm home. The whole process took about 4.5 hours, and <u>the worst part was the needle stick into my port</u>. With the exception of one little scream when that happened, <u>I think I was a pretty good patient</u>. I have a private room with a private bathroom and my own TV. Tracey stayed with me the whole time and my mom came by too. I even had a visit from Larry Shyatt, one of the UF basketball coaches and player David Lee.
> Jackie (January 21, 2005)

In contrast, Anecdotes are stories that report a remarkable event, characterized by an evaluative punch line.

> Then I was subjected again to the blue STIRRUPS where I had another color Doppler ultrasound. There is a large flat panel color screen right over your head and you can see what the doctor sees. Last time I had this procedure there were several red clusters all over my prostate that indicated the blood flow that was feeding the cancer. <u>This time NADA!!! I can tell you that it was a powerful image for me. NADA cancer!</u>
> Dan (March 27, 2006)

I suggest that rather than forming a unified narrative that follows a single teleological progression, the blog posts contain a myriad of Recounts and Anecdotes that capture the author's fluctuating experiences of cancer interwoven with his or her everyday life. Both women and men used a range of story genres in their cancer blogs. However, men tended to use more Recounts, while women made greater use of Anecdotes. The difference in the use of story genres is important, for the function of Anecdotes is to generate a shared affectual response to an event, leading to solidarity between narrator and audience (Martin and Plum 1997, 310) while the emphasis of a Recount is simply the retelling of events. The women's greater use of Anecdotes hints at a more affective style of storytelling, in line with their overall greater use of evaluation and tendency to promote solidarity through online interaction.

The material marked out as "tellable" reinforces this gendered difference. Although not exclusively so, the men tended to use evaluation in a dispersed way to describe events, whereas the women often used evaluation to highlight an emotional response or to reveal their internal thought processes. The contrast between a masculine focus on events and feminine self-disclosure is demonstrated in the following extracts where the narrators describe getting their initial diagnosis:

JIM'S DIAGNOSIS
1. I was diagnosed with prostate cancer on the Friday before Memorial Day, 2004.
2. This was completely unexpected and has turned my life upside down.
3. The whole affair started when my doctor referred me to a local urologist because my PSA blood test was slightly above normal (4.9).
4. I got another blood test a few weeks later that came back 6.6.
5. Next was a prostate biopsy that took 20 minutes and was not very comfortable.
6. I found out the bad news three days later.
7. Cancer detected on both sides of my prostate with a Gleason level of 7.
8. That scale indicates the cancer is growing and active and needs to be dealt with quickly.
   Jim, (June 28, 2004)

The male narrator, Jim, evaluates the external events such as the diagnosis (line 2): "This was completely unexpected"; treatment (line 5): "a prostate biopsy that . . . was not very comfortable"; and cancer itself: "the cancer is growing and active"; but he does not then provide any internalized reaction to these events other than that these have "turned my life upside down," locating the impact of the illness externally on "my life" rather than introspectively on him.

The women's accounts tend to be different, with evaluation that highlights both their emotions and thought processes. An eloquent example of this is found in the writing of Sylvie Fortin. The full account of her initial diagnosis is lengthy (1,487 words). I include here a small extract from what she describes as the "internal dialogue" that occurred during her diagnosis:

SYLVIE'S DIAGNOSIS

Modified Scarff Bloom Richardson Grade: 3/3 with a Total Score of 8/9

OK, this doesn't sound good at all. So, let me understand this correctly. You're saying that out of all the types of breast cancers, mine is the worst it can get? I have to look this up when I get home to see what this really means. (*Please tell me this didn't spread to my lymph nodes*)

(update: I did look it up when I got home. It means I have a 50% chance of surviving another 5 years.)

Lymphatic/Vascular Invasion: Extensive

Oh crap! It spread to my lymph nodes! Oh my god, oh my god, oh my god! OK, now what? What does this mean? Does this mean I'm going to die? Is that what this means? (*Please tell me you can fix me!*)
Sylvie (October 20, 2006; underlining
and italics in the original)

The evaluation in this example is extensive, again including intensifiers (repetition, ritual utterances, exaggerated quantifiers) and comparators (superlatives, negatives, questions, modals). What is significant is the way that these dramatize Sylvie's internal reaction to the diagnosis, juxtaposing the official terminology with her attempts to understand what is being said and her hope that the medical profession will be able to treat her, graphically intensified by her use of bold font, italics, and parentheses. The focus is not on the event itself but rather on Sylvie's attempt to come to terms with the diagnosis.

The women's use of evaluation is not limited to highlighting remarkable events but also characterizes further stretches of reflective commentary that are interwoven with their narratives. I give typical examples of these evaluative passages below, indicating evaluation through underlining:

Another recent conversation with another person. . . . In a reference to a male worker in a workplace—"He chases after anything with breasts." Granted, I found this to be a comment that I have heard in various forms over the years. This time when I heard it, I couldn't help but take note. It was the criteria and the plural; breasts. Once again I found myself mulling over the role a woman's breasts (yep, there is that plural again) play in our society. Yes, I have always been aware of this, but now it is taking on a much different slant as I [sic] my unilateral mastectomy is approaching a week from today.

Jeanette (May 30, 2005)

This, my dears, is not a life. This is a drudge, a waste of energy. I am not a wonderful, caring, lovely, all encompassing mother with my arms open wide for my darling babies, I am a ghost, a bald spectre who is barely moving around the rooms, whose path barely disturbs the flow of air.

Minerva (February 14, 2007)

His words shattered my confidence and belief in my own ability to live forever. In a single moment, my life flashed in front of me, my plans for the future were called into question, and the happiness I had begun my day with was suddenly and completely overshadowed by these terrifying words.

Sylvie (August 9, 2006)

The women's reflections are rich in evaluative devices, particularly the subtype described by Labov as comparators. These are characterized by modality, negation, metaphor, questions, superlative, and comparative forms and function by comparing present events "with events which might have happened but did not" (1972, 381). The implicitly dual nature of comparators makes them an apt device for narrating the fragmentation of self undergone by those experiencing severe illness. The change in perspective articulated by Jeanette and despairing frustration of Minerva seems typical of the illness narrative as a genre described by Frank, where the author is dislocated from the illusions of their previous "normal experience" and instead forced to recognize their own lack (1994, 15). What is significant about these passages is that they do not readily conform to the

heuristic typology set out by Martin and Plum (1997), nor do they occur at all in the blogs written by men in this sample.

What emerges from these women's stories is a distinctive subgenre I am calling the Reflective Anecdote. As the name suggests, this is most closely related to Martin and Plum's Anecdote, for the evaluation is typically located following the report of a narrative event and may be tied cohesively to it. In the earlier examples, this is signaled by the cataphoric references (italicized): "I found *this* to be a comment" (Jeanette), "*This*, my dears, is not a life" (Minerva). However, the excess of evaluation extends far beyond the evaluative punctuation described by Martin and Plum, and the reflective passages are marked by a deictic shift from the past event to the present time of narration: "*now* it is taking on a much different slant" (Jeanette), "and *now*, I face an uncertain and frightening future" (Sylvie). In narrative terms, the evaluation signals that the raison d'être of the story lies not so much in the reported events but with the act of narration itself. These Anecdotes are thus reflective both in their content (emphasizing introspection), in their pivotal structure (interfacing between events and evaluative narration), and their linguistic concentration of comparators, all of which illustrate the liminal boundaries of the narrator's past, present, and future in critical flux (Rimmon-Kenan 2002, 20).

It remains to explain why Reflective Anecdotes are absent from the cancer blogs written by men. Far from being dismissed in derogatory terms as a feminine digression, Reflective Anecdotes perform an important social purpose. Minerva explains the motivation behind her writing as follows:

> So why am I going on about this? It isn't, surprisingly to those who know me, (*grin*), a cry for attention but I want you, you on the other side of this fence to understand what it is like if you have someone going through this and where their anger and frustration comes from.
>
> Minerva (February 16, 2007)

The point of the Reflective Anecdote is thus to provide emotional education for the audience. Unsurprisingly, the emphasis on emotional disclosure is similar to that of Anecdotes generally, which are told so as to share an affectual response. While it is certainly not the case that Anecdotes are a gender-specific genre, emotional solidarity especially as constructed

through self-disclosure has been found typical of conversational stories told between women friends and rare in all-male talk (Coates 2003). The absence of self-disclosure from the men's blogs might then be interpreted as means of reinforcing hegemonic masculinity. As Coates writes, in men's stories, emotional vulnerability is usually concealed behind what she describes as the "masculine mask of silence," a discourse strategy that promotes a view of conventional masculinity as being "tough" and "achievement focused" (2003, 75). It is too strong to state that men do not self disclose at all in their narratives of illness. Nonetheless, in this sample the absence of Reflective Anecdotes, primary use of Recounts and the overall lesser use of evaluation by the men combined together point to gendered discourse styles being carried over into online personal storytelling. As one of the male bloggers puts it, in a blog post tellingly headed by an image of a disintegrating mask:

> Men suffering PCa do not speak up.
> Men suffering PCa remain silent.
> Men suffering PCa hide their disease.
> . . .
> Hundreds of thousands of men die every year from Prostate Cancer.
> In silence.
> Manuel (December 27, 2005)

Conclusion

In summary, it seems that gender does make an important difference to the ways people narrate their experiences of illness in personal blogs. In this study, the women's cancer blogs were characterized by a larger number of comments, with more hyperlinks to and from the blog than were the men's. The greater engagement between the women bloggers and their audience was also manifest in the narrative features. Women employed more evaluation than men, used this to foreground emotional response, and created an emergent story genre of Reflective Anecdotes used to promote solidarity through affective self-disclosure. In contrast, the men favored Recounts, emphasized events, and did not use any Reflective Anecdotes in this sample. Contrary to findings from corpus-based studies that found little evidence of gender difference in writing on blogs

(Herring and Paolillo 2006), this study suggests that women and men tell online narratives of illness in subtly contrasting ways. The question of gender difference in storytelling still remains open and will require further empirical analysis from a range of perspectives yet to be covered.

Despite its prominent use here by women, the Reflective Anecdote should not be understood as a feminine form. Usage alone cannot form the basis of a definitive relationship between gender and genre. Indeed, I would stress that the relationship between gender and *any* narrative feature cannot be essentialist or universal. Rather, my argument is that offline values and communicative styles that support gendered behavior in this case contribute to the production of the Reflective Anecdote. The role of self-disclosure and collaboratively sharing personal experience as a means of sustaining hegemonic femininity (and not masculinity) is critical and aligns readily with both the personal, emotive subject matter of these narratives and a medium that facilitates connection with others online. Thus, the Reflective Anecdotes as they appear in this data are shaped by the synergy of offline gendered behavior, the nature of illness narratives, and the interactive features of the blog. Whether this will reinforce or challenge subsequent patterns of storytelling in the blogosphere remains to be seen. What is clear is that digital media matters a great deal in the emergence of new narrative genres, and that as we seek to understand this, our analysis cannot be divorced from content or wider contextual factors such as gender.

Notes

1. The blogs in this sample are freely available within the public domain. Blogger's names or pseudonyms have been retained as a reflection of their authorship. Where possible, permission to reproduce excerpts from the blogs has been sought.

2. The analysis of the comments cannot account for the profile of the audience who "lurk," that is, who read the blog (even regularly) but do not leave any comment.

References

Beaulieu, Anne. 2005. "Sociable Hyperlinks: An Ethnographic Approach to Connectivity." In *Virtual Methods: Issues in Social Research on the Internet*, ed. Christine Hine, 183–98. Oxford: Berg Publishers.

Bowen, Deborah S. 2004. *Towards an E-criture Feminine: Woolf, DuPlessis, Cixous and the Emerging Discursive Tradition in Women's Online Diaries*. Ann Arbor: University of Michigan Press.

Cixous, Hélène. 1989. "Sorties: Out and Out: Attacks/Ways Out/Forays." In *The Feminist Reader: Essays in Gender and the Politics of Literary Criticism*, ed. Catherine Belsey and Jane Moore, 101–16. London: Macmillan.

Coates, Jennifer. 1996. *Women Talk*. Oxford: Blackwell.

———. 2003. *Men Talk*. Oxford: Blackwell.

Eggins, Suzanne, and Diana Slade. 1997. *Analysing Casual Conversation*. London: Cassell.

Frank, Arthur W. 1994. "Reclaiming an Orphan Genre: The First-Person Narrative of Illness. *Literature and Medicine* 13, no. 1:1–21.

Herring, Susan C., Inna Kouper, Lois Ann Scheidt, and Elijah L. Wright. 2004. "Women and Children Last: The Discursive Construction of Weblogs." In *Into the Blogosphere: Rhetoric, Community, and Culture of Weblogs*, ed. Laura J. Gurak, Smiljana Antonijevic, Laurie Johnson, Clancy Ratliff, and Jessica Reyman. Available at http://blog.lib.umn.edu/blogosphere/women_and_children.html (accessed September 24, 2007).

Herring, Susan C., and John C. Paolillo. 2006. "Gender and Genre Variation in Weblogs." *Journal of Sociolinguistics* 10, no. 4:439–59.

Herring, Susan C., Lois Ann Scheidt, Sabrina Bonus, and Elijah Wright. 2004. "Bridging the Gap: A Genre Analysis of Weblogs." In *Proceedings of the 37th Hawai'i International Conference on System Sciences*. Los Alamitos CA: IEEE Computer Society Press.

Labov, William. 1972. *Language in the Inner City*. Philadelphia: University of Pennsylvania Press.

———. 1997. "Some Further Steps in Narrative Analysis." *Journal of Narrative and Life History* 7, nos. 1–4:395–415.

Lanser, Susan. 1986. "Toward a Feminist Narratology." *Style* 20, no. 3:341–63.

Martin, Jim, and Gunther A. Plum. 1997. "Construing Experience: Some Story Genres." *Journal of Narrative and Life History* 7, nos. 1–4:299–308.

McLellan, Faith. 1997. "'A Whole Other Story': The Electronic Narrative of Illness." *Literature and Medicine* 16, no. 1:88–107.

Nilsson, Stephanie. 2007. "The Function of Language to Facilitate and Maintain Social Networks in Research Weblogs." D-essay, Umeå University. Available at http://www.eng.umu.se/stephanie/web/LanguageBlogs.pdf (accessed January 7, 2011).

Nowson, Scott, and Jon Oberlander. 2006. "Identity and Openness in Personal Blogs." Conference paper presented at the AAAI Spring Symposium, Computational Approaches to Analyzing Weblogs, Stanford University.

Rimmon-Kenan, Shlomith. 2002. "The Story of 'I': Illness and Narrative Identity." *Narrative* 10, no. 1:9–27.

Ryan, Marie-Laure. 2006. *Avatars of Story*. Minneapolis: University of Minnesota Press.

Sorapure, Madeleine. 2003. "Screening Moments, Scrolling Lives: Diary Writing on the Web." *Biography* 26, no. 1:1–23.

Walker, Jill. 2003. "Fiction and Interaction: How Clicking a Mouse Can Make You Part of a Fictional World." D. Art. thesis, University of Bergen.

13 Using the Force

LEGO Star Wars: The Video Game, *Intertextuality, Narrative, and Play*

JAMES NEWMAN AND IAIN SIMONS

Even though *Star Wars* did not become a video game until 1983, we contend that it was a richly playable experience from its very first exposure to the public. The popular assumption of the *Star Wars* canon as one primarily seeded by a series of six films is one that is ripe for challenge. *Star Wars*, in its broadest sense is, and always has been, richly transmedial. Collectible cards, licensed novels, themed LEGO sets, and the "Expanded Universe" of characters and stories reach out, extend, and sometimes run parallel to the purely cinematic experience of *Star Wars*. These are not trivial additions to cinematic "primary texts." Rather, these extrafilmic texts are vital parts of the storytelling system adding weight, richness, depth, and dimension to the resources of the canon. While action figures, merchandising, and the "Expanded Universe" are comparatively well documented in writings on *Star Wars* (e.g., Kapell and Lawrence 2006; Brooker 2002), video games have been largely neglected within scholarly discussions of transmedia storytelling.

From their first appearance in the arcades to the current raft of home console titles, *Star Wars* video games have offered opportunities to play as and with different characters, swapping between the Rebellion in *X-Wing* or the Empire in *Tie-Fighter* and *Dark Forces*, for instance. However, for all their playfulness, *Star Wars* video games usually operate within the strict bounds of the canon (or the "Expanded Universe" as with *Shadow of the Empire*). Raph Koster, developer of the *Star Wars Galaxies* online role-playing game, perhaps suggests one reason (see Jenkins 2007). *Star Wars* is so beloved by its fans that possess an intimate knowledge of its minutiae that it might be reasonably assumed that they would be critical of any deviation from canonically sanctioned authenticity.

However, in our case study of the LEGO *Star Wars* video game series, we see levels of canonical abandon that allow characters from the different film episodes to coexist on screen. Moreover, we witness the dissolution of the central narrative tenet of good versus evil as Jedi and Sith characters are forced to cooperate to overcome the series of puzzles that compose the gameplay. Here, we encounter a video game that is infused with the playful spirit of LEGO and, as such, is not simply a video game of a film but rather a video game that exists in the continuum of *Star Wars* toys. It is not that the LEGO *Star Wars* video games present the first chance to remix the elements of this much loved saga, as action figures and plastic bricks have long facilitated this. Rather, through their structure and status as "official" texts, the video games effectively sanction these inventions. However, what makes the LEGO *Star Wars* video games so fascinating as texts is that while they offer freedom far beyond that of other *Star Wars* video games, their playfulness and inventiveness remains located within carefully policed boundaries. Their virtual world is far from a *Star Wars* sandpit where anything goes, and like any (video) game, their rules, restrictions, and limitations still contain the possibilities and govern what is permissible. By exploring the development processes of the LEGO *Star Wars* teams and their engagements with Lucasfilm, we gain a glimpse of the unexpected freedoms offered the games' designers in working with the otherwise fiercely protected *Star Wars* canon (see Jenkins 1992).

Transmediality

In this chapter, we wish to explore the concept of transmedia storytelling as outlined by Henry Jenkins (e.g., 2003, 2004, 2006, 2007) with reference to a set of specific *Star Wars* games by examining their surfaces and boundaries and considering their place and function within the *Star Wars* canon and universe. *Star Wars* and its franchised range of coordinated media assets have always been beacons of transmediality. As Jenkins notes, "We might also see performance taking centre stage in the release of action figures which encourage children to construct their own stories about the fictional characters or costumes and role playing games which invite us to immerse ourselves in the world of the fiction. In the case of *Star Wars*, the Boba Fett action figure generated consumer interest in a character that had otherwise played a small role in the series, creating pressure for giving that character a larger plot function in future stories" (2007).

Transmediality and *transmedia storytelling* are voguish yet slippery terms whose contours shift depending on the position one adopts. Here, we consider transmedia storytelling as the process by which a narrative might be dispersed throughout multiple, differentiated but contingent spaces such that, according to Jenkins (2007) there is no singular "ur text" in which resides all of the information required to fully know or make sense of the totality of the narrative universe. This broad concept finds a number of names in the work of different theorists. Ito's discussion of the Yugioh and Pokémon phenomena describes the way in which "linking content in multiple media forms such as video games, card games, television, film, manga books, toys, and household objects, Pokemon created a new kind of citational network that has come to be called a 'media mix'" (2005, 4). Similarly, Hanson offers "screen bleed" to describe "a modern narrative condition where fictive worlds extend into multiple media and moving image formats" (2003, 47). In addition to this terminological confusion, we might also be tempted to simply deride the term *transmediality* as an unnecessary neologism that seeks to replace rather less glamorous terms such as *multimedia, entertainment supersystem* (Kinder 1991), or perhaps even *horizontal integration*. Certainly, with regard to this latter concept, we would do well to remember that it is precisely because of the shifts in the industries and institutions of contemporary media that the array of media channels through which popular narratives might be distributed exists at all. In the pragmatic hands of the rights holder, transmediality is principally a complex and potentially lucrative set of intellectual property agreements and transactions.

We should note that there is a clear financial advantage to media organizations in spreading their message across a wide range of media. Offering audiences a range (if not a choice) of places and opportunities to engage with the narrative universe and, in the process, consume more and more voraciously, as they search for the complete story through their mobile phones, online, and in their inboxes, makes obvious economic sense. However, there is more to transmedia storytelling than just the exploitation of intellectual property. Similarly, what we are interested in here is more than multimedia per se. Without doubt, and in keeping with multimedia texts and products, the transmedia narrative is inherently multimodal in that it is one that is deliberately and self-consciously distributed throughout a system of channels that each offer parts of a whole. Perhaps more importantly, however, the decentralized mode of storytelling that Jenkins documents as characteristic of the contemporary media environment is one in which each channel of communication may contribute something to the telling of the story or the ability of the audience to engage with it as the particular affordances of the medium are harnessed. It is this characteristic of transmediality that most clearly separates it from "multimediality" in which a single, self-contained text might comprise a variety of different elements, including audio, still and moving images, and text. Transmedial texts may be multimedia texts, but it is their relationship to other texts in a wider system of storytelling that sets them apart.

Dena identifies a situation in which "content can be repurposed, adapted and stretched across platforms. A story can start in one medium and finish in another" (2007, 2). Dena's observation is interesting and apparently has much in common with transmediality. However, it differs in that there is a suggestion that the narrative may not merely exist or flow across multiple media forms but that it also may be told in a sequential manner with consecutive sequences delivered via different forms. Our position here is more closely aligned with Jenkins's, in that while the various texts within the storytelling system are distinctive and bring specific opportunities as a consequence of the affordances of the medium, each is capable of standing alone. Each video game, television program, LEGO brick, or action figure is located within the context of the totality of texts in the storytelling system and gains something from this situation and proximity; each has a self-contained set of meanings and does not rely on other materials in the system to bestow meaning upon it. Elsewhere (e.g., Dena 2006), this sequential multimodality is termed "transfiction" to differentiate it from Jenkins's system. "In transfiction . . . the story is dependent on all the pieces on each medium, device or site to be read/experienced for it to be understood. Basically, no single segment will be sufficient" (Dena 2006). The transmedial storytelling system, in our (and Jenkins's) conceptualization, is one in which texts are multiple and contingent but not reliant or dependent on one another for continuity of meaning. As such, slavish recreation of the canonical narrative is not inevitable. As Jenkins says, "The *Star Wars* game may not simply retell the story of *Star Wars*, but it doesn't have to in order to enrich or expand our experience of the *Star Wars* saga. We already know the story before we even buy the game and would be frustrated if all it offered us was a regurgitation of the original film experience. Rather, the *Star Wars* game exists in dialogue with the films, conveying new narrative experiences through its creative manipulation of environmental details" (2004, 124).

Playing with *Star Wars*

In this chapter, we are specifically concerned with three recent *Star Wars* video games that exemplify transmedial storytelling at its most powerful and playful. The LEGO *Star Wars* (LSW) series of video games, developed by UK developer Traveller's Tales and published by family games specialist TT Games publishing have been remarkably successful both critically and commercially—finding audiences well beyond the "young players" at which they target their work (each of the games is rated as suitable for ages three and up in accordance with Pan European Game Information, or PEGI).[1] The games cast the player within a *Star Wars* built entirely from LEGO, and invite the player to explore the narrative of the film by manipulating the bricks and the environments and happenings that they model with audacious abandon. The game is designed to enable parents and children to play together, a focused sociality specifically encouraged through a multiplayer experience.

The first game, LSW: *The Video Game*, was released in 2005, just prior to the much anticipated release of *Revenge of the Sith*, the last link in the *Star Wars* chain. Players who purchased LSW: *The Video Game* were privileged to play the full denouement of Anakin's journey to the Dark Side. That such an unveiling would be allowed to happen in a video game speaks volumes of director George Lucas's attitude toward this "new" media form.[2] A sequel to this game was released a year later, LSW: *The Original Trilogy*, which developed the aesthetic and gameplay styles of the first game and applied them to *Episodes IV–VI* of the *Star Wars* saga. LSW: *The Complete Saga* was released in 2007 and combines the two previous titles with some new levels and modes.

LEGO *Star Wars: The Video Game* is not a single brand but a compound formed from a number of separate elements. LEGO is a play system, comprising plastic bricks. *Star Wars* is a series of films created by George Lucas. LEGO *Star Wars* is a subset of the LEGO play world, featuring LEGO characters and vehicles that recreate those featured in the *Star Wars* films. LEGO *Star Wars: The Video Game* is a further, distinct conceptual leap. Unlike Dena's (2006) sequential transfiction, which requires that each part be engaged with and decoded, the transmedial experience of *LSW* does not demand, but is certainly enriched when, the complex sum of its parts are understood by its player(s). Importantly, this extends beyond intimate awareness of the details of the canon to include knowledge of the qualities and characteristics of the media through which the constituent elements are delivered. Not least of these tacit understandings is the reverence in which *Star Wars* is held by fans of a certain age. *Star Wars* and the introduction to it has become an important rite of passage for fathers and sons (Brooker 2002). Like the passing down of precious books or toys, the handing of the baton (lightsaber?) down to the child is a moment loaded with a nostalgic gravitas.

Playing with LEGO . . . with *Star Wars* . . . with Video Games . . . with a Child

Throughout the course of our research, we observed and interviewed a number of parents and their children playing the various *LSW* games. Here, we will focus on the responses of one specific familial pair of players: a father (age thirty-three) and his son (three). The father held the original (*Episodes IV*, *V*, and *VI*) films as significant markers of a particular moment in his childhood. In order to ensure the integrity of these valuable cultural artifacts, he was anxious that his son have the best possible introduction to the canon: "The first watching together of *Star Wars* should be something boys remember. Like their first kiss." Almost immediately following an enthusiastic viewing of the original trilogy, the universe exploded into being a place to play. Even thirty years after the original film, toy lightsabers are still regular stock in toy shops, and one was duly purchased. A gift of some *LSW* spaceships with associated minifigures provided a new form within which the story could be replayed. The *LSW* video game was introduced shortly after that, providing the child's first video game experience.

Utilizing a "drop-in, drop-out" multiplayer mechanic, with which a player can enter or leave the game at any time without disadvantaging the other or interrupting the action, *LSW* makes cooperative play easy. It is worth noting that cooperation is not commonplace in video game design, and multiplayer experiences usually revolve around competitive play in which players are cast in a combative relationship and in which success typically comes at the expense of another's failure. Unusually, there are numerous sections and sequences in the games that not only benefit from collaborative play but demand it. For the parent/child player pairs in our research, this emphasis on teamwork opened up a (virtual) environment ideally suited to the nurturing, supportive parental role. As such, the *Star Wars* legacy was handed down from father to son in a manner that allowed parents to hold the hand of their child as they guided them. The impact of this collaboration was particularly keenly felt by those (older) players well versed in the cultures and conventions of video gaming, for whom competition was the norm. As one player put it: "Having played the game myself a few years ago, it's only when re-playing it with [my son] that it really shines . . . working together on puzzles, showing, encouraging and helping him to do stuff were things I hadn't really appreciated were in the game before."

The *LSW* games make some radical design decisions, perhaps the most audacious of which was to remove the possibility of "death" from the game. From the earliest days of video games, players have learned that their opportunities for interactive engagement are portioned out in a series of attempts that are coded as "lives" that are lost as the onscreen character plunges to its electronic death only to be miraculously reborn, often at the beginning of the level or sequence. The absence of a finite number of "lives" and the impossibility of the player(s)' onscreen death has a great impact on the way the game plays out, in that it is considerably less fractured than a typical gaming experience that is punctuated by the series of deaths and rebirths. Moreover, and perhaps of even greater consequence, the mechanic means that there is no enforced game-over. Upon running out of health, the player explodes into a haze of LEGO studs, before reforming moments later to continue from the same point. While this kind of failure is something to be avoided, the player is not explicitly punished, as they can continue their journey from the precise point in the game world at which they broke apart and may be infinitely rebuilt (just like their real-world, plastic brick counterparts). According to Jonathan Smith, development director of TT Games (formally Giant Entertainment) who oversaw the LEGO *Star Wars* video games, "It came quite specifically from learning that children play best in the real world when they feel safe. Generally speaking, a game designer's orientation is toward putting the player in jeopardy—which is a driver of challenge and excitement. But from a LEGO perspective it makes you wonder if there's an alternative that can still be exciting, without necessarily being dangerous."[3]

This game mechanic clearly assists the player in moving through the gameworld but also has the effect of retaining the integrity of the characters and narrative. To remain within canon, Han and Luke surely cannot die. Interestingly, in our study, we noted that the radical nature of this design decision was felt only by those sufficiently experienced in gaming. For younger players less aware or even unaware of the prevalence of finite lives and the "Game Over" message, this infinitely continuous play was understood not as liberating but as the norm. One father explained: "It was when we came to play other games that there were problems. He couldn't understand why Mario was lying down and not moving. Suddenly being confronted with 'game over' was at first crushingly brutal—and frankly, difficult for a parent to explain."

The child's understanding and familiarity with both the three "original trilogy" movies and the LEGO toys allowed him to invest in the game and the *Star Wars* story with an extraordinary enthusiasm. However, by alighting on the LSW video game series as the point of entry into video gaming, we find the young boy's understanding and appreciation of the form is complicated by the radical design decisions and modes of play.

LSW: *The Video Game* and its sequels divide each of the three films of their respective trilogies into six chapters. These are themselves designed to be played in two explicitly different modes, each offering very different ways of engaging with the *Star Wars* world (additionally, the most recent title, LSW: *The Complete Saga* offers a third mode as we will see).

Story Mode

In the very first play through of a chapter of the games, the player is confined to "Story Mode." Within Story Mode, the player(s) make their way through the *Star Wars* stage, swapping characters, reconfiguring scenes, and traveling through a beautifully rendered LEGO mise-en-scène. Story Mode is concerned with a broad replication of the narrative of the films. The core exposition of the story is delivered principally through non-playable sections of the game. Most explicitly, each chapter is introduced by the familiar, anticipation-building "crawl text" featured in the movies, which roots them firmly in the storybook tradition. Following this text, further exposition is delivered by cut-scenes that bookend the action (and occasionally interrupt it). In these witty reductions of the story, this epic saga is reduced to its absolute minimum component beats. Much knowing comedy is generated from moments of intense, operatic emotion being played out by small yellow LEGO figures with severely limited facial expressions.

Freeplay Mode

Having played through a chapter in Story Mode, the game unlocks a new option—"Freeplay." Here, players are at liberty to swap and change between multiple characters—not necessarily those that are scenically or canonically "correct." Importantly, in Freeplay Mode, LSW video games are more closely allied with LEGO *Star Wars* bricks than with the filmic texts. The playful subversions that arise from mixing and matching characters and scenes are transferred from the bedroom floor to the screen. Thus, two Darth Vaders might find themselves allied in assisting Yoda, or the Emperor might assist Luke in his journey back home on Tatooine. The simultaneous onscreen appearance of multiple "instances" of the same character is a staple of video game genres such as the beat-'em-up in which two or more functionally identical characters, differentiated only by the color or design of their costumes, battle against one another with no sense of schizophrenia or identity crisis. For those already immersed within the aesthetic and representational world of video games, the presence of two Darth Vaders presents no conceptual challenge. However, for younger players or video game non-acolytes, this potentially poses a challenge to the narrative integrity of this story. Yet, our participants and players did not appear to undergo any jolt or shock of disbelief. The answer is perhaps to be found in the qualities of LEGO itself and the configurability of the characters and minifigures. Although in Freeplay Mode, LSW video games might have their ludic roots in LEGO bricks; it is their ability to "authorize" these playful excursions from the canonical norms that separates them in the transmedial storytelling system.

Challenge Mode

LSW: *The Complete Saga* offers a third mode of play. In "Challenge Mode," players are required to perform specific tasks within a time limit, such as collecting 1,000 LEGO studs. In this mode, the individual abilities of characters and the specific locations in the *Star Wars* universe are deemphasized as they give way to types of play and objectives drawn from the canon of video gaming.

These three modes represent a spectrum of emphasis, beginning with Story Mode's commitment to the narrative origin, through to Challenge Mode's total emphasis on more recognizable gamelike systems. While still taking place within a recognizably *Star Wars* locale and featuring canonical characters, Challenge Mode reduces the relationship with the source narrative to one of providing a context for playing out simple challenges.[4] This subtle but declared rebalancing of the relationship between the source-text and the concern of the game design reveals new potential for the transmedial enjoyment of the experience. One might also read this shift of emphasis as a journey from the source-text toward a particular kind of LEGO-ness, as the trappings of the canon are gradually stripped away to reveal the pieces of a LEGO play-set, inviting us to reconfigure it.

This literal reconfiguration of the world as so many constituent bricks is made explicit in the central "hub" area of the game, the Cantina/Dexter's Diner. This area functions as an orientation area for the player, where he or she can rehearse moves and controls, purchase items from the "bar," and have full permission to explore the boundaries of what an LSW video game world is. The Cantina declares the intent of the designers' treatment of the canon with startling clarity. Here, characters who would never meet within the narrative collide with each other, items collected within chapters can be assembled into new vehicles, and, most playfully, entirely new characters can be created from constituent parts. The "Bacta tank" offers the player the ability to swap the different elements of the minifigure characters to playfully create new ones. This exploding of characters into constituent elements is referenced as a visual joke within both *Episodes II* and *V* of the movie trilogy. In *Episode V*, C-3PO finds himself disassembled by a team of Ugnaughts, only to be reconstructed later on with his head facing the wrong way. Yet more playfully, *Episode II* sees Threepio broken into two and remade as parts of the evil Droid army. Fighting against the Rebels and against his will, he appears onscreen both as the body to a clone trooper head and the reluctant head atop a Droid trooper body, profusely apologizing for the attacks his lower-half is carrying out against his friends and allies.

The video game is untroubled by shy reverence in its treatment of the *Star Wars* canon, having no difficulty conflating narrative elements for its own purposes, but the game takes no such liberties with the rendering of the brick components. LEGO itself is the most highly prized currency within this world. The LEGO models that populate it are reproduced with a fastidious continuity to their real-world counterparts, with complex vehicles and structures within the game world being animated and constructed from exactly the same constituent bricks as they would be in real LEGO. Utterly intoxicated by the near-infinite possibilities of the colored bricks, the game hammers its ideology home in a witty design joke. As Smith comments, "There's a moment in the videogame where we recreate a scene from *Episode II*, and the location is a clone factory designed for the production of cloned beings. In the game we recreate this environment—where in the movie there are tiny foetuses in glass jars, we have the irreducible 1x1 Lego stud. It's a stem cell, it can grow into anything."

This Is Not a Simulation

Jonathan Smith oversaw the development of the three games in the LSW series. The earliest stages of the creation of the game were concerned not with an understanding of any narrative universe but of LEGO itself. The apparent goal was simultaneously intuitively clear and rationally obtuse: to understand, codify, and thus be able to create at will LEGO-ness. Much of the early work that led to the project focused on answering that "simple" question: what is LEGO-ness? It was clear that becoming mired down in observational data and ontological doublespeak could easily become crippling to a creative project. Smith noted, "If you've had any kinds of dealings with a modern large institution, you can find that the challenges you face are often couched in a very heavily coded, internal language— people start to talk of brand values. Particularly the use of the word 'brand' comes with a whole set of interlocking terminology. We spent some time throwing those terms around, but of course ultimately you're only referencing one term to another term. There are only so many ways in which you can say 'fun' and 'quality'—and they don't necessarily progress you in terms of actually doing anything."

The design document to which all collaborators on a project refer can be an essential tool, much like the story bible employed in the development of long-term, character driven narrative projects. Having experimented with manifestos, commandments, and recommendations, the hope that a clear, reproducible formula would appear from the fog of research questions began to evaporate. In its place, however, came a richer articulation of the hallmarks, qualities, and traits of LEGO-ness. "You can analyse anything, break it down and then build it back up again," says Smith, "but the best criterion for us was to simply ask, is it LEGO?"

There is a set of clear conclusions that anyone with a passing affinity with the plastic bricks might assume when codifying its essence. Colorful, fun, creative . . . These specific qualities of LEGO-ness are rather more obvious than the more philosophical, cultural, or ethical qualities. Of course, there had been LEGO video games before, most notably *LEGO Island* (1997) and *LEGO Racers* (1999), both of which sold well and were held in high regard by Smith and his collaborators. The titles signposted some of the themes and qualities that the team were attempting to develop. This was a particular kind of freedom; a *permission* to play. Smith notes: "LEGO island was a place to play in and with. It wasn't LEGO rollercoaster, or LEGO amusement park—it was an island, to explore. On that island, lots of different things are going to happen."

Perhaps looking at non-LEGO licensed video games might offer some clues as to the nature of LEGO-ness? The notion of total freedom of player choice, instigated by *Elite* and most popularly exemplified by *Grand Theft Auto* is a clearly LEGO quality. Smith espouses a zen of LEGO: "Within the spectrum of videogames, we can categorise them all along a spectrum of more or less LEGO."

We see that the *Grand Theft Auto* series, with its freedoms, variety, and (most importantly) sense of discovery is an archetypal LEGO game. The endless customization of vehicles in racing game *Gran Turismo 4* is "highly LEGO" (the television campaign for that title specifically emphasized the sheer volume of possible configurations of cars as a key selling point). Importantly then, discovering LEGO-ness is not a quest to simulate playing with LEGO. Rather, it is a quest to translate the feelings, sensations, and ideologies of physical LEGO into something that might have meaning and resonance onscreen. Most importantly, to create an onscreen experience that young people might want to buy (into). With this objective, development reached a point of comfortable clarity, Smith recalls: "Everyone playing it enjoyed it and was happy, but we came to the realisation that there was no reason for anyone to buy it. We didn't have any connection with the audience. Someone said . . . well . . . *Star Wars*?"

Alone, LEGO was insufficient to engage the young audience, but coupled with the narrative universe of *Star Wars*, the possibilities of transmedial play were intoxicating. Smith is clear that it is only when the philosophical concerns of LEGO were fused with the "entertainment proposition" of the *Star Wars* frame that the project came to life: "When we went to Lucas at the start, their initial response was, well we're already doing *Star Wars* games. We had to emphasise the LEGO experience, just how special this is going to be. This isn't the game of the movie. This is the game where you play with the movie."

An End of Sorts . . .

Ultimately, what we see in the LSW video games is a clear example of the way in which the *Star Wars* universe continues its journey across a transmedial landscape. No longer can the canon be thought of as a series of films with allied multimedia extensions that support and reinforce the brand or that drive consumers toward the cinematic experience. Rather, we see a complex series of narratives and contexts laid out across a sprawling web of interconnected messages and channels, each adding to the audience's experiential opportunities and repertoire. In our exploration of the LSW video games, we have seen how their design, structure, and aesthetic encourage an engagement with the materials of *Star Wars* that renders them malleable resources for play. Indeed, LSW situates itself within a transmedial network. To assist in the collection of the various characters and vehicles in the game, a number of secret codes (sometimes known as "cheat codes" [see Consalvo 2007]) are available. However, as the printed instruction manual points out, while these codes may aid those lacking in the requisite skill to unlock the secrets for themselves, they are not given away lightly. Players are required to expend some effort in finding them in magazines or online, for instance. "Secret codes can be entered here. But you won't find these codes in the game—you'll need to search for them elsewhere!" (LSW 2007, 6).

This virtual Easter Egg hunt resonates strongly with Jenkins's (2003) observations on the ways in which transmediality is transforming the media consumption habits of a generation of audiences. "Younger consumers have become information hunters and gatherers, taking pleasure in tracking down character backgrounds and plot points and making connections between different texts within the same franchise," notes Jenkins

(2003). Indeed, the transmediality of the *lsw* video game world does not even end with the *Star Wars* universe however "Expanded" this may be. During a demonstration of *lsw: The Complete Saga* in 2007, Jonathan Smith disclosed one of the many secrets of the game. To an enthusiastic audience, he both revealed one of the new unlockable characters and pushed the transmedial and intertextual boundaries of the project into new frontiers. As a lovingly rendered LEGO Indiana Jones whip-cracked his way through *Episode IV*'s Cantina, the audience members were left to ponder a narrative that spanned and connected not just Lucas's *Star Wars* canon but his entire oeuvre.

Notes

1. Both Traveller's Tales and TT Games were acquired by Warner Bros Home Entertainment Group in November 2007 for in excess of £100 million. At the time, a *LEGO Batman* video game was in development. PEGI is a content-based age-ratings system for video games. See www.pegi.info.

The *LEGO Star Wars* games have sold over 12 million copies worldwide (http://www.gamasutra.com/php-bin/news_index.php?story=16158) and were awarded consistently high review scores (75–86 percent). See http://www.metacritic.com/search/process?sort=relevance&termType=all&ts=lego+star+wars&ty=0&x=0&y=0.

2. In 2008 LucasArts—the game development arm of Lucas's organization—produced *The Force Unleashed*, the first officially sanctioned new chapter in the *Star Wars* canon.

3. As part of our research project, we interviewed Jonathan Smith immediately before the release of the first *lsw* video game in 2005. All of the direct quotations from Smith in this chapter date from these interviews.

4. *lsw: The Complete Saga* also offers an "Arcade Challenge" mode, in which unlocked characters can fight one another within selectable canonical locations. Here the narrative trappings are wholly disregarded, and Luke can find himself locked in combat with Obi-Wan, or even himself.

References

Brooker, W. 2002. *Using the Force*. New York: Continuum.
Consalvo, M. 2007. *Cheating: Gaining Advantage in Videogames*. Cambridge MA: MIT Press.

Dena, C. 2006. "Writing Predictions for the Next Decade." *Cross-Media + Transmedia Entertainment*. Available at http://www.cross-mediaentertainment.com/index.php/2006/01/06/writing-predictions-%20for-the-next-decade/ (accessed December 1, 2007).

———. 2007. "Patterns in Cross-Media Interaction Design: It's Much More Than a URL . . . (Part 1)." *Cross-Media + Transmedia Entertainment*. Available at http://www.cross-mediaentertainment.com/index.php/2007/03/10/cross-media-interaction-design-cmid/ (accessed October 31, 2008).

Hanson, M. 2003. *The End of Celluloid: Film Futures in the Digital Age*. Hove: Rotovision.

Ito, M. 2005. "Intertextual Enterprises: Writing Alternative Places and Meanings in the Media Mixed Networks of Yugioh." In *E.T. Culture: Anthropology in Outerspaces*, ed. D. Battaglia, 180–99. Durham NC: Duke University Press.

Jenkins, H. 1992. *Textual Poachers*. London: Routledge.

———. 2003. "Transmedia Storytelling." *Technology Review*, January 15, 2003. Available at http://www.technologyreview.com/Biotech/13052/ (accessed November 3, 2007).

———. 2004. "Game Design as Narrative Architecture." In *First Person: New Media as Story Performance, and Game*, ed. N. Wardrip-Fruin and N. Harrigan, 118–30. Cambridge MA: MIT Press.

———. 2006. *Convergence Culture*. New York: New York University Press.

———. 2007. "Transmedia Storytelling 101." Available at http://www.henryjenkins.org/2007/03/transmedia_storytelling_101.html (accessed July 8, 2007).

Kapell, M., and J. Lawrence. 2006. *Finding the Force of the Star Wars Franchise Fans, Merchandise, and Critics*. New York: Peter Lang.

Kinder, M. 1991. *Playing with Power in Movies, Television, and Video Games*. Berkeley: University of California Press.

LEGO *Star Wars: The Complete Saga*. 2007. Instruction manual. Traveller's Tales.

14 Digital Narratives, Cultural Inclusion, and Educational Possibility

Going New Places with Old Stories in Elementary School

HEATHER LOTHERINGTON

Introduction

I am reading a revised version of *Goldilocks and the Three Bears* as an underwater tale, written by a little girl in grade 2 (age seven to eight) who has clearly borrowed heavily from Disney's animated movie rendering of *The Little Mermaid* to create this context. In her story, Goldilocks has become a mermaid, and she has invaded the home of three fish to find three bowls of . . . fish food. I question her on the menu—"What would Goldilocks like to eat?" "Carrots?" she enquires tentatively. "Well, they don't grow underwater," I respond. She looks at me, and frowns. "It is a 'once upon a time' story," she replies rather disdainfully. "Maybe mermaids like fish food!"

She is absolutely correct. I agree with her, smile broadly at my folly, and move on. This is an educational research project in which elementary schoolchildren reimagine narratives through their own cultural understanding to give traditional stories contemporary digital makeovers: *Goldilocks* living underwater or in outer space, told in hypertext; *The Little Red Hen* making a Kraft macaroni and cheese dinner or a birthday cake with Prince Charming, scripted as a play, acted and videotaped for other children to watch; *The Gingerbread Man* on the loose in the hallways of the school where he is spotted dashing cheekily into a computer screen, before ending up in the kindergarten classroom, captured in digital photography and programmed into a slide presentation; *The Three Little Pigs* created in multilingual Claymation, bringing the languages of the home into the school.

Emergent Multiliteracies in Theory and Practice is a funded collaborative university–school research project bringing together primary and junior grade teachers at Joyce Public School (JPS) in the greater Toronto area (GTA) with researchers at York University to develop multiliteracies pedagogies.[1] The study is motivated by the challenges faced by contemporary urban children living in multicultural proximity who are acquiring literacy in an era of complex digitally mediated, globalized communication but are constrained educationally by standardized assessments that fundamentally limit literacy to reading and writing on paper in English. Our collaborative teacher–professor research takes up the challenge posed over a decade ago by the New London Group "to extend the idea and scope of literacy pedagogy to account for the context of our culturally and linguistically diverse and increasingly globalized societies, for the multifarious cultures that interrelate and the plurality of texts that circulate . . . [and] account for the burgeoning variety of text forms associated with information and multimedia technologies" (New London Group 1996, 61).

Our objective is to engage a highly multicultural population socialized into interactive multimodal communications in narrative learning with a twist. Following Freire's ideology of literacy education as writing the word through the world (Freire and Macedo 1987), we are developing ways of teaching emergent literacy that engage children who are relatively new to Canadian society in writing themselves into the narratives they are learning to read. This dimensional shift is facilitated by digital technology that allows the story to be picked off the page, reshaped, and retold in another voice.

Theoretical Framework

Narrative Learning as Socialization

Stories form the bedrock of educational experience. As Davis and colleagues explain, the narrative is not simply an aide-mémoire, it is a memory structure: "Cognitive science researchers typically identify two sorts of conscious long-term memories: *episodic* (event-based, autobiographical, and narratively structured), and *semantic* (fact-based, rote, and often lacking an integrated structure). The former tend to be more stable and easily recalled than the latter—hence the effectiveness of the ancient teaching practice of embedding factual knowledge in rich images and narratives" (Davis, Sumara, and Luce-Kapler 2008, 13).

Folk and fairy tales were originally created by adults for adults, who by oral recitation, "instructed, amused, warned, initiated and enlightened" one another, and further "opened windows to imaginative worlds inside that needed concrete expression outside in reality" (Zipes 2007, 2). They have evolved into bedtime stories forming assumed common knowledge acquired in childhood. Children are expected to know how the prince tracked Cinderella down, who the seven dwarfs were, and what Aladdin's lamp could do.

Zipes caustically notes that one can buy everything from bathing suits to ashtrays to pornographic films based on folk and fairy tale motifs (2002, 2). Children's traditional stories are social tropes, surfacing in contemporary political, social, commercial, and philosophical commentary. For example, an advertisement posted on YouTube depicts the *Goldilocks and the Three Bears* narrative extended to Hummer vehicles, where Baby Bear exclaims: "Someone has taken my Hummer!"[2]

But how do children acquire the assumed cultural knowledge of traditional folk and fairy tales when their preschool socialization has been in a refugee camp, or locked in a small high rise apartment with the television set as babysitter while parents frantically search out employment? How culturally naïve are our expectations of the universality of the bedtime story (Heath 1982)? How much of the children's literature canon is actually encountered these days in Disney animations and associated merchandise?

Luke describes childhood culture as fabricated from commoditized narratives that are interwoven in "TV, toys, fast-food packaging, video games, T-shirts, shoes, bed linen, pencil cases, and lunch boxes" (New London Group 1996, 70). The elementary schoolchildren in our research project, born in the twenty-first century, grow up in a technologically saturated environment that they understand better than their parents. These children may recognize the fractured and commoditized Disney-mediated images of fairy tale characters without always knowing the stories behind them.

Narratives, Literacy Education, and New Media

Bruner (2004) sees narratives as fundamentally constructivist, played out in dual landscapes of action and consciousness in which the narrator creates a world as a function of mind, not as a description of objective phenomena. The narrative offers a transformative educational possibility: the creator as agent. Literacy in this scenario has the potential of critical activism.

Ryan notes that the study of narratives transcends media to embrace "language, image, gesture, and further, spoken language, writing, cinema, radio, television, and computers" (Ryan 2004b, 1). Herman discusses this multimodality as "the what and the way" of the narrative where the "what" is seen as medium independent but the "way," as the story conveyance, is not (2004, 51). Narrative theorists have varying visions of new media in narrative construction, from Murray's *Hamlet on the Holodeck* where new media transcribe old stories on new stages, to Landow, who sees new media as conscripting the reader as coauthor to change what might be described as the "how" of narrative experience (Ryan 2004c, 337).

Our multiliteracies project uses a multimodal rewriting process to invite the literacy learner into narrative construction as coauthor. In this process, with the self as incipient reader and, later, cowriter of an established traditional story that is personally or collectively reconstructed, Bruner's (2004) landscapes of action and consciousness are concurrently engaged.

Emergent Literacy in a Multicultural Society

Literacy education assumes a linear progression from orality to literacy. This requires the learner to understand the language encoded in text, despite the inevitable presence of new words. Though the great literacy debate has long argued the merits of a sound-based (phonic) versus a meaning-based (whole language) approach to emergent literacy instruction, a combined approach is needed for alphabetic literacy (Stanovich and Stanovich 1995). This means that for children to read alphabetic writing, there must be a basis for decoding—for connecting sound and symbol, and for associating a meaning with the text form. For most children in Toronto, learning to read means learning how to read in English.

Nearly half of the children in the Toronto District School Board do not speak English as mother tongue, however, so the majority of children in school are learning to read by attempting to decode words and associate a meaning to an oral counterpart they do not necessarily recognize.

Children's canonical literature is typically conceptualized in terms of the editions captured in print by nineteenth-century European authors such as Hans Christian Andersen and the Brothers Grimm, though folk and fairy tales are, in fact, far more international in origins than their reified Eurocentric print forms would suggest. *Cinderella* with her diminutive feet, for instance, though best known as she has evolved from Charles Perrault's portrait of *Cendrillon*, has roots in China in the story of Ye Xian in *You Yang Za Zu*, told a thousand years before European print versions (Lai 2007; Louie 1999). Lai (2007, 50) further notes that the Chinese Cinderella story draws from an earlier Egyptian prototype. Zipes extends this history, quoting August Nitschke's theory that the *Cinderella* story evolved after the last ice age (2002, 194). Twentieth-century story reproductions prominently include Disney's screen animations that reposition cultural stereotypes through an American lens (cf. Dorfman and Mattelart 1991; Zipes 1995).

For children entering public school in the GTA, literacy will be introduced through stories, songs, and chants in English.[3] For the most part, the storybooks that children will encounter will not mirror their faces or languages, implying subtextually that the world in print is not their world but an exclusive world they must learn to access.

Exclusive text in education is not a new invention: many of us learned to read with mid-twentieth-century texts in which women were seldom if ever acknowledged in pronouns, and families were white, two-parent, and middle class. Harré and Moghaddam theorize social positioning psychologically, stating that "a position implicitly limits how much of what is logically possible for a given person to say and do" (2003, 5). Phillips, capturing his own negative positioning in a Eurocentric classroom, states, "If the teaching of English literature can feed a sense of identity then I, like many of my black contemporaries in Britain, was starving" (1987, 2). Though the perennial white picket fence of primers has long been dismantled, we still have some distance to go to create welcoming stories for the multicultural children who populate contemporary classrooms.

Norton (2000) argues the importance of identity in language learning, critically noting how uniformly language learners tend to be framed. She argues that absent from research perspectives are "the voices of particular learners, their distinctive histories, their unique desires for the future" (2000, 47–48). Cummins outlines the pedagogical importance of encouraging children to create texts that acknowledge and celebrate their diverse linguistic and cultural views at school (Cummins 2006; Cummins et al. 2005), which he describes as "*identity texts* insofar as students invest their identities in these texts (written, spoken, visual, musical, dramatic, or combinations in multimodal form) that then hold a mirror up to students in which their identities are reflected back in a positive light" (Cummins 2006, 60). Cummins's identity texts facilitate positive social positioning in the classroom, an aim our project pursues by revising literacy education to incorporate children's languages and ideas of cultural relevance in multimedia narration.

Critical Multiliteracies

The Brazilian educator Paulo Freire once said, "I have always insisted that literacy, thought of in terms of reading words, must necessarily, be preceded by the reading or deciphering of the world around us. Learning to read and write is tantamount to 're-reading' the world of our experience" (cited in Campos 1990). Freire was inspired to rethink literacy teaching as critical pedagogy in the 1960s and 1970s, working with adults for whom learning to read was a process of submission rather than emancipation. In Freire's vision of literacy as emancipatory, the reader develops a critical consciousness ("conscientização"), rather than sinking into the negative positioning of oppressive literacy education practices (Freire 1998). Freire outlined two diametrically opposed approaches to literacy education. In the "banking system," "education . . . becomes an act of depositing, in which the students are the depositories and the teacher is the depositor. Instead of communicating, the teacher issues communiqués and makes deposits which students patiently receive, memorize, and repeat" (1998, 53). He proposed as an alternative to the anaesthetizing banking approach to learning, "problem-posing education," in which students and teachers participate through dialogue as subjects in the reenvisioning, critical intervening, and reconstituting of their social realities (1998, 60).

Our research utilizes a critical literacy perspective in which the learner learns stories by becoming a part of them, which facilitates taking ownership of the story. Our discursive, project-based orientation is the natural concomitant of technology-enhanced learning that invites problem-solving learning, provides creative collaborative opportunities, and offers individualized multimodal expression.

Digital Epistemologies

Our project moves traditional narratives into digital spaces where inclusive multiliteracies can be experimentally taught and learned. Following the New London Group's 1996 programmatic manifesto to explore and develop multiliteracies pedagogies, researchers have stressed the need to develop digital epistemologies to account for the new literacies occasioned by digital technologies (Kellner 2002, 2004; Lankshear and Knobel 2003, 2006). Prensky (2006) points out that basic literacy in the twenty-first century requires a knowledge of programming, which children develop socially in computer-mediated communication, video game play, and use of cell phones and MP3 players.

The envisioning of the electronically mediated global village we inhabit in the twenty-first century was predicted by Marshall McLuhan over four decades ago (1964). Walter Ong subsequently developed the concept of secondary orality (1980, 1982) to account for the postliterate orality created by electronic technologies such as television and video recorders. The possibilities for secondary orality theorized by Ong in an era of relatively unsophisticated electronic technologies lacked the interactivity of primary orality (Ryan 2004a); however, avenues to interactivity proliferate in the digital era of the twenty-first century, where powerful, portable networked communications technologies have redefined communication, community, culture, and literacy.

Taking these theoretical directions, our project works toward layering text, oral language development, and digitally mediated, multilingual narration to revive and extend storytelling. In our multiliteracies project, children retell traditional stories, using their voices and interpretations, enabled by new media. In so doing, they acquire agency in storytelling and develop critical consciousness as literacy acquisition.

Context

Toronto is a testament to Canada's immigration policy. The GTA is a multicultural metropolis of international note. The school system serving Toronto is, however, provincially governed by a languages-in-education policy catering to English and French bilingualism that is seriously out of step with the multilingual population of the province's capital city, which is also the country's largest city. Funding cutbacks have seriously eroded support for ESL assistance and reduced the teaching of languages other than English and French to continuing education programs, available, for the most part, after school to multilevel classes. Critical province-wide tests benchmarking literacy achievement are exclusively on paper in English (or French).

The community attending Joyce Public School, as in other public schools in inner-city contexts, does not fit the colonial profile of students' backgrounds that grounds provincial curricular expectations. With well over 90 percent of the JPS community being immigrants to Canada,[4] children have little access to the preschool socialization into English and literacy imagined in provincial curricula.

Method/Aims

Donaldo Macedo once wrote: "Far from the democratic education we claim to have, what we really have in place is a sophisticated colonial model of education designed primarily to train teachers in ways in which the intellectual dimension of teaching is devalued. The major objective of a colonial education is to further deskill teachers and students to walk unreflectively through a labyrinth of procedures and techniques" (2000, 3).

The Emergent Multiliteracies in Theory and Practice project engages in a collaboratively guided action research methodology: participating teachers are steered to develop, implement, document, and present narrative interventions designed to teach literacy through personalized stories. The project provides a multidimensional learning experience, bringing together theory and practice in the classroom context. Our focus is to invite into the educational process the multilingual capabilities and digital literacies of the students, and to bring their cultural vantage points into the reading process, allowing them to interpret text from what they know, and retell it so that it makes sense in their worlds.

The project aims to update and democratize literacy education toward the possibilities of a culturally plural society in the twenty-first century. Within this aim, we educate ourselves, building a learning community of teacher-researchers in mutually informing teacher education. The creative process toward building multiliteracies pedagogies is complex and highly individuated, and the media available are ever changing. As such, what we have created is a climate of living experimental pedagogy that invites perspectives critical to children's improved education that are currently not well served by the provincial curriculum.

Once upon a time the children made a gingerbread man.

16. Making gingerbread men. Photo by Michelle Holland.

Children's New Narratives

Linda Hutcheon notes, "An emphasis on process . . . permits us to think about how adaptations allow people to tell, show, or interact with stories" (2006, 22). In our project teachers choose a story from the traditional Western canon of children's literature and familiarize their students with the story as told in English.[5] This is a lengthy process of story reading and retelling, including associated multimodal arts and crafts activities. As the narrative becomes familiar, the children are invited to take ownership of the story, revising it to their time and place. Different technologies are used to shape the narrative retelling process.

Learning What a Story Is from the Inside Out:
The Gingerbread Man *in Michelle's Kindergarten*

What is a story? Many children entering kindergarten at JPS have not experienced bedtime stories as a cultural practice at home; some children do not have books to call their own. Yet the provincial curriculum assumes that children come to school having heard stories in English. For many children at JPS, this socialization must be fostered in kindergarten.

The gingerbread man was gone. He left a message. Run, Run as fast as you can! You can't catch me, I'm the Gingerbread Man.

17. Gingerbread note. Photo by Michelle Holland.

In Michelle's combined junior and senior kindergarten class (ages four to six), the children discovered the story of *The Gingerbread Man* from the inside out as a collective experience. Having learned the story in successive readings, they made their very own gingerbread men (figure 16).

But when the gingerbread men were being baked in the staff room kitchenette, they escaped! The children found a note in place of the baking tray (figure 17), and a cookie crumb trail (a tactic functionally borrowed from *Hansel and Gretel*) left behind by the runaway gingerbread men (figure 18).

Of course in kindergarten, children cannot yet read and write. However, the gingerbread man's repetitive refrain—"Run, run, as fast as you can. You can't catch me, I'm the gingerbread man!"—was easily recognizable with a little guidance. The trail led the children through a treasure hunt of clues that they had to decode, following the antics of the real/virtual gingerbread man who appeared in a computer screen darting over the shoulder of an educational assistant (figure 19), leaving evidence in several classrooms (figure 20).

Finally, the clues led the children back to their home classroom, where

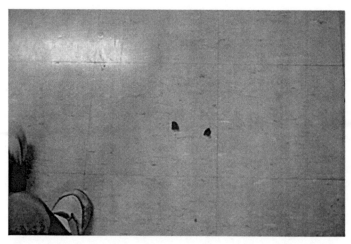

The children saw cookie crumbs on the ground. They followed them to the library.

18. Gingerbread cookie crumbs. Photo by Michelle Holland.

they each caught their own gingerbread man and decorated him (figure 21). Michelle notes that many children scolded their gingerbread man for being such a bad boy!

Michelle captured the children inside the story of *The Gingerbread Man* using digital photography, and then inserted captioned pictures of the children at different stages of the unfolding story into a slide show (using Microsoft PowerPoint). The children, in this way, became part of the story they were learning: it was their personal gingerbread man who had been so naughty, and they each exacted their own yummy revenge.

In this learning experience, Michelle brought *The Gingerbread Man* to life in the context of the school, dashing around hallways and into computers, and in so doing, inserted the children into the narrative they were learning as protagonists: a true story experience. *The Gingerbread Man* was recast as local, tangible, and immediate, rather than as an abstract character in a book. The children, likewise, were repositioned as agentive in creating their own gingerbread man who could be touched and smelled and decorated . . . and eaten! They took part in the action of the story creating, chasing, and then exacting their just desserts, so to speak, on a character who had escaped from the confines of a book into their

Brian said he saw the Gingerbread Man. Brian said the Gingerbread Man jumped on his back! Poor Brian! The Gingerbread Man said, "Run, Run as fast as you can. You can't catch me I'm the Gingerbread Man." The children ran on.

The children saw Mr. M. and asked, "Did you see the Gingerbreadman?" Mr. M. saw the Gingerbread Man. The Gingerbread Man said, "Run, Run as fast as you can. You can't catch me I'm the Gingerbreadman!" The children ran on.

19 and 20. Following the gingerbread man. Photos by Michelle Holland.

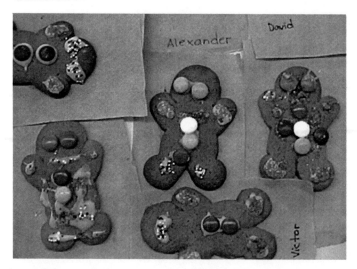

The children went to room 102 and saw the Gingerbread Man on the table. They decorated him and ate him up!

21. Gingerbread men decorated by the children. Photo by Michelle Holland.

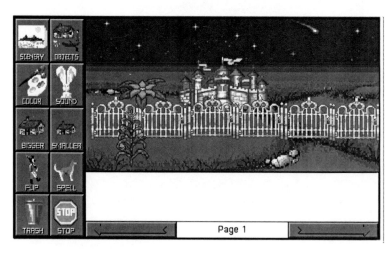

22. A child's revised story setting using Storybook Weaver. Created by Sandra Chow.

own hands. In this way, Michelle positioned children who are developing basic literacy proficiencies as critical agents (Freire 1998).

Genre-Bending: The Little Red Hen *in Sandra's Grade 2*

Having pioneered the first successful multiliteracies project—a rewriting of *Goldilocks and the Three Bears* (Lotherington and Chow 2006)—Sandra chose a well-known folk tale for her next grade 2 (ages seven to eight) narrative adventure: *The Little Red Hen.* This story was selected for a number of reasons, including the narrative's prosocial message of contributing and sharing, the logical sequencing of narrative events, and the relatively simple setting.

Sandra began by reading the story in the traditional version, eventually followed by versions in which other animals were involved and other baked goods were created. She guided her students to compare the fundamental elements of the story, using graphic organizers. As the children moved into planning individual adaptations, they explored and interlinked real and virtual resources, including puppets, and digital storyboards for creating revised story settings and programming retold stories (see figure 22).

The story updating brought the moral lessons of the traditional story into sharper focus. Instead of barnyard animals baking bread and harvesting the wheat to do so, the scene changed to magic castles where the princess, given a decidedly feminist slant, decided to bake a birthday cake for herself, and in the process needed a real live cookbook to follow the instructions—a literacy lesson normally considered far above the reading level of children in grade 2. The story settings were generally fantastical: castles, deserts, and under the sea, pointing to the place of small- and large-screen adaptations of children's literature in the children's repertoires. The protagonists included wild animals, such as tigers and eagles, and sea creatures such as crabs and jellyfish, as well as the usual storybook royalty. However, Prince Charming got into the act by helping out with baking the birthday cake (from scratch!). What was distinctly localized was the food that the characters were making and eating: birthday cakes, hot dogs, and instant macaroni made with the instructions cut from the back of a package of Kraft dinner.

After the children's stories had been planned, mapped onto a digital storyboard (using HyperStudio), and enhanced through digital means, the children voted on the best of the story revisions, which were then translated into dramatic form. They collaboratively scripted and staged their rewritten versions of *The Little Red Hen* in small groups, using both real and digital twenty-first-century contexts. The children created their own scenery and costumes for their adaptations, learned their lines, organized a story narrator, and timed scenery changes with accompanying musical interludes. The rewritten plays were performed before a live audience; every class in the school was invited in to view their plays, which were greeted with enormous approval by all. The plays were videotaped live and converted to iMovie, where the students were able to do their own voice-overs.

The Little Red Hen story familiarization and retelling adventure crossed genres from story to stage play to movie, and wove together paper, material, and digital forms as students took ownership of the narrative, writing themselves and their classmates into their retold versions. The children learned a vocabulary of genre (Lacey 2000), and experienced many aspects of the "way" of a narrative (Herman 2004) by reinterpreting this traditional story into multiple genres, and into contexts that made sense to them.

Bridging Home and School Language and Literacy Development:
The Three Little Pigs *Claymation in Shiva's Grade 1*

A multiliteracies approach to emergent literacy instruction fundamentally involves a broad and inclusive notion of what constitutes literacy. In urban schools where community members may not have a strong command of the English language, they are often not easily able to follow what their children are learning in school, and may feel alienated from their children's academic progress. In Shiva's grade 1 class (six to seven years old), however, the children's home languages have been welcomed into everyday classroom interactions, and into our narratives project.

Grade 1 is a critical year in emergent literacy acquisition: children are learning to write connected text, though they start with different levels of English socialization, story familiarity, and maturation. For many, literacy in English is a double hit of learning both the spoken and the written language. Fortunately, Shiva is professionally invested in multilingualism, teaching Farsi in continuing education classes in addition to her grade 1 homeroom.

23. *The Three Little Pigs* in the classroom. Photo by Heather Lotherington, with permission of Shiva Sotoudeh.

Shiva chose *The Three Little Pigs* for her grade 1 class, as it incorporated aims from across the curriculum, including language, art, mathematics, social studies, and science. The story introduces children to comparative environmental materials: which house is stronger and why?

After the children became familiar with the story of *The Three Little Pigs* through a highly multimodal approach (see figure 23), they were invited to adapt the characters and the setting, modeling their story retelling on the teacher's storyboard.

The individual stories, when worked out, were shared with parents, many of whom volunteered to produce written or taped translations of their children's retold stories. The children then created their personalized stories in modeling clay, depicting each "page" as a frame in a box (see figures 24 and 25).

The frames of each story were photographed and input into iMovie, where they were viewable as Claymation, narrated by the children. Moviemaking software can handle multiple soundtracks, so multilingual versions are possible, though Shiva encountered technical problems

24. *The Three Little Pigs* in finger puppets, story books, masks, and games. Photo by Heather Lotherington, with permission of Shiva Sotoudeh.

25. *The Three Little Pigs* plasticine storyboards. Photo by Heather Lotherington, with permission of Shiva Sotoudeh.

synchronizing multilingual storytelling and image files. This was an important point of learning for the research collective: multilingual versions require tandem programming, as the teacher does not speak every language in the class. This, in turn, spurs other queries about where in the storytelling process we can invite community languages. The pedagogical choices deeply affect programming options and learning possibilities (see Lotherington 2007).

In Shiva's narrative project, children created multimodal stories incorporating knowledge across the curriculum. Many of their stories were taken home for intergenerational translations. This invited immigrant parents, who are marginalized in the school system through their lack of cultural capital (Bourdieu 1991), into their children's learning, strengthening communication between home and school, and broadening children's conceptual understanding of literacy. The revised stories showcase not only the emerging literacies of children who have authored their very own versions of a traditional story but also include the family and the community in this literacy building.

Conclusion: Telling Old Stories in New Ways

Bruner notes that "as Henry James once put it, stories happen to people who know how to tell them" (2004, 691). These are the narrative worlds created by multicultural, multilingual, urban children in the primary grades as they learn English, acquire emergent literacy, and find out how a story works. The stories they are building utilize the technologies of today to learn stories of long ago. In Freire and Macedo's (1987) terms, they are learning to write the word through the world—as they understand it.

Bruner believes that "any story one may tell about anything is better understood by considering other possible ways in which it can be told" (2004, 709). The teachers utilize a variety of digital technologies to create opportunities for kids to rewrite themselves into the stories they are learning. The technologies are motivational, facilitating, and equalizing: digital culture is a common cultural thread with children whose preschool understanding of both Canadian culture and narratives owes much to electronic media, such as television and video games.

Mackey approaches literacy in the digital age from an asset model that recognizes individuals' involvements with multiple text types, broadly categorized as text on paper, audiovisual text, audio, electronic images, electronic text, wireless text, and online text (2002). Her definition of literacy as the "interpretation of recorded symbolic representation" (Mackey 2002, 199) positively acknowledges students' arrival in school classrooms with "experience in a rich matrix of multimedia engagements" (214) that offer many opportunities for classroom learning. These opportunities require teachers to rethink literacy epistemologically as well as pedagogically.

Our ongoing research to develop multiliteracies pedagogies through narrative learning has implemented the New London Group's (1996) agenda to interconnect the "what" and "how" of literacy pedagogy in *situated practice* (rewriting traditional stories through local understanding using contemporary media), *overt instruction* (teaching story structure, reading and writing, English, genres, and new media applications), *critical framing* (revising characters, reimagining story settings), and *transformed practice* (involving community languages and cultural vantage points in digitally mediated stories). The project has taught us much about responsive literacy teaching and learning in an urban, multicultural community. We have come to realize the overwhelming place of digital culture in children's Canadian enculturation. This sense of culture is at odds with the adult perception of culture as rooted in ethnic traditions that grounds notions of multiculturalism in Canada, and it is a world apart from what is assessed in the conservative, paper-based provincial literacy tests children write at grades 3, 6 and 10 (Lotherington 2003).[6]

The teachers' exploratory pedagogies are opening up important avenues for inclusive language learning, which is critical for successful language and literacy development, and for the cultural awareness and respect that underpins antiracist pedagogy. Their evolving multiliteracies pedagogies for narrative learning are repositioning minority children under the multicultural umbrella as coauthor and agent in literacy acquisition rather than as outsider at the margins of the story.

Part of this repositioning involves using the languages of the community in the classroom, which is challenging, though difficulties encountered are grist for problem-posing education. Public schools tend to have anything but the latest hardware, and even at JPS, which has won awards for its sustained and innovative technological integration, technical problems can all too often derail good intentions. Children in schools where digital technologies are nativized learn how to read machines as well as the information they are seeking on the screens (Lotherington and Sinitskaya Ronda 2009). This is a part of twenty-first-century literacy according to scholars such as Prensky (2006).

We have discovered in this project that learning how to tell a story is difficult learning. To adapt a story, the children must first thoroughly understand the plot of the story: the "what." They must understand the story to adapt it without destroying the essential narrative thread. This is a sophisticated undertaking.

As Hutcheon points out, "multiple versions of a story in fact exist laterally, not vertically" (2006, 169). The upshot of children's adaptations is that they understand intimately the characters they create: they are responsible for clarity of motive in their revisions. The *The Little Red Hen* making Kraft dinner is not a lesser telling of this story; it is contemporary, relevant, comprehensible, and tangible. Rewriting stories through their own young eyes and mouths has allowed children who begin school as marginalized populations to take center stage in their own learning.

Notes

1. I gratefully acknowledge the Social Sciences and Humanities Research Council of Canada for awarding standard research grant 410-2005-2080 in support of the research project Emergent Multiliteracies in Theory and Practice: Multicultural Literacy Development at Elementary School.

2. See http://www.youtube.com/watch?v=NviBNiwbRbM&feature=related for the video advertisement.

3. French medium public schools are available in Ontario for those whose mother tongue is French.

4. Personal communication, Cheryl Paige, principal of Joyce Public School, February 8, 2010.

5. The stories shared here were created in Michelle Holland's kindergarten class; Shiva Sotoudeh's grade 1 class; and Sandra Chow's grade 2 class at Joyce Public School in Toronto.

6. The Education Quality and Accountability Office (EQAO) administers mandatory province-wide literacy and numeracy tests across Ontario (http://www.eqao.com/).

References

Bourdieu, Pierre. 1991. *Language and Symbolic Power*. Trans. Gino Raymond and Matthew Adamson. Cambridge MA: Harvard University Press.

Bruner, Jerome. 2004. "Life as Narrative." *Social Research* 71:691–710.

Campos, Marcio D. 1990. "Reading the World—Interview with Brazilian Educator Paulo Freire." *UNESCO Courier*, December. Available at http://findarticles.com/p/articles/mi_m1310/is_1990_Dec/ai_9339028/print (accessed January 9, 2011).

Cummins, Jim. 2006. "Identity Texts: The Imaginative Construction of Self through Multiliteracies Pedagogy." In *Imagining Multilingual Schools: Languages in Education and Glocalization*, ed. Ofelia García, Tove Skutnabb-Kangas, and Maria E. Torres-Guzmán, 51–68. Clevedon: Multilingual Matters.

Cummins, Jim, Vicki Bismilla, Patricia Chow, Sarah Cohen, Frances Giampapa, Lisa Leoni, Perminder Sandhu, and Padma Sastri. 2005. "Affirming Identity in Multilingual Classrooms." *Educational Leadership* 63:38–43.

Davis, Dennis Sumara, and Rebecca Luce-Kapler. 2008. *Engaging Minds: Changing Teaching in Complex Times*. 2nd ed. New York: Routledge.

Dorfman, Ariel, and Armand Mattelart. 1991. *How to Read Donald Duck: Imperialist Ideology in the Disney Comic*. Trans. David Kunzle. New York: International General.

Freire, Paulo. 1998. *Pedagogy of the Oppressed*. Trans. Myra Bergman Ramos. 20th anniversary edition. New York: Continuum. (Orig. pub. 1970.)

Freire, Paulo, and Donaldo P. Macedo. 1987. *Literacy: Reading the Word and the World*. South Hadley MA: Bergen and Garvey.

Harré, Rom, and Fathali Moghaddam. 2003. "Introduction: The Self and Others in Traditional Psychology and in Positioning Theory." In *The Self and Others: Positioning Individuals and Groups in Personal, Political, and Cultural Contexts*, ed. Rom Harré and Fathali Moghaddam, 1–11. Westport CT: Praeger.

Heath, Shirley Brice. 1982. "What No Bedtime Story Means: Narrative Skills at Home and School." *Language in Society* 11:49–76.

Herman, David. 2004. "Toward a Transmedial Narratology." In *Narrative across Media: The Languages of Storytelling*, ed. Marie-Laure Ryan, 47–75. Lincoln: University of Nebraska Press.

Hutcheon, Linda. 2006. *A Theory of Adaptation*. New York: Routledge.

Kellner, Douglas M. 2002. "Technological Revolution, Multiple Literacies, and the Restructuring of Education." In *Silicon Literacies: Communication, Innovation and Education in the Electronic Age*, ed. Ilana Snyder, 154–69. London: Routledge.

———. 2004. "Technological Transformation, Multiple Literacies and the Re-visioning of Education." *E-Learning* 1:9–37.

Lacey, N. 2000. *Narrative and Genre: Key Concepts in Media Studies*. Houndmills: MacMillan.

Lai, A. 2007. "Two Translations of the Chinese Cinderella Story." *Perspectives: Studies in Translatology* 15:49–56.

Lankshear, Colin, and Michele Knobel. 2003. *New Literacies: Changing Knowledge and Classroom Learning*. Buckingham: Open University Press.

———. 2006. *New Literacies: Everyday Practices and Classroom Learning*. Maidenhead: McGraw Hill/Open University Press.

Lotherington, Heather. 2003. "Emergent Metaliteracies: What the Xbox Has to Offer the EQAO." *Linguistics and Education* 14:305–19.

———. 2007. "Rewriting Traditional Tales as Multilingual Narratives at Elementary School: Problems and Progress." *Canadian Journal of Applied Linguistics* 10:241–56.

Lotherington, Heather, and Sandra Chow. 2006. "Rewriting *Goldilocks* in the Urban, Multicultural Elementary School." *The Reading Teacher* 60:244–52.

Lotherington, Heather, and Natalia Sinitskaya Ronda. 2009. "Gaming Geography: Educational Games and Literacy Development in the Grade 4 Classroom." *Canadian Journal of Learning and Technology* 35. Available at http://www.cjlt.ca/index.php/cjlt/article/view/542/265 (accessed March 2, 2011).

Louie, Ai-ling. 1999. *Yeh-shen: A Cinderella Story from China*. New York: Puffin.

Macedo, Donaldo. 2000. Introduction to *Chomsky on Miseducation*, ed. Donaldo P. Macedo, 1–14. Lanham MD: Rowman and Littlefield.

Mackey, Margaret. 2002. "An Asset Model of New Literacies: A Conceptual and Strategic Approach to Change." In *Digital Expressions: Media Literacy and English Language Arts*, ed. Roberta F. Hammett and Barrie R. C. Barrell, 199–215. Calgary: Detselig.

McLuhan, Marshall. 1964. *Understanding Media: The Extensions of Man*. New York: McGraw-Hill.

New London Group. 1996. "A Pedagogy of Multiliteracies: Designing Social Factors." *Harvard Educational Review* 66:60–92.

Norton, Bonny. 2000. *Identity and Language Learning: Gender, Ethnicity and Educational Change*. Harlow: Pearson Education.

Ong, Walter. 1980. "Literacy and Orality in Our Times." *Journal of Communication* 30:197–204.

———. 1982. *Orality and Literacy: The Technologizing of the Word*. London: Routledge.

Phillips, Caryl. 1987. *The European Tribe*. New York: Vintage.

Prensky, Marc. 2006. *Don't Bother Me Mom, I'm Learning*. St. Paul: Paragon House.

Ryan, Marie-Laure. 2004a. "Face-to-Face Narration." In *Narrative across Media: The Languages of Storytelling*, ed. Marie-Laure Ryan, 41–46. Lincoln: University of Nebraska Press.

———. 2004b. Introduction to *Narrative across Media: The Languages of Story-telling*, ed. Marie-Laure Ryan, 1–40. Lincoln: University of Nebraska Press.

———. 2004c. "Will New Media Produce New Narratives?" In *Narrative across Media: The Languages of Storytelling*, ed. Marie-Laure Ryan, 337–59. Lincoln: University of Nebraska Press.

Stanovich, Keith E., and Paula J. Stanovich. 1995. "How Research Might Inform the Debate about Early Reading Acquisition." *Journal of Research in Reading* 18:87–105.

Zipes, Jack. 1995. "Breaking the Disney Spell." In *From Mouse to Mermaid: The Politics of Film, Gender, and Culture*, ed. Elizabeth Bell, Linda Haas, and Laura Sells, 21–42. Bloomington: Indiana University Press.

———. 2002. *Breaking the Magic Spell: Radical Theories of Folk and Fairy Tales*. Rev. ed. Lexington: University Press of Kentucky.

———. 2007. *When Dreams Came True: Classical Fairy Tales and Their Tradition*. 2nd ed. New York: Routledge.

Glossary

anachrony: Nonchronological narration, in which the reported events are told in an order other than that which they are presumed to have taken in the "real" or "storyworld."

analepsis: The equivalent of a flashback in a story, where the events A-B-C are narrated in the order B-A-C.

API: An Application Programming Interface is a set of data structures or protocols provided by an organization for building applications.

blending: A cognitive account of the ways in which individuals subconsciously create new meanings by integrating elements of meaning from two or more distinctive scenarios. This theory was developed by Mark Turner and Gilles Fauconnier.

blog: A frequently updated web page in which the entries appear in reverse chronological order.

blogosphere: A composite of all extant blogs.

born digital: Materials that have developed in the digital realm only and have no print or analog counterpart. In criticism of digital fiction, used to distinguish between texts created on CD-ROM and those that are native to the World Wide Web.

canon: An authoritative list, for example of the works of an author or group of authors.

cross-media: A story distributed across more than one media platform, such as video game, DVD, or web page.

existent: "The objects contained in story-space [as opposed to discourse-space] . . . namely character and setting" (Chatman 1978, 107).

fanfiction: Stories written by fans based on preexisting texts or fictional worlds.

fanon: A fan-derived alternative to the "canon" whereby aspects of plotting, background information, or characterization become "fanonical" due to uptake and dissemination within fan communities.

first- and second-wave theory: Distinguishes between successive trends in literary criticism of digital media. First-wave theory is typically associated with the work of writers/theorists from Eastgate publishers. Second-wave theorists draw on empirical, contextualized perspectives.

focalization: The perspective from which events are narrated. Classically distinguished as "who sees" in contrast to "who speaks" (Genette 1980).

geoblogging: Geographical mapping of blogs, achieved by attaching geographical metadata such as altitude, latitude, and longitude coordinates. This data can also be added to photos, videos, and websites.

geocaching: An outdoor treasure-hunting game in which the participants use a GPS receiver or other navigational techniques to hide and seek containers (called "geocaches" or "caches") anywhere in the world.

GIS: A Geographic Information System integrates hardware, software, and data for capturing, managing, analyzing, and displaying all forms of geographically referenced information.

GPS: The Global Positioning System is a satellite navigation system developed by the U.S. Department of Defense that enables receivers to determine their location, speed, direction, and time.

graphical user interface: Enables a user to interact with a computer or similar hand-held device by manipulating icons rather than text-based labels.

implied reader: The constructed audience presupposed by the norms and values of a text. Usually treated in distinction from real readers. The concept was developed by Booth (1983).

LED: Light Emitting Diodes are lighting devices that emit light when an electric current is passed through them.

lexia: A block of text linked electronically to other blocks of text in a network. In hypertext theory, Barthes's concept of the lexia is extended by Nelson (1981) and Landow (1997).

metafiction: A type of fiction that draws attention to itself as a fictional artifact, severing the traditional mirror-like connections between art and life.

MOO: A MUD that uses object-oriented techniques to organize its systems.

MUD: A Multi-User Domain is a multiplayer virtual world created in text, often in the form of a computer role-playing game.

multiliteracies: Refers to the variation in literacy practices related to specific cultural or social domains. A second usage incorporates the various literacies enabled by differing forms of technologies. Both uses are current in pedagogic literature.

node: A connection point within a communication network.

Oulipo: A writing project founded in the 1960s by Raymond Queneau and François Le Lionnaise that encouraged writers to create new works of literature governed by mathematic and ludic constraints.

PDA: A Personal Digital Assistant is a hand-held computer, also known as a palmtop.

personalization: The customizing or tailoring of a text or product to the user's specification.

phenomenology: A philosophical method devoted to the study of structures from the first person perspective.

prolepsis: The equivalent of flashforward in a story where the events A-B-C are narrated A-C-B.

qualia: Term used by philosophers of the mind to refer to the sense of "what it is like" for someone or something to have a given experience.

RFID: A Radio Frequency Identifier tag is an object that can be applied to or incorporated into a product, animal, or person for the purpose of identification and tracking using radio waves.

synesthesia: Used in literary theory to describe when one sensory mode is described in terms of another, such as "her eyes searched hungrily through the pages."

tellability: The quality of events that makes them reportable, usually in distinction from an everyday backdrop.

transmedia(l): The study (usually comparative) of narratives across more than one medium.

virtual reality: A computer-generated simulation with which a user can interact. These are usually highly visual, often three-dimensional displays. The user's interaction can be via a keyboard or a haptic tool.

VKB: Virtual Knowledge Builder, a spatial hypertext system developed by Frank Shipman.

VRML: Virtual Reality Modeling Language.

wifi: The name of a popular wireless network that provides high speed Internet and networking connections by using radio waves.

wiki: A web page that is available for anyone to edit. From the Hawaiian word meaning "quickly quickly."

Wikipedia: A free online encyclopedia collaboratively written using wiki software.

WIMP GUI: Windows-Icon-Mouse-Pointer device is a type of Graphic User Interface, now usually known just as a GUI. The user can employ a number of devices (touchpad, keyboard, mouse) to send information to the computer, which represents the position of the "pointer" (e.g., a cursor or arrow) on the screen monitor.

(w)reader: A blend of "writer" and "reader" coined by Landow (1997) to reflect the empowered status of the hypertextual audience as they manipulate and so co-construct examples of digital writing (usually fiction).

References

Booth, Wayne C. 1983. *The Rhetoric of Fiction.* Chicago: University of Chicago Press.

Chatman, Seymour. 1978. *Story and Discourse: Narrative Structure in Fiction and Film.* Ithaca: Cornell University Press.

Genette, G. 1980. *Narrative Discourse: An Essay in Method*. Trans. J. E. Lewin. Ithaca NY: Cornell University Press.

Landow, G. P. 1997. *Hypertext 2.0: The Convergence of Contemporary Critical Theory and Technology*. Baltimore: Johns Hopkins University Press. (Orig. pub. 1992).

Nelson, Theodor H. 1981. *Literary Machines*. Swarthmore PA: Self-published.

Contributors

Alice Bell is a senior lecturer in English language and literature at Sheffield Hallam University. Her research interests include narrative theory, digital literature, stylistics, and Possible Worlds Theory. She is the principal investigator of the Digital Fiction International Network (funded by The Leverhulme Trust). She is the author of *The Possible Worlds of Hypertext Fiction* (Palgrave-Macmillan, 2010). Her other publications include a contribution to *Contemporary Stylistics*, edited by Marina Lambrou and Peter Stockwell (Continuum, 2007), and she coedited with Astrid Ensslin "New Perspectives on Digital Literature: Criticism and Analysis," a special issue of *dichtung-digital*, http://www.dichtung-digital.de/ (2007).

Paul Cobley, reader in communications at London Metropolitan University, is the author of a number of books, including *The American Thriller* (Palgrave, 2000) and *Narrative* (Routledge, 2001). He is the editor of *The Communication Theory Reader* (Routledge, 1996), *Communication Theories*, 4 volumes (Routledge, 2006), *The Routledge Companion to Semiotics* (Routledge, 2009), and *Realism for the 21st Century: A John Deely Reader* (University of Scranton Press, 2009) among other books; coedits two journals, *Subject Matters* and *Social Semiotics*; and is associate editor of *Cybernetics and Human Knowing*. He is the series editor of Routledge Introductions to Media and Communications and co–series editor (with Kalevi Kull) of Semiotics, Communication and Cognition (Mouton de Gruyter).

Astrid Ensslin is senior lecturer in digital humanities at the School of Creative Studies and Media, Bangor University. Her main research interests are in the areas of digital literature (especially fiction), discourse analysis, games and virtual environments, and language in the (new) media. She is principal editor of *Journal of Gaming and Virtual Worlds* and founding editor of the MHRA *Working Papers in the Humanities* and has guest edited (with Alice Bell) the 2007 issue of *dichtung-digital*. Her further publications include *Canonizing Hypertext: Explorations and Constructions* (Continuum, 2007), *Language in the Media: Representations, Identities, Ideologies* (coedited with Sally Johnson; Continuum, 2007), *Creating Second Lives: Community, Identity, and Spatiality as Constructions of the Visual* (coedited with Eben Mose; Routledge, 2011), as well as articles in *Language and Literature*,

Corpora, Journal of Literature and Aesthetics, Language Learning Journal, Gender and Language, and *Sprache und Datenverarbeitung.* She is coinvestigator of the Leverhulme-funded Digital Fiction International Network.

Brian Greenspan is associate professor in the Department of English and the Institute of Comparative Studies in Literature, Art and Culture at Carleton University in Ottawa, where he teaches contemporary literature and new narrative media. He is the founding director of the Hypertext and Hypermedia Lab, a facility for interdisciplinary graduate and postdoctoral research in the digital humanities, located in Carleton's HCI Institute. His published research comprises topics ranging from American and Australian fiction to hypertext narratives, video games, and interface design. Lately, his research interests have included New World utopian and dystopian narratives, digital culture, and the intersections between them.

Nick Haeffner is senior lecturer in communications at London Metropolitan University. He is the author of *Alfred Hitchcock* (Pearson, 2005) and has published a range of articles on film, media, and cultural theory. In 2006 he cocurated a traveling interactive new media exhibition inspired by Hitchcock's *Vertigo.* He is currently working on a book about the British film director Michael Winterbottom, titled *In this World: Michael Winterbottom and Revolution Films.*

David Herman, who serves as the editor of the Frontiers of Narrative book series and the journal *Storyworlds,* teaches in the English department at Ohio State University in the United States. He has published widely in the areas of interdisciplinary narrative theory and storytelling across media. Recent projects include an edited volume titled *The Emergence of Mind: Representations of Consciousness in Narrative Discourse in English* (University of Nebraska Press, 2011) and a 2011 special issue of the journal SubStance, "Graphic Narratives and Narrative Theory," co–guest edited by Jared Gardner.

The *New York Times* termed **Michael Joyce's** *afternoon* (Eastgate, 1987) "the granddaddy of hypertext fictions," and he since has published numerous hypertext fictions on the web and on disk, as well as print collections of short fictions, prose pieces, and essays. His poems have been published in *nor/, The Iowa Review, New Letters, Parthenon West,* and elsewhere, and his most recent novel, *Was: Annales Nomadique, a novel of internet,* was published by Fiction Collective 2 in 2007. Another novel, *Liam's Going* (2002), has recently been reissued in paperback by McPherson and Company. He has been collaborating in multimedia work with Venezuelan video artist Anita Pantin and Canadian composer Bruce Pennycook; and, more recently, in another project with Los Angeles visual artist Alexandra

Grant, which has been widely exhibited, including at the Museum of Contemporary Art in Los Angeles. He is currently professor of English and media studies at Vassar College, where he cofounded the latter program.

Heather Lotherington is professor of multilingual education at York University in Toronto, Canada, where she teaches in the fields of both education and linguistics. She is the principal investigator in a collaborative research project to design pedagogies leading to the development of multimodal literacies at Joyce Public School, an elementary school in northwest Toronto, where researchers and teachers have been engaged in codesigning multilingual, digitally mediated narrative projects since 2003. The research, which is grounded in the challenges that contemporary urban children experience in acquiring literacy across home, school, community, and societal contexts, focuses on the creation of narrative projects that provide socially relevant elementary literacy education for culturally diverse and digitally socialized children. This research, which contributed to a national technology award for Joyce Public School in 2006, has been published in numerous journal articles and book chapters and will be published as a book by Routledge: *Pedagogy of Multiliteracies: Rewriting Goldilocks*. This project-based approach to contemporary, inclusive literacy learning can be viewed in more detail at http://www.multiliteracies4kidz.ca.

Nick Montfort is associate professor of digital media at the Massachusetts Institute of Technology. Montfort has collaborated on the blog *Grand Text Auto*, the sticker novel *Implementation*, and *2002: A Palindrome Story*. He writes poems, text generators, and interactive fiction such as *Book and Volume* and *Ad Verbum*. Most recently, he and Ian Bogost wrote *Racing the Beam: The Atari Video Computer System* (MIT Press, 2009). Montfort also wrote *Twisty Little Passages: An Approach to Interactive Fiction* (MIT Press, 2003) and coedited *The Electronic Literature Collection*, volume 1 (ELO, 2006) and *The New Media Reader* (MIT Press, 2003).

James Newman is a professor in media communications at Bath Spa University. He conducts research on a variety of subjects, including video gaming and gaming cultures, media preservation, and media fandoms. His recent books include *Playing with Videogames* (Routledge, 2008), *100 Videogames* (BFI Publishing, 2007), *Teaching Videogames* (BFI Publishing, 2006), and *Videogames* (Routledge, 2004). He is currently writing books on the materiality of game cultures and on media decay, obsolescence, and preservation strategies. Newman is a cofounder of the National Videogame Archive, which, with the National Media Museum, is the United Kingdom's first official archive of video games and the ephemera of gaming culture.

Ruth Page is a lecturer in the School of English at the University of Leicester. She has published numerous articles and essays that bring together the interests of language and gender studies and narrative theory along with her monograph, *Literary and Linguistic Approaches to Feminist Narratology* (Palgrave, 2006). She is editor of *New Perspectives on Narrative and Multimodality* (Routledge, 2010) and is currently working on the story genres found in the everyday writing that use Web 2.0 technologies.

Daniel Punday is professor of English at Purdue University Calumet. He is the author of *Narrative after Deconstruction* (SUNY Press, 2002), *Narrative Bodies* (Palgrave, 2003), and *Five Strands of Fictionality: The Institutional Construction of Contemporary American Writing* (Ohio State University Press, 2010). His contribution to this volume reflects his current interest in contextualizing contemporary definitions of multimedia within a broader historical and aesthetic framework. This research is part of a larger project on how the contemporary American novel draws on and appeals to other media.

Scott Rettberg is associate professor of humanistic informatics in the Department of Linguistic, Literary, and Aesthetic Studies at the University of Bergen, Norway. Prior to moving to Norway in 2006, Rettberg directed the new media studies track of the literature program at Richard Stockton College in New Jersey. Rettberg is the author or coauthor of works of electronic literature, including *The Unknown, an Anthology* (Spineless Books, 2002), *Kind of Blue* (Trace, 2003), and *Implementation* (2004–5). Rettberg is cofounder and served as the first executive director of the Electronic Literature Organization. Rettberg is a contributor to the collaborative digital culture web log *Grand Text Auto*. He is currently working on a book about contemporary electronic literature in the context of the twentieth-century avant-garde.

A native of Geneva, Switzerland, **Marie-Laure Ryan** is scholar in residence at the University of Colorado, Boulder. She is the author of *Possible Worlds, Artificial Intelligence and Narrative Theory* (Indiana University Press, 1991), which received the 1992 Prize for Independent Scholars from the Modern Language Association; of *Narrative as Virtual Reality: Immersion and Interactivity in Literature and Electronic Media*, which received the 2001 Aldo and Jeanne Scaglione Prize for Comparative Literature Studies, also from the Modern Language Association; and of *Avatars of Story: Narrative Modes in Old and New Media* (University of Minnesota Press, 2006). She has edited *Cyberspace Textuality: Computer Technology and Literary Theory* (Indiana University Press, 1999) and *Narrative across Media* (University of Nebraska Press, 2004) and coedited the *Routledge Encyclopedia of Narrative Theory* (Routledge, 2005), with David Herman and Manfred Jahn. Her home page currently resides at http://spot.colorado.edu/~marielau/.

Andrew Salway is a researcher at Uni Computing in Bergen, Norway. He works on the computer-based analysis of multimedia documents, with a focus on the formal manifestation of their narrative and multimodal properties. He contributed a chapter on this topic to *New Perspectives on Narrative and Multimodality*, edited by Ruth Page (Routledge, 2010). Through the Television in Words project (2002–5) he pioneered the corpus-based analysis of audio description, and he has subsequently enjoyed collaborations with colleagues from a range of academic disciplines and industry. He has published over thirty papers and given invited talks on multimedia computing, audiovisual translation, multimodal semiotics, narratology, and corpus linguistics.

Iain Simons produces live and published content about video games and tech-culture for a wide variety of media outlets, including *New Statesman*, *Design Week*, *Gamasutra*, and BBC *Focus*. In 2005 he curated the first weekend of video game events at the National Film Theatre and in 2006 founded the annual GameCity festival. His published work includes *Difficult Questions about Videogames* (Suppose Partners, 2004) and *100 Videogames* (BFI Publishing, 2007), both cowritten with James Newman, and *Inside Game Design* (Laurence King Publishing, 2008). Iain is the director of the GameCity festival at Nottingham Trent University and a cofounder of the National Videogame Archive.

Bronwen Thomas is senior lecturer in linguistics and literature in the Media School at Bournemouth University in the United Kingdom. She is the author of a chapter on dialogue in *The Cambridge Companion to Narrative* (2007), and she has contributed entries on dialogue to the *Routledge Encyclopedia of Narrative Theory* (2005) and to the *Blackwell Encyclopedia of the Novel* (2010). Thomas has presented several conference papers on digital narratives and has previously published articles on both hypertext fiction and fanfiction. She has also contributed a chapter on television-based fanfiction to *New Perspectives on Narrative and Multimodality*, edited by Ruth Page (Routledge, 2010) and is currently completing a monograph called *Fictional Dialogue: Speech and Conversation in the Modern and Postmodern Novel*, to be published by the University of Nebraska Press.

To order or obtain more information
on these or other University
of Nebraska Press titles, visit
www.nebraskapress.unl.edu.